PSYCHOLOGICAL ASSESSMENT AND TREATMENT OF PERSONS WITH SEVERE MENTAL DISORDERS

THE SERIES IN CLINICAL AND COMMUNITY PSYCHOLOGY

PSYCHOLOGICAL ASSESSMENT AND TREATMENT OF PERSONS WITH SEVERE MENTAL DISORDERS

Edited by

Jeffrey R. Bedell, Ph.D.
*Albert Einstein College of Medicine of Yeshiva University
and Montefiore Medical Center
Bronx, New York*

Taylor & Francis
Publishers since 1798

USA	Publishing Office:	Taylor & Francis 1101 Vermont Avenue, N.W. Suite 200 Washington, DC 20005-3521 Tel: (202) 289-2174 Fax: (202) 289-3665
	Distribution Center:	Taylor & Francis 1900 Frost Road, Suite 101 Bristol, PA 19007-1598 Tel: (215) 785-5800 Fax: (215) 785-5515
UK		Taylor & Francis Ltd. 4 John St. London WC1N 2ET Tel: 071 405 2237 Fax: 071 831 2035

PSYCHOLOGICAL ASSESSMENT AND TREATMENT OF PERSONS WITH SEVERE MENTAL DISORDERS

1 2 3 4 5 6 7 8 9 0 B R B R 9 8 7 6 5 4 3

This book was set in Times Roman by Innodata, Inc. The production supervisor was Peggy M. Rote. Cover design by Michelle Fleitz. Printing and binding by Braun-Brumfield, Inc.

A CIP catalog record for this book is available from the British Library.⊗The paper in this publication meets the requirements of the ANSI Standard Z39.48-1984 (Permanence of paper)

Library of Congress Cataloging-in-Publication Data
Psychological assessment and treatment of persons with severe mental
    disorders / edited by Jeffrey R. Bedell.
        p. cm. — (The Series in clinical and community psychology)
    Includes bibliographical references.

    1. Mentally ill—Rehabilitation. 2. Chronically ill—
Rehabilitation. I. Bedell, Jeffrey R. II. Series.
    [DNLM: 1. Mental Disorders—rehabilitation. 2. Personality
Assessment. 3. Psychotherapy. 4. Rehabilitation, Vocational. WM
29.1 P9748 1993]
RC439.5.P84 1993
616.89'03—dc20
DNLM/DLC
    for Library of Congress   93-11643
ISBN 1-56032-292-6   CIP
ISSN 0146-0846

Dedicated to Charles Spielberger, for teaching me the science and profession of psychology, and to Ruth Bedell, for helping me understand persons with handicaps.

Contents

Contributors

William A. Anthony, PhD
Professor and Director, Center
  for Psychiatric Rehabilitation,
  and Director, Rehabilitation Research
  and Training Center,
Sargent College of Allied
  Health Professions,
Boston University,
Boston, Mass.

Leona L. Bachrach, PhD
Research Professor of Psychiatry,
Department of Psychiatry,
University of Maryland School
  of Medicine, and international
  consultant on rehabilitation
  program development.

Jeffrey R. Bedell, PhD
Associate Professor of Psychiatry
  (Psychology) and Director, Behavior
  Therapy Program,
Department of Psychiatry,
Albert Einstein College of Medicine of
  Yeshiva University and Montefiore
  Medical Center,
Bronx, N.Y.

Bertram J. Black, MSW
Professor Emeritus of Psychiatry
  (Rehabilitation), Epidemiology, and
  Social Medicine,
Albert Einstein College of Medicine,
Bronx, N.Y.

Andrea K. Blanch, PhD
Director, Community Support Programs,
New York State Office of Mental Health,
Albany, N.Y.

Mikal R. Cohen, PhD
Associate Research Professor,
Department of Rehabilitation
  Counseling and Associate Executive
  Director,
Center for Psychiatric Rehabilitation,
Boston University,
Boston, Mass.

Barry A. Edelstein, PhD
Professor and Chair,
Department of Psychology,
West Virginia University,
Morgantown, W.V.

Marianne D. Farkas, ScD
Associate Professor,
Department of Rehabilitation
  Counseling, and Director of Training,
Center for Psychiatric Rehabilitation,
Boston University,
Boston, Mass.

John V. Flowers, PhD
Professor of Psychology,
Chapman University,
Orange, Calif.

Jeffrey A. Frank, MA
Sound View Throgs Neck Community
  Mental Health Center,
Albert Einstein College of Medicine of
  Yeshiva University,
Bronx, N.Y.

Robert Gervey, PsyD
Assistant Professor,
Department of Psychiatry (Psychology),
Albert Einstein College of Medicine,
  and Director of Behavior Therapy Unit,
Sound View Throgs Neck Community
  Mental Health Center,
Bronx, N.Y.

Joseph S. Lechowicz, PhD
Associate Professor of Education and
  Director, Rehabilitation Counselor
  Education,
Hofstra University,
Hempstead, N.Y.

Shelley S. Lennox, PhD
Assistant Professor,
Department of Psychiatry (Psychology),
Albert Einstein College of Medicine,
  and Director, Central Intake Unit,
Sound View Throgs Neck Community
  Mental Health Center,
Bronx, N.Y.

Barry J. Naster, PhD
Department of Community
  Mental Health,
Florida Mental Health Institute,
University of South Florida,
Tampa, Fl.

William F. O'Brien, MS
Senior Training Associate,
Center for Psychiatric Rehabilitation,
Boston University,
Boston, Mass.

Janice E. Pace
Department of Community Mental
  Health,
Florida Mental Health Institute,
University of South Florida,
Tampa, Fl.

Peter Provet, PhD
Director, Adolescent Programs and
  Clinical Support Services,
Phoenix House, Inc.,
New York, N.Y.
Visiting Assistant Professor,
Department of Psychiatry,
Albert Einstein College of Medicine,
Bronx, N.Y.

Richard C. Surles, PhD
Commissioner,
New York State Office of
  Mental Health,
Albany, N.Y.

Dennis Upper, PhD
Director, Outpatient Services,
Northeast Psychiatric Associates,
Nashua, N.H.

John C. Ward, PhD
Associate Professor and Associate Chair,
Department of Community Mental
  Health,
Florida Mental Health Institute,
University of South Florida,
Tampa, Fl.

Paula K. Whitaker, MA
Department of Community Mental
  Health,
Florida Mental Health Institute,
University of South Florida,
Tampa, Fl.

Jerome Yoman, PhD
Director of Behavioral Programming,
Psychosocial Rehabilitation Unit,
Community Support Program,
Brockton/West Roxbury VA
  Medical Center
Brockton, Mass.

Preface

For many years, patients with severe and long-lasting disorders were considered to be unsuitable for psychological treatment and were treated primarily by means of long-term hospitalization and psychotropic medication. Hospitalization protected these patients from neglect and abuse by providing shelter and custodial care, and medication helped relieve debilitating symptoms such as intense anxiety and depression. Unfortunately, these types of treatments were frequently only partially effective, and did not lead to the development of adaptive social skills. Moreover, such treatments sometimes stabilized the individual at far less than an optimal level of social functioning.

Recent efforts to improve the therapeutic outcome for patients with severe mental disorders have adapted treatment approaches from behavioral and rehabilitation therapies and social skills training. A wide array of effective psychological assessment and treatment approaches have been conceived, tested, and refined over the last decade. While hospitalization and psychotropic medication are still important, the newly developed psychological approaches have greatly increased treatment effectiveness. Using innovative behavioral and rehabilitation treatments, patients previously believed to be hopelessly disabled have shown significant improvement. For example, social skills training has been repeatedly demonstrated to result in dramatic reductions in the need for hospitalization among individuals with schizophrenia.

Unfortunately, effective psychological assessment and treatment approaches, often derived from disparate sources, have not been well integrated in the rehabilitation of patients with severe and long-lasting disorders. The development and delivery of effective and well-integrated treatments to individuals with these types of disorders is considered by many to be a mental health priority in this country. For this reason, the current volume provides a comprehensive and integrated presentation to the reader.

This current volume describes psychological assessment and treatment practices specifically designed for use with patients with severe and long-lasting mental disorders. This book comprises three sections: Assessment and Treatment Planning, Social and Vocational Skills Development, and Group and Family Therapy in Rehabilitation. A brief overview of the content of each of the chapters is provided in the Introduction. The topics covered in each of the sections were selected by determining the most fundamentally important issues regarding assessment and treatment planning, social and vocational skills development, and group and family therapy. Individuals with established expertise in each subject area were invited to describe an assessment or treatment approach. Specifically, they were asked to describe procedures that would be useful to the clinical practitioner, as well as empirical information regarding the effectiveness of the approach. The editor is very grateful to these authors for contributing their expertise, and often their patience, to the creation of this book.

It is hoped that the reader will find this book useful as a guide to clinical practice, as a classroom text, and for other similar purposes. Professionals such as psychologists; psychiatrists; social workers; rehabilitation counselors and psychiatric nurses working with patients with schizophrenia, major depression, and other severe, long-term disorders should find the assessment and treatment techniques described in this book relevant to their clinical work. The volume is intended as a handbook that can be kept conveniently available as a reference on the fundamental psychological approaches that are effective with patients having severe disabilities. This volume also has the potential to be used as a textbook. The editor used it in a seminar on the topic of psychosocial approaches to the assessment and treatment of severely disabled patients. This book proved to be extremely useful since it covers many of the fundamental issues relevant to this topic. The students, consisting of psychologists, social workers, nurses, and activity therapists, gave it a very positive rating because it provided information in sufficient detail that they could use it as a guide to clinical practice.

Jeffrey R. Bedell, Ph.D.

Introduction

This volume is designed to familiarize practitioners with assessment and treatment approaches that have been shown to be effective in the rehabilitation of psychiatric patients. The psychological procedures that are described have been selected because of their effectiveness with patients having severe and long-term mental disorders such as schizophrenia and major depression. An integrated description of these psychological treatments for use with these types of patients is needed. These assessment and treatment methods have also been applied to individuals having other chronic disorders such as substance abuse, and less severe problems such as anxiety disorders, school adjustment, and marital difficulties.

In order to assist the reader in understanding the overall focus and scope of this volume, the content of each chapter will be briefly described, along with information to help integrate the various topics. The first major section, on Assessment and Treatment Planning, consists of four chapters. Several interrelated and complementary methods of evaluation are described that have not previously been presented together in one place. By seeing these assessment techniques together, the reader can better understand and integrate the compatible elements of each approach.

In the first chapter of Part I, Farkus, O'Brien, Cohen, and Anthony present a detailed overview of the principal elements of the "Boston University Model" of assessment and treatment planning. This chapter provides a concise yet comprehensive presentation based on many years of work by the authors with their innovative model. The essential elements of the model that make this approach effective are highlighted. The Boston University Model, which has been employed by practitioners nationwide, represents one of the most comprehensive, well-developed, and widely accepted approaches to treatment planning, especially for individuals with severe and long-lasting mental disorders.

Functional assessment is the cornerstone for assessment and treatment planning in the Boston University model. Because functional assessment is of central importance, an entire chapter is devoted to this topic. Yoman and Edelstein present an exceptionally clear and practical explanation of functional assessment, show how it is a crucial element in treatment planning, and give detailed examples that will help the practitioner to understand and effectively use this method of assessment.

Once effective functional assessment techniques are put into practice, standardization of procedures is desirable. Standardized assessment makes the information gathered on patients at different times and places more comparable. Many severely handicapped patients receive treatment in a variety of settings over time. Therefore, increasing the comparability of assessment information makes evaluations more useful as patients move to new programs or receive treatment from different therapists.

Bedell and Lennox describe the development of standardized procedures for social skills assessments. As shown by these authors, a major benefit of standardized assessment includes the ability to compare the performance of the psychologically handicapped with that of normal individuals. Moreover, as described in this chapter, standardized assessments comparing normal and handicapped groups yield clinically useful and often unexpected findings. These assessments also provide information that contributes to the determination of which psychological treatments should be employed in rehabilitating patients with particular skill deficits.

No matter what types of evaluation techniques are used, mental health practitioners have increasingly recognized that both assessment and treatment planning should include input from the patients themselves. Because of their lengthy and varied treatment experiences, many patients with severe and long-lasting disorders become knowledgeable regarding different types of mental health treatment. Patients have been writing about their experiences in mental health and rehabilitation programs for many years. In Chapter 4, Bachrach examines this patient-authored literature with the goal of identifying points of agreement between patient-authors and professionals who are involved in assessment and mental health planning. Her poignant review identifies areas of agreement between consumers and professionals, and important areas overlooked by the professionals.

The second major section of this volume, which includes five chapters, examines Social and Vocational Skills Development. Adaptive social and vocational skills are emphasized because the development of such skills is the primary goal of the most effective psychological approaches to the rehabilitation of severely disabled psychiatric patients. There are well over 100 published articles and several books describing applications of social skills training techniques with a wide range of psychological disorders. In his chapter on social skills training, Bedell emphasizes applications with patients having severe mental disorders. He presents a detailed description of a social skills training model that integrates both cognitive and behavioral skill development, and emphasizes the fundamental role of "skill concepts" in assisting the patient to define, organize, and guide adaptive behaviors.

Bedell's chapter provides a number of examples of cognitive-behavioral skill training methods, such as how to teach patients to make effective requests and how to respond to requests from others. Flow charts are provided that illustrate the processes being taught, and material is presented in sufficient detail to be useful to the practitioner interested in using this social skills training model.

Social skills training is a flexible therapeutic approach that may be applied in many innovative formats. Ward, Naster, Pace and Whitaker, in Chapter 6, describe in detail an application of a social skills training program that involved novel modification of traditional recreational and activity therapies. An important advantage of the methods described in this chapter is that these procedures can be used with patients who are more decompensated and functioning at a lower level than is possible with more traditional social skills training approaches. These methods, which facilitate self-awareness, communication, and problem-solving skills, also result in more rapid stabilization and recovery of patients.

For many patients, developing effective social skills greatly enhances the potential for vocational placement. Chapters 7 and 8 provide an in-depth consideration of the topic of vocational rehabilitation. In Chapter 7, Black and Lechowicz describe a number of programs that have been successfully employed in contemporary vocational rehabilitation of psychiatrically disabled persons. Based on their extensive experience and understanding of vocational rehabilitation, these authors identify the therapeutic elements that are essential for effective treatment. An innovative and controversial model of vocational rehabilitation is described in Chapter 8. This approach to vocational rehabilitation, which is referred to as Supported Employment, advocates the rapid employment of the handicapped person, with the vast majority of the skill training taking place in the workplace.

Supported employment approaches reflect a radical divergence from traditional models of vocational treatment, which typically emphasize extensive periods of "job readiness training" prior to placing an individual on the job. In Chapter 8, Gervey and Bedell describe the contemporary developments in vocational rehabilitation that have contributed to the current emphasis on supported employment. After describing the major models of supported employment, noting their similarities and differences, Gervey and Bedell report the results of the first published controlled evaluation of a supported employment program with psychiatric patients that they have carried out over the past three years. Factors that contributed to the dramatic superiority of the supported employment program as compared with the traditional sheltered workshop treatment are discussed.

Patients in need of rehabilitation often have a wide array of services available to them. As can be seen from the variety of treatment programs described in the previous chapters, however, these services are usually enmeshed in a bureaucratic system that is complex and confusing to the mental patient. In order to negotiate the system of mental health and social services available to them, many patients benefit from effective case management. Case management is intended to assist patients in making effective use of the complicated system of rehabilitation services that may be available to them. As patients make better use of available treatment, they generally experience reduced frequency of relapse and hospitalization. Blanch and Surles describe a statewide system of intensive case management that is currently implemented in New York, and present research findings evaluating the effectiveness of this program. The results of this research are enlightening in providing some interesting insights into the skills and supports patients need to beneficially utilize the mental health system.

Part II of this book comprises two chapters that focus on group and family therapy in psychiatric rehabilitation. Any serious application of psychological approaches to treatment must take into consideration the unique learning environment created when patients and families are treated in groups. In Chapter 10, Upper and Flowers describe a Behavioral Group Therapy model that uses learning principles to maximize the effectiveness of group process variables such as group-cohesiveness and self-disclosure. Based on their clinical experience and extensive research, these authors present and discuss a series of recommendations for improving group therapy in the rehabilitation of psychiatric patients.

In the final chapter, Bedell, Provet, and Frank present a model for multiple family therapy that has been shown to stimulate and facilitate effective family problem solving. The rationale for multiple family therapy and the unique learning opportunities that are provided by this model are described in detail based on their extensive experience with the multiple family therapy model. The authors identify the seven principal elements that comprise the essence of this type of treatment. Several interesting case presentations are also provided to illustrate the application of this therapy technique in the rehabilitation of psychiatric patients.

Of the wide range of topics that are covered in this volume, the specific chapters in each of the three sections were selected to examine the most fundamental and important issues that are encountered in the assessment and treatment of patients with severe disabilities. Hopefully the topics that are considered will contribute to enhancing the skills of practitioners, while stimulating interest in working more effectively with patients with severe and long-lasting psychological difficulties.

Part One

Assessment and Treatment Planning

Chapter 1

Assessment and Planning in Psychiatric Rehabilitation

Marianne D. Farkas, William F. O'Brien,
Mikal R. Cohen, and William A. Anthony

Many mental health settings have begun to develop psychiatric rehabilitation programs to enhance or replace existing, more traditional programs (e.g., Allen & Velasco, 1980; Bachrach, 1982; Beard, Propst, & Malamud, 1982). Some are adopting rehabilitation services as a complement to existing services (Anthony, Buell, Sharratt, & Althoff, 1972), while others are moving from no services for persons with severe psychiatric disabilities to a psychiatric rehabilitation approach (Lamb, 1982; Anthony & Liberman, 1986). As psychiatric rehabilitation becomes more widely used as a concept, it becomes necessary to clarify what psychiatric rehabilitation is, and how it differs from other approaches to providing effective services to persons with psychiatric disabilities. This chapter will first clarify the psychiatric rehabilitation approach. Second, it will focus on the unique contributions of the rehabilitation diagnosis and planning process to services for persons with severe psychiatric disability.

Parts of this chapter are adapted, with permission, from: Anthony, W. A., Cohen, M. R., Farkas, M. D. (1990). *Psychiatric Rehabilitation.* Boston: Boston University. Center for Psychiatric Rehabilitation; and Farkas, M. D., & Anthony, W. A. (1989). *Psychiatric Rehabilitation Programs: Putting Theory into Practice.* Baltimore: Johns Hopkins University Press.

As the term "psychiatric rehabilitation" has become widely used, misconceptions about the term have also become common. The term "psychiatric" does not refer to psychiatrists as providers, nor does it reflect the notion that psychiatric treatment techniques are used. It refers rather to the population served, persons with psychiatric disabilities. The term "rehabilitation" does not refer to a state agency providing the service, nor does it reflect a unique emphasis on helping people to obtain employment. It does refer to improving functioning in a specific environment. Psychiatric rehabilitation is best defined by its mission or overall purpose, which is to enable persons with psychiatric disabilities to increase their functioning in their chosen environments so that they can be successful and satisfied with the least amount of professional intervention possible (Anthony, 1979; Anthony, Cohen, & Cohen, 1984). Although there are many program settings (e.g., psychosocial clubhouses, supported apartments, supported work) and many techniques (e.g., social skills training, advocacy, job coaching) used in the rehabilitation of persons with psychiatric disability, all of them share a common model and philosophy.

THE REHABILITATION MODEL

The rehabilitation model, as practiced with persons who have severe physical disabilities (e.g., persons with quadriplegia), serves as a conceptual model for the basic goals and treatment process of psychiatric rehabilitation (Anthony, 1980). Despite the obvious differences between difficulties of those with severe psychiatric disabilities and those with physical disabilities, there are similarities as well. Persons with either disability require a wide range of services, exhibit limitations in their role performance, may receive services for a long period of time, and often do not experience complete recovery from their disabilities (Anthony, 1982).

The concepts of impairment, disability, and handicap have been used to describe the domains of rehabilitation (physical or psychiatric) as compared to those of traditional treatment (Wood, 1980; Frey, 1984). Table 1-1 illustrates the rehabilitation model based upon these concepts.

Treatment techniques focus on either eliminating illness or controlling its symptoms. A reduction in pathology or the impairment may not necessarily lead to an improvement in disability. For example, a person's hallucination may be controlled without improving that person's ability to hold a job or return to school—particularly if that person has never held a job or has had great difficulty in remaining in school. As Leitner and Drasgow (1972) pointed out, mental health treatments have focused on minimizing sickness, rather than maximizing functioning and health.

Similarly, improving functioning may not automatically reduce pathology, although such a possibility could occur (Strauss, 1986). Persons may learn to be better students and still have as many psychotic episodes as they always had.

Table 1-1   The Focus of Rehabilitation

	Impairment	Disability	Handicap
Definition	Any loss or abnormality of psychological, physiological, or anatomical function (resulting from underlying pathology)	Any restriction or lack (resulting from an impairment) of the ability to perform an activity in the manner or within the range considered normal	A disadvantage for a given individual (resulting from an impairment or disability) that limits or prevents the fulfillment of a role that is normal (depending on age, sex, social, cultural factors) for that individual.
Example	Hallucinations Ideas of reference Somatic complaints	Lack of conflict resolution skills, planning skills, social skills, daily living skills	Housing Discrimination, Work disincentives
Interventions	Treatments focused on alleviating or reducing pathology (e.g., chemotherapy, behavior modification)	Clinical rehabilitation focused on developing skills and environmental supports	Societal rehabilitation focused on changing the system/society

Note. From Anthony, W. A., Cohen, M. R., & Farkas, M. D. (1990). Psychiatric Rehabilitation. Boston: Boston University, Center for Psychiatric Rehabilitation. Adapted by permission.

They may simply be better able to warn their instructor of an impending episode and develop techniques to protect themselves and their fellow students during the episode. Further, a chronic or severe impairment does not always mean a chronic disability. For example, a person with chronic diabetes may or may not also have a severe disability (Anthony & Liberman, 1986).

The basic philosophy of physical rehabilitation provides direction to the psychiatric rehabilitation process: That is to say, persons with disabilities need skills and supports to function in the living, learning, social, and working environments of their choice. The clinical practice of psychiatric rehabilitation contains two interventions: the development of persons' skills and the development of environmental supports that enable them to fulfill a chosen role in their preferred living, learning, social, or working settings. The use of these interventions is guided by basic rehabilitation philosophy. Rehabilitation philosophy assumes that changing individuals' use of critical skills or supports in a specific environment results in their being better able to fulfill the demands of their chosen role. In addition, they become more successful and satisfied in the process. In other words, changing a person's skills and/or environmental supports will benefit both the person (client satisfaction) and society (improved educational and working status) (Anthony, Kennard, O'Brien, & Forbess, 1986; Farkas, Anthony, & Cohen, 1989).

The practice of societal rehabilitation is focused on eliminating barriers in the environment that prevent persons from performing their chosen role (Anthony et al., 1972). The barrier produces a handicap that can prevent those whose impairment has lessened, and whose disability is minimal, from performing their chosen role. Job discrimination, welfare or Medicaid benefit regulations that limit the salary a recipient can earn, and community prejudice are examples of barriers that produce handicaps. Changes in legislation, stigma reduction programs, and rights advocacy programs are examples of societal rehabilitation interventions that can reduce handicaps. Clinical and societal rehabilitation interventions are not mutually exclusive (Stubbins, 1982).

Just as clinical and societal rehabilitation interventions are complementary, so too are rehabilitation and treatment interventions. Treatment and rehabilitation can be complementary approaches because each one is focused on a different target (i.e., impairment vs. disability/handicap), and therefore each one uses different criteria for success. Treatment focuses on the reduction of pathology while rehabilitation focuses on improved role performance in an environment.

THE REHABILITATION PROCESS

The key values of the rehabilitation process emerged from the historical developments that shaped psychiatric rehabilitation as a field. For example, the moral therapy era, the post–World War II development of vocational rehabilitation, and the emergence of psychosocial rehabilitation centers (Beard et al., 1982; Grob, 1983) all contributed to its development (Anthony & Liberman, 1986). These historical trends led to psychiatric rehabilitation's emphasis on pragmatism and the notion of "doing everyday activities"; the importance of people taking on valued roles in the real-world environment (such as work); a belief in the potential productivity of persons with the most severe disabilities; and the primacy of client involvement or ownership of the process.

More recent contributors to the emergence of key psychiatric rehabilitation values include the community mental health center and deinstitutionalization movements. Both the deinstitutionalization movement and the Community Mental Health Centers Act of 1963 underscored the concept that persons could be treated and supported outside hospitals in the natural communities from which they came (i.e., the real-world environment).

The parallel development of the community support initiative (Turner & TenHoor, 1978; Parrish, 1988) strengthened the notion that mental health was in the business of supporting *people* in the community rather than simply providing paid professionals to treat patients or clients. Persons with disabilities began to understand their right to make choices and to be treated as full citizens, participating within society (Funk, 1987; Ward, 1988).

These historical trends, in summary, resulted in nine key values (Table 1-2). The first value is that of *person orientation.* The rehabilitation process uses techniques designed to diagnose, plan, and intervene with the person in a holistic manner rather than narrowly focusing on emotional deficits or standard symptoms as the most meaningful aspect of the "case." The person is viewed as one who has physical, emotional, and intellectual strengths and deficits in relation to the types of housing, employment, and social and educational opportunities that he or she prefers. Because of the primary values of *self-determination* and *involvement,* the rehabilitation process focuses on "enabling techniques" designed to empower persons with disabilities to become successful and satisfied in their chosen environment—rather than on techniques that promote compliance with the demands of environments assessed by others to be appropriate for that person's placement. The rehabilitation process helps people to make their own choices about their goals and then gives them the tools they need and want to achieve these goals.

Proponents of rehabilitation value not only the full participation or involvement of the person with disability in the process but also *individualization.* Individualization is attained when the practitioner is able to tailor interventions to the unique needs of the individual. Practitioners often espouse this value without having a well-defined way to put the value into practice. For example, treatment goals across clients often look alike: "to leave the hospital," "to control aggressive behavior," "to take medications appropriately." When a skill assessment is included in the battery of assessment instruments, it is often an instrument that assesses skills according to a standard list. The list has little to do with clients' unique situations or the unique demands of their chosen environment. Techniques that allow specific descriptions of individuals in relation to their specific environments, rather than descriptions of functioning in general categories of behaviors, are one important means of addressing individual differences. Further, since clients' full participation in the rehabilitation process is valued, the process must be flexible in its duration and intensity. Each person has a different rate of progress in overcoming disability. Each person is unique in learning style, preference for intimacy, and tolerance for intense interventions. The rehabilitation process, while clearly systematic, respects these individual differences and paces itself accordingly.

Since the rehabilitation model focuses on overcoming disability (Table 1-1), psychiatric rehabilitation values *functioning* and techniques that develop functioning rather than those that reduce symptoms or develop insights. Psychiatric rehabilitation methods develop positive behaviors as opposed to controlling negative behavior. Interventions that improve a person's repertoire of skills and environmental supports are the predominant means for increasing functioning.

Table 1-2   Key Psychiatric Rehabilitation Values

Person orientation
A focus on the person rather than on the disease; belief in the importance of viewing
   the person holistically, as one with strengths, and preferences, rather than as
   a "case" exhibiting symptoms of disease

Self-determination
A focus on the person making his or her own decisions

Involvement
A focus on the importance of the person being empowered to participate in all
   aspects of the rehabilitation process

Individualization
A focus on respecting the unique differences among persons with psychiatric
   disabilities; tailoring all aspects of the rehabilitation process to the person's specific
   needs and wants

Functioning
A focus on performance of everyday activities

Environmental specificity
A focus on the importance of a person's specific living, learning, working, or social
   context in the "real world"

Outcome orientation
A focus on evaluating rehabilitation in terms of its impact on specific results valued
   by the person

Support
A focus on providing assistance with dignity, for as long as it is needed and wanted

Growth potential
A focus on the inherent capacity of any person to improve functioning and status,
   given the appropriate opportunity and support

Note. From Farkas, M. D., Anthony, W. A., & Cohen, M. R. (1989). Psychiatric rehabilitation: The Approach and Its Programs. In M. Farkas & W. Anthony (Eds.), *Psychiatric Rehabilitation Programs: Putting Theory into Practice.* Baltimore; John Hopkins University Press. Adapted by permission.

Environmental specificity reflects the understanding that people in general function differently in different environments. For example, a person may be able to express negative opinions at home but unable to express them at work. Psychiatric rehabilitation focuses on assessing persons in relationship to the demands of the particular environments they have chosen. In addition, the value placed on the concept of environmental specificity suggests that psychiatric rehabilitation focus on the "real world" or "natural environments" rather than on treatment environments. For example, the competencies identified as necessary to participate regularly in group therapy reflect some of what is required to be a successful client in a treatment program. "Participation in groups" is a competency that reflects the demands of the treatment environment. Clients' rehabilitation success is measured, however, in terms of the extent to which they improve in the areas of functioning required by the *natural* environments that they have selected.

While rehabilitation programs are most frequently located in community-based or natural settings, the rehabilitation process can begin in a treatment setting. Regardless of location, however, rehabilitation interventions are designed with a focus on the "real world." For example, a rehabilitation program based in a hospital may organize activities to help clients leave the hospital grounds and explore various alternative community environments in order to assist them in making a choice about where they want to live, learn, socialize, or work in the future. This hospital program may further its real-world focus by arranging for its assessment activities and interventions to occur in the community (Craig, Peer, & Ross, 1989). In addition, a hospital-based rehabilitation program may look for vocational or educational opportunities in the community, even though the clients may still be clients in the hospital.

The emphasis on functioning and environmental specificity contributes to a strong *outcome orientation*. Practitioners with outcome orientation evaluate their practice based on evidence of real-world results rather than on adherence to "good theory." An evaluation of adherence to a rehabilitation approach includes process measures (e.g., the number of skills assessed or taught, the number of hours of interviewing time taken to create a plan). For most people, these measures have little meaning or perceived impact on their daily lives. An evaluation of real-world results includes outcome measures such as an "increase in the person's functioning that was perceived as important to his or her success and satisfaction" or "time spent performing a preferred role in a setting the person has chosen."

The rehabilitation value that is shared by most mental health approaches is *support*. Most practitioners see themselves as offering support to their clients. In the psychiatric rehabilitation process, support is given for as long as it is needed and wanted. Rehabilitation practitioners do not view dependency with alarm. "Dependency is not a dirty word" (Anthony & Nemec, 1984 p. 392). In the field of physical rehabilitation the notion has been accepted that supporting dependency in one area can often increase a person's independence in another. For example, someone who is dependent upon a personal care attendant and a wheelchair, and who receives that support consistently, can hold a job. In psychiatric rehabilitation, support is mostly given in the emotional realm. The support is considered to be constructive if the support is wanted at the time it is given, if the intensity with which it is given is the desired intensity, and if the support frees the person to perform a role in some other environment.

The last key rehabilitation value is *growth potential*. The aim of rehabilitation is more than stabilizing or maintaining people in the community. Stabilization and maintenance of gains are important. The overall aim of rehabilitation, however, is growth. This involves an increase in the client's functioning that is critical to success and satisfaction, and a reduction in the amount of *professional* support and an increase in *natural* supports. Persons with serious psychiatric disabilities are often highly aware of their limitations. Professionals also fall into the trap of focusing on limitations in the guise of being "realistic." Research, however, indicates that our ability to predict who will or will not improve and succeed in the community is no better than chance (Miles, 1967; Anthony, 1979). A client's lack of success therefore may be more an indication that sufficient rehabilitation techniques have not been developed than an indication that growth is not possible for an individual. In the absence of tools that can accurately predict success, the rehabilitation value placed on growth potential leads practitioners to be hopeful rather than pessimistic.

The rehabilitation model, the mission of rehabilitation, and these nine values are the underlying philosophy that guides the psychiatric rehabilitation process. The overall focus of psychiatric rehabilitation is to enable persons to choose, get, and keep their preferred environments (Danley, Rogers, & Nevas, 1989). The process of psychiatric rehabilitation involves three phases: rehabilitation diagnosis, rehabilitation planning, and rehabilitation interventions (Table 1-3) (Anthony, Cohen, & Cohen, 1983; Farkas et al., 1989; Anthony, Cohen, & Farkas, 1990).

Rehabilitation diagnosis, the first phase, enables a client to choose a specific environment (e.g., living at home with family). Only once the choice has been made does the diagnosis involve the person in an assessment of critical skills and resources. The assessment identifies the skills and resources that the person currently has or does not have in relation to being successful in the chosen environment.

The second phase of the process, rehabilitation planning, enables the practitioner and the client to assign priorities to the deficits to be corrected and to identify the type of intervention that would best address the particular deficit. The planning phase also involves assigning responsibility for the interventions and identifying timelines. The third phase of the approach, rehabilitation interventions, includes skill development (i.e., skill teaching, programming skill use) and resource development (i.e., resource linking, modification or creation of new resources capable of providing the client with needed supports).

The practitioner knowledge, attitudes, and skills needed to diagnose, plan, and intervene with persons who have severe psychiatric disability have been defined (Cohen et al., 1986, 1989). Furthermore, the approach details the program structure needed to support practitioners in assisting clients through the rehabilitation process (Farkas et al., 1989). Lastly, the components of a mental health system that incorporates a rehabilitation philosophy in its operations have been defined (Cohen, 1989; Anthony et al., 1990; Cohen, Anthony, & Farkas, 1991). Although in practice the practitioner, program, and system dimensions are important to supporting the psychiatric rehabilitation process, this chapter will focus on discussing in detail only the first two phases of the process, rehabilitation diagnosis and planning.

Table 1-3   Psychiatric Rehabilitation Process: Practitioner Activities

PHASE I: Rehabilitation diagnosis	Setting the overall rehabilitation goal Conducting a functional assessment Conducting a resource assessment
PHASE II: Rehabilitation planning	Selecting priority skill or resource objectives Organizing responsibilities Projecting timelines Monitoring the plan

PHASE III: Rehabilitation intervention	Skill Development
	  Direct skill teaching
	  Programming skill use
	Resource Development
	  Resource coordination
	  Resource modification

Note: From Anthony, W. A., Cohen, M. R., & Farkas, M. D. (1990). *Psychiatric rehabilitation.* Boston: Boston University, Center for Psychiatric Rehabilitation. Adapted by permission.

REHABILITATION DIAGNOSIS

Psychiatric rehabilitation diagnoses enable persons with psychiatric disabilities to identify where they want to live, learn, socialize, or work and what they must do and have in order to achieve their goal. A psychiatric rehabilitation diagnosis and a traditional psychiatric diagnosis are two different forms of assessment. The goal, process, and tools of each are different and provide different types of useful and meaningful information (Cohen & Anthony, 1984; Anthony, Cohen, & Nemec, 1987). There were three basic reasons for the development of a psychiatric rehabilitation diagnostic process, as distinct from that of psychiatric diagnoses: (a) psychiatric diagnosis was designed to provide information about the impairment, not the disability or the handicap; (b) psychiatric diagnosis does not predict rehabilitation outcomes; and (c) psychiatric diagnosis was not designed to give direction to the psychiatric rehabilitation process.

Psychiatric Diagnosis was Designed to Provide Information about the Impairment, not the Disability or the Handicap   The goal of the typical psychiatric diagnostic procedure is to assign a diagnostic label to describe a person's pathology or symptoms based on a history and observation of behavior, affect, and reactions in the diagnostic interview (Anthony et al., 1987). Although psychiatric diagnoses (e.g., those in the revised third edition of the *Diagnostic and Statistical Manual of Mental Disorders* [American Psychiatric Association, 1987]) do include a limited amount of global information about functioning, the emphasis is, as it was designed to be, on categorizing the symptoms of the impairment.

On the other hand, rehabilitation focuses on the disability. Several reviews of the literature have indicated that (a) clients can learn skills regardless of symptoms and (b) skill and resources that provide integrated support in the community can positively impact on clients' rehabilitation outcome or their ability to perform chosen roles in a preferred environment (Anthony, 1980; Anthony, Cohen, & Vitalo, 1978; Anthony et al., 1984; Anthony & Jansen, 1984; Cohen & Anthony, 1984; Dion & Anthony, 1987). Given that rehabilitation outcome is a function of client skills and resources, it follows that rehabilitation assessments must evaluate present and needed levels of client skills and resources in order to provide meaningful information to the rehabilitation process.

The goal of a rehabilitation diagnostic process is, therefore, to describe clients' skill functioning and environmental supports with respect to their impact on the clients' success and satisfaction in a particular setting.

The information about skill and resources includes information about clients' strengths as well as deficits. The assessment is expressed in specific behavioral terms and is related to a specific environmental goal. Increasingly, psychiatric diagnostic instruments are also focusing on skill and resource assessment in addition to assessment of symptoms and pathology; however, these instruments are still limited by their lack of environmental specificity. For example, a standardized instrument might provide information relevant to employment, in general, rather than a specific job situation (et al., 1987.

Psychiatric Diagnosis does not Predict Rehabilitation Outcomes   Even though psychiatric diagnoses were designed to evaluate the level of impairment rather than the disability, psychiatric diagnostic procedures have often been used, in practice, to provide information about potential rehabilitation outcomes. Case conferences used symptom descriptions to predict how successful or unsuccessful a person might be in a future environment. Citing many reviews of the research literature, Anthony and Cohen (1990) reported that little or no relationship exists between rehabilitation outcome and psychiatric diagnostic labels or descriptions of clients' symptom patterns. For example, Townes and colleagues (1985) classified psychiatric clients into six groups, according to their unique pattern of strengths and deficits, and found that the classification was essentially independent of reported psychiatric symptomatology and diagnosis. Similar results were reported by Dellario et al., (1984). They correlated 16 different symptom measures with 19 different measures of function taken on the same psychiatric inpatients. Only eight of the 304 correlations were statistically significant. There was no discernible pattern. A number of other studies illustrate the lack of relationship between a variety of assessments of psychiatric symptomatology and future ability to live and work independently (e.g., Gaebel & Pietzcker, 1987; Möller, von Zerssen, Werner-Eilert, & Wuschenr-Stockheim, 1982; Strauss & Carpenter, 1972, 1974). Although occasional studies do report a relationship between a type of symptom and rehabilitation outcome (McGlashan, 1987), the overwhelming majority do not. Even the belief that persons with bipolar affective disorder have drastically better rehabilitation outcomes than those with many other psychiatric impairments has been questioned. Rehabilitation outcomes for persons with multiple hospital admissions due to bipolar affective disorder approximate the rehabilitation outcomes of persons with multiple hospitalizations due to schizophrenia (Dion, Cohen, Anthony, & Waternaux, 1988).

Psychiatric Diagnosis was not Designed to Give Direction to the Psychiatric Rehabilitation Process   The goal of a psychiatric diagnosis is to prescribe a course of treatment that will address an impairment. The psychiatric diagnosis allows the practitioner to assess impairment-related information provided by the client and others, and then to make a determination about the meaning of the information. The degree of client involvement in the diagnostic procedure is often a function of the perceived level of pathology. Less ill clients are more reliable informants about their history and symptomatology than are more ill clients. Since pathology is the focus of the assessment activities, it is reasonable that the role of the client be that of providing information whenever possible rather than participating in the analysis of the meaning of the information. The information can also be gathered from observations of the client or others' reports if the client is an insufficiently reliable source of information. The diagnosis can therefore be produced in a relatively brief time, over a number of interviews through data-gathering activities conducted by the treatment practitioner or team. The client's involvement in the diagnostic process is encouraged because good medical practice recognizes that compliance with treatment is increased when the client is more involved.

In psychiatric rehabilitation, the involvement and full participation of the person in the overall process is the sine qua non of the approach. The client is seen as the major participant in the process, and the effectiveness of the process is directly linked to the degree to which the person takes ownership of the goal, the assessment, the plan, and the interventions. The values of person orientation, self-determination, involvement, and environmental specificity (Table 2-2) require that the person be the driving force in not only the data-gathering process but also the analysis of the meaning of that data. A rehabilitation diagnosis derives its meaning from clients' choice of which role they want to play in a preferred environment. The rehabilitation diagnosis is *part* of the process, rather than a *precursor* to the process. The psychiatric rehabilitation diagnostic process is often completed over a lengthy period in order to ensure the active participation of even the most disabled client in choosing a goal and assessing skills and resources. The psychiatric rehabilitation diagnostic process conforms to the value system underlying the approach.

In summary, a review of practice in the field of mental health and the research literature suggests that psychiatric diagnosis provides a procedure and information that are not the critical information or procedure necessary to facilitate the rehabilitation process. A unique psychiatric rehabilitation diagnosis was needed to describe what people with severe psychiatric disabilities want and the extent to which they have the skills and resources to achieve their goals.

COMPONENTS OF A PSYCHIATRIC REHABILITATION DIAGNOSIS

The psychiatric rehabilitation diagnosis contains three components: an overall rehabilitation goal, a functional assessment, and a resource assessment (Anthony et al., 1990).

Overall Rehabilitation Goals

The overall rehabilitation goal identifies a particular environment in which the person chooses to live, learn, work, or socialize during the following 6 to 24 months (Cohen, Farkas, Cohen, & Unger, 1992). These four types of environments (i.e., living, learning, working, and social) are the focus of the goal-setting process because they are the types of environments many clients have been reported as wanting (e.g., Ball & Havassy, 1984; Hutchinson, Lord, Savage, & Schnarr, 1985; Ridgway, 1988). Some examples of overall or self-determined rehabilitation goals follow: "I intend to live with a roommate, in my own apartment by November." "I intend to complete my Certified Public Accountancy program by May." "I intend to work as a short-order cook at McDonalds restaurant until January." "I intend to serve as the treasurer of the Drop In Center until December." Clients may choose to stay in the current environment and work toward increasing their success and satisfaction there, or they may choose to move to another environment within the following year or two. The goal drives the rest of the rehabilitation process in that it is the basis upon which plans and interventions are made. The overall rehabilitation goal identifies, as much as possible, both the role and the specific setting preferred by the person. For example, the client intends not only to work in a restaurant—but to work as a "short-order cook at McDonald's" restaurant. This specificity helps to make the goal concrete and therefore more real to clients. It also provides clear guidelines against which clients can later assess whether or not they have the necessary skills and resources. The goal-setting process helps to answer the question Where does the client *want* to live, learn, work, or socialize in the next year or two? rather than the question Where *should* the client live, learn, work, or socialize in that period?

The necessity of setting overall rehabilitation goals as the initial phase of psychiatric rehabilitation is consistent with the philosophy of psychiatric rehabilitation and its emphasis on individualization, self-determination, and involvement (Anthony, 1982; Cnaan, Blankertz, Messinger, & Gardner, 1988). In general practice, clients are seldom asked about what services or assistance they need (Merwin & Ochberg, 1983). Not only are clients seldom asked about what they need or want, their assessment and those of their practitioners are often at odds. There is often little to no agreement on items as diverse as potential for recovery (Blackman, 1982); desired outcomes (Berzinz, Bednar, & Severy, 1975); rehabilitation issues (Leviton, 1973); perceptions of problems that contribute to the handicapping condition (Tichenor, Thomas, & Kravetz, 1975; Mitchell, Pyle, & Hatsukami, 1983); and the existence of skills (Dellario, Anthony, & Rogers, 1983). For example, Dimedale, Klerman, and Shershow (1979) studied a group of hospital clients in which the staff viewed "insight" as their primary goal. The clients, however, placed insight at the bottom of their list of goals. Dimsdale and his colleagues concluded that if there were a greater convergence of goals, clients might be more satisfied and their length of hospitalization might be reduced. Other research indicates that when clients' and therapists' goals are incongruent, they do not appear to profit from therapy, are disappointed with their care, and often fail to comply with the rest of their treatment activities (Goin, Yamamoto, & Silverman, 1965; Lazare, Eisenthal, & Wasserman, 1975; Mitchell et al., 1983).

The reasons for not establishing clients' choices about their needs or goals seem to stem from the prevailing belief that clients are unable to make decisions or choices. Some authors suggest that the inability of clients to make choices is related to the treatment environments in which they are placed. For example, Ryan (1976) suggests that the treatment environment itself can take away the clients' abilities to make important life decisions and that the process of institutionalization results in a loss of initiative, an assumption of deviant values, and an inability to make decisions (Schmieding, 1968; Goffman, 1961).

Others hold the view that the lack of decision-making ability or goal setting is inherent in the pathology of mental illness. The three major groupings of problems associated with schizophrenia, for example, include positive symptoms, negative symptoms, and disordered relationships. Of these three, negative symptoms (which include withdrawal, lack of motivation, and lack of goal-directed behavior) are the ones considered to be prognostically most important and are viewed as the source or results of chronicity (Keith & Matthews, 1984; Strauss, Carpenter, & Bartko, 1974; American Psychiatric Association, 1987).

Apart from the conflicting opinions about why clients have not been involved in making their own choices or stating their own needs, there is little disagreement that setting goals is important, in and of itself (Locke, Shaw, Saari, & Latham, 1981; Carkhuff & Anthony, 1979). Some research evidence exists that goal setting itself impacts outcome (Smith, 1976) and that the attainment of goals affects satisfaction and recidivism (Willer & Miller, 1978).

Setting goals from the clients' perspective has neither been well understood nor become common practice in mental health (Holroyd & Goldenberg, 1978; Farkas, Cohen, & Nemec, 1988). To respond to this lack in the field, the Center for Psychiatric Rehabilitation developed a technology to assist in enabling clients to make such choices. The technology for setting overall rehabilitation goals was developed so that even persons with severe psychiatric disabilities could participate (Cohen et al., 1992). Each component of the technology is derived from an analysis of research results.

The goal is established through a series of interviews designed to first help clients understand their own criteria for making a choice. Clients' judgments about the degree of fit between a setting and their own preferences have been shown to be strongly related to outcomes, as measured by levels of functioning and adaptation (Coulton, Holland, & Fitch, 1984). This finding held even for instances in which raters viewed the consumer's judgment as unrealistic. Segal, Everett-Dille, and Moyles (1979) demonstrated that a person's perceptions about the quality of the environment was the strongest predictor of increased participation in that environment, regardless of the perceptions of the staff.

In addition to identifying personal criteria, the goal-setting technology is designed to help clients become knowledgeable about alternative environments. Successful problem solving has been linked to the degree to which the person making the choice fully understands the alternatives. Lastly, the technology assists clients in completing a structured decision-making process. In nonclinical literature, the choice of a goal seems to have some relationship to the presence of a supportive person (Locke et al., 1981; Hannon, 1975). A supportive person, according to these studies, appears to be one who listens to what is being said, demonstrates understanding, and asks encouraging questions. Several authors in the clinical literature have described the skills needed by practitioners to provide this type of support in rehabilitation as well as in treatment relationships (Carkhuff & Anthony, 1979; Goering & Stylianos, 1988; Anthony et al., 1990). These "connecting skills" have been incorporated into the goal-setting technology (Cohen et al., 1992) so that both consumer and practitioner may enter into a collaborative relationship as a means of setting mutually agreed upon goals.

Functional Assessment

After determining where the client wants to live, learn, work, or socialize, the diagnostic process next focuses on answering the question What critical skills does the person have or need in order to be successful and satisfied in that environment? Functional assessment is an evaluation of the physical, emotional, and/or intellectual skills necessary to achieve the overall rehabilitation goal. The assessment describes the skills in observable terms and then measures the frequency with which the person performs these skills in the chosen environment (Cohen, Farkas, & Cohen, 1986). Functional assessment identifies, therefore, both strengths and deficits, rather than focusing on problems or deficits alone.

The importance of assessing functioning is not in dispute in the field. For example, in every study in which work adjustment skills were assessed, they were found to be significantly related to future work performance (e.g., Distefano & Pryer, 1970; Cheadle & Morgan, 1972; Griffiths, 1973; Watts, 1978).

Similarly, ratings of social disabilities or skills have also been found to predict vocational performance (Griffiths, 1974; Strauss & Carpenter, 1974). Despite the general consensus about the importance of conducting functional assessments, the majority of the methods used proved to be problematic. Anthony and Farkas (1982) reviewed instruments that have been used in outcome studies of psychiatric rehabilitation interventions, with a specific focus on research studies of skills training, drug therapy, and community support interventions. Thirty-one functional assessment procedures were reviewed in terms of who conducts the assessment, the presence of reliability and validity data, the client population on which the instrument was developed, and the primary reference source for information about the instrument. In general, the authors noted that the literature lacks specificity in the description of the instruments, the populations for which they are appropriate, their validity, and their reliability. Most of these instruments were developed out of specific institutional needs, as indeed are most functional assessment instruments, and reflect the unique interests and capacities of a particular setting rather than an individual's needs (Frey, 1984). Most functional assessments tend to operationalize behaviors in the physical and intellectual area much better than in the emotional-interpersonal area of functioning (Cohen & Anthony, 1984). This problem is particularly glaring in psychiatric rehabilitation assessments because the target of the rehabilitation intervention is more likely to be in the emotional-interpersonal area.

Some researchers, in attempting to improve on existing instruments, have suggested that psychological and neuropsychological instruments be used with a rehabilitation perspective (Erickson & Binder, 1986). Rather than using these instruments to document psychiatric illnesses, positive symptoms, and organicity, neuropsychological tests have been viewed as helpful in profiling a person's cognitive competencies and deficits, among other intellectual competencies, with obvious implications for rehabilitation interventions (Townes et al., 1985). In general, however, the many instruments that now are available to evaluate overall functioning and resources have, unfortunately, proved more useful to researchers and program evaluators than to practitioners because of their lack of specificity and individualization (Anthony et al., 1987).

Liberman (1982) has categorized five different kinds of assessment technology used in assessing social skill: (a) self-report questionnaires; (b) interviews; (c) naturalistic in vivo observations; (d) role-play situations; and (e) permanent products of interactions. A psychiatric rehabilitation functional assessment uses these same methods not only for social skills but also for intrapersonal skills, intellectual skills, and physical skills. The technology developed for conducting a functional assessment involves a series of interviews and observations that involve the person in identifying the skills that are critical from the perspective of the preferred environment as well as those that are critical from the person's own perspective (Cohen et al., 1986). The interviews require practitioners to use their ability to orient the clients to the assessment tasks and demonstrate empathy or understanding of clients' perspective as well as the more traditional skills of asking questions and making observational comments. Table 1-4 presents an example of the end product of this process.

Just as an assessment of the client's skills is critical for later skill development, a resource assessment is crucial to developing the person's supports. A resource is a person, place, object, or activity that is supportive to the person's achievement

Table 1-4   A Functional Assessment.

Assets (+) Deficits (−)		Skill Functioning[b]					
		Spontaneous Use		Prompted Use		Performance	
± Critical Skills[a]	Skill Use Descriptions	Present Use	Needed Use	Yes	No	Yes	No
	***Overall Rehabilitation Goal for Joan:*** **Joan wants to live in the Pine Valley Supervised Apartments for the next year.**
− Organizing Tasks	Number of weeks per month Joan writes a "task by timeline" list after residential chore assignment meetings	0	4	—	X	—	X
+ Scheduling Appointments	Percentage of times per month Joan arranges a date and time for a service provider visit when her schedule indicates that the agreed-upon interval since the last service provider's visit has elapsed	90%	90%	—	—	—	—
− Requesting Social Contacts	Percentage of times per month Joan asks someone to spend time with her, when she has no other activities planned	0%	50%	X	—	—	—
− Offering Help	Percentage of times per month Joan asks if she can help when other residents request assistance	25%	75%	—	—	—	—

Client agreed to assessment and initialed.

[a]The client's skill level is evaluated in three different ways. Spontaneous Use indicates the highest present frequency of appropriate use in the chosen environment as compared to what is needed or required in that environment. Prompted Use indicates whether a client can (Yes) of cannot (No) perform the skill at least once in the chosen environment. Performance indicates whether a client can (Yes) or cannot (No) perform the skill in a simulated environment. These last two evaluations are done only if the present level of spontaneous functioning is 0.

Note. From Cohen, M. R., Farkas, M. D., & Cohen, B. F. (1986). *Psychiatric Rehabilitation Training Technology: Functional Assessment* (Trainer Package). Boston: Center *for Psychiatric Rehabilitation.*

Table 1-5 Example: Resource Assessment.

			Resource Evaluation[b]					
			Resource Actual Use		Resource Available		Resource Exist	
Assets(+) Deficits(−)	Critical Resources[a]	Resource Use Description	Present Use	Needed Use	Yes	No	Yes	No
Overall Rehabilitation Goal: **Joan wants to live in the Pine Valley Supervised Apartments for the next year**								
+	Empathic Residential Counselor	Percentage of times per week Joan's supervisor paraphrases Joan's feelings and the reasons for those feelings when Joan stops doing her morning chores and stares at the ceiling	60%	60%				
−	Supplementary Food Coupons	Number of times per month the residential counselor issues supplementary food coupons to Joan at the beginning of the week, before food shopping has been scheduled	0	4	x			

[a]Client agreed to assessment and initialed.

[b]Resources are evaluated in three ways. Resource Use indicates the highest present level of spontaneous delivery to the client of the resource in the chosen environment as compared to what is needed or required in that environment. Resource Availability indicates whether a resource is willing or available (Yes) or not (No) to provide the described support in the chosen environment. Resource Existence indicates whether a resource exists at all (Yes) or not (No) to provide the described support in the chosen environment. These last two evaluations are done if the present level of resource use is 0.

Note. Adapted from Cohen, M.R., Farkas, M.D., & Cohen, B. F., *Phyciatric Rehabilitation Training Technology: Functional Assessment.* Copyright 1991 by Center for Psychiatric Rehabilitation, Boston University. Adapted by permission.

of the overall rehabilitation goal. The process of conducting a resource assessment is similar to that of conducting a functional assessment. The person is engaged in identifying the resources that are critical to success and satisfaction. The resource is described in observable terms. The description of the resource involves an observable and specific statement that clarifies the use of the support and the circumstances of the use of the support. The resource is then evaluated, as described, using in vivo procedures. Table 1-5 presents an example of the end product of this process.

REHABILITATION PLANNING

Rehabilitation planning is the second phase of the psychiatric rehabilitation process. Planning is a systematic process resulting in practitioner and client agreement about the rehabilitation interventions needed to achieve an overall rehabilitation goal. The rehabilitation plan suggests a strategy for developing the skills and supports needed to ensure success and satisfaction in a particular environment (Anthony et al., 1983; Anthony et al., 1982).

Rehabilitation planning responds to four basic problems that arose in the attempt to use traditional service plans for rehabilitation purposes. These problems were the following: (a) traditional plans often reflect a confusion about the definition of rehabilitation services; (b) traditional plans typically reflect the agency's program philosophy and expertise, rather than a systematic rehabilitation process; (c) traditional planning is often an event rather than a process; and (d) traditional plans often do not reflect the relationship between the prescribed interventions and the attainment of an overall goal.

Traditional Plans Often Reflect a Confusion about the Definition of Rehabilitation Services   It is not uncommon for treatment, basic support, enrichment, case management, and other services to be described in a plan as rehabilitation. Rehabilitation problems that are described in the plan often are to be addressed by other service interventions. The outcome of these other interventions is not necessarily resolution of the original rehabilitation problem. For example, a plan may indicate that a hospitalized young woman wants to return to the community but is unclear about where to live. This "rehabilitation plan" may prescribe psychotherapy. This treatment service is not likely to assist the client in getting sufficient experience of herself and the possible alternatives that exist in order to make a sound residential decision.

The outcome of rehabilitation is separate and distinct from the outcomes of other service interventions.

Rehabilitation is an environmentally specific service that focuses on developing the skills and supports needed for success and satisfaction in a chosen environment (Cohen et al., 1989). Rehabilitation is different from other services in its mission, focus, and activities (rehabilitation is compared to other services in Table 1-6). The outcomes differ as well. Basic support services are designed to ensure safety and survival. Enrichment services are designed to enhance quality of life and general satisfaction. Treatment is designed to stabilize and provide relief. Rehabilitation is designed to help people to achieve valued roles in society. Psychiatric treatment and rehabilitation services are ideally provided simultaneously (Anthony et al., 1990), and can be delivered by the same program. However, it is important for the practitioner to understand the difference between services in order to prescribe the appropriate interventions.

Traditional Plans Typically Reflect the Agency's Program Philosophy and Expertise, Rather than a Systematic Rehabilitation Process   Plans may vary as a result of differing program philosophy (Paul & Lentz, 1977; Pelletier, Rogers, & Thurer, 1985; Mitchell et al., 1983). The goals, objectives, and methods

Table 1-6   Key Services That Can Be Provided by Psychiatric Facilities

	Basic Support	Treatment	Psychiatric Rehabilitation	Enrichment
Mission:	Maintains and/or gains for clients the things required for survival	Decreases clients' emotional distress and symptoms of illness	Increases clients' success and satisfaction in environments of their choice with the least amount of professional help	Achieves and maintains a satisfactory quality of life for clients
Focus	Providing the things required for survival	Reducing symptoms	Developing skills and supports	Enjoyment and self-development
Activities	• Financial support • Providing shelter • Meals • Clothing • Health care • Protecting physical safety	• Psychiatric diagnosis • Treatment planning • Psychotherapy • Chemotherapy	• Setting an overall rehabilitation goal • Functional assessment • Resource assessment • Rehabilitation planning • Skills teaching • Skills programming • Resource coordination • Resource modification	• Socialization • Continuing education • Health promotion • Leisure-time activities

Note. From Cohen, M.R.,Nemec, P.B., Farkas, M.D., & Forbess, R. (1989). *Psychiatric Rehabilitation Training Technology: Case Management* (Tainer Package). Boston: Boston University, Center for Psychiatric Rehabilitation. Copyright 1991 by Center for Psychiatric Rehabilitation, Boston University. Adapted by permission.

of a plan often provide an indication of a program's underlying philosophy. For example, how the plan refers to the client ("patient," "consumer," "resident") may reflect a philosophical orientation. Also, the most cited interventions on the plan tend to indicate the particular expertise of the practitioners (such as skill teaching, milieu therapy, psychotherapy). Since there is often no overt value base to service plans, the choice of specific priority objectives and interventions is often standardized rather than individualized.

On the other hand, the rehabilitation planning process is value driven. The ideal rehabilitation plan systematically reflects the key values of the rehabilitation approach (Table 1-2). First, it emphasizes *self-determination.* All rehabilitation plans are developed as a result of clients' specific decision to try to achieve their desired goal. Second, based on the value of *involvement,* clients are primary participants in the planning process, rather than simple signatories to an already-decided service plan. Third, the plan focuses on *functioning,* or the performance of everyday activities. Rehabilitation plans specify particular interventions that enable clients to increase the use of physical, emotional, and intellectual skills needed in actual "real-life" environments. Fourth, the plan is *environmentally specific.* Guided by the overall goal or the choice of environment in which clients want to live, learn, work, or socialize, the plan identifies specific interventions designed to maximize success and satisfaction there. This value *individualizes* the plan and assures that the interventions chosen are not simply the standard menu of activities offered in a program. For example, learning to negotiate conflict is a helpful rehabilitation intervention only if it allows a client to negotiate conflict in a real-life environment more effectively and if the lack of negotiation skills on the person's part has led to specific difficulties with environmental demands or personal satisfaction. Finally, the plan is *outcome oriented* and focuses on interventions that are designed to meet the requirements of significant others in the clients, world, as well as the requirements for the clients' own satisfaction. The objectives of the plan are not, therefore, participation in the intervention. The psychiatric rehabilitation plan is concerned with behaviors demonstrated as a result of an intervention. For example, a traditional plan and a rehabilitation plan may state the following objectives:

> Traditional objective: Joe W. will attend the assertiveness skills class two times per week.
> Rehabilitation objective: Joe W. will ask his boss for clarification when he is unclear about a particular request.

The rehabilitation objective may require Joe W. to attend the assertiveness class two times per week. It is the outcome of that class in relation to Joe's job, however, that concerns the rehabilitation practitioner during planning. Personal satisfaction is an important rehabilitation outcome. A client's lack of motivation to "follow through" on a rehabilitation plan may be due to the plan's lack of appeal. If clients cannot clearly identify their potential satisfaction in the expected outcomes of the plan, it may be difficult for them to become engaged in implementing the plan. Lastly, the timelines for support in a rehabilitation plan reflect the provision of assistance for as long as it is needed and wanted. A client's success is obtained through a combination of increased functioning and dependence on supports needed to ensure success. Support goals suggest the involvement of significant others. For example, organizing prescribed medications may require ongoing emotional support from a mental health professional, family member, or peer. Giving emotional and interpersonal support specifically to assist with medication compliance may be a necessary intervention, and as such is included in the plan. Also, the support intervention may not have a fixed timeline of 1 month, 3 months, or a year. It may be a support that is needed and wanted with varying amounts of intensity for an indeterminate amount of time. Rehabilitation resource development interventions may be open-ended in their use; however, they do require fixed timelines for review and revision.

Traditional Planning is Often an Event Rather than a Process   Traditional planning is often conceptualized as a meeting that is held at regular intervals. The activities of a planning meeting often include diagnosing client problems, debate and discussion on the reasons for client problems, and the development of strategies for resolving the client's problem. It is not unusual for a traditional planning meeting to include 20 minutes of diagnosis, 8 minutes of problem solving, and 2 minutes for planning. Rehabilitation planning occurs over time, and only after goals, strengths, and problems have been assessed.

Rehabilitation planning is a systematic process. It is more than a meeting held at regular intervals. It is, rather, a process that involves the client and practitioner in prescribing a set of interventions designed to ensure goal achievement. The actual planning activity incorporates the client in a process of selecting high-priority objectives, organizing responsibilities, and estimating timelines for monitoring and completion. In a systematic planning process, planning occurs after an assessment and before any skill or support development interventions begin. The planning process may take place over a series of meetings. Rehabilitation planning may be best incorporated into traditional planning meetings by using the time to update the team on the current status of a person's rehabilitation.

Traditional Plans Often do not Reflect the Relationship Between the Prescribed Interventions and the Attainment of an Overall Goal   The relationship between clients' goals and the interventions they receive is at times ambiguous. It is often difficult to determine how an intervention will actually result in the accomplishment of a goal. For example, a plan may state that "Joe M. will get a job." His planned intervention will be to "attend the vocational group." The plan may in addition state Joe's goal as "eventual placement into a structured residence." His corresponding intervention may state "attend and participate three times in an ADL group" (i.e., activities of daily living group). Traditional plans often describe how clients will complete program requirements rather than accomplish a personal goal. Achieving the overall rehabilitation goal is the primary reason for and focus of the rehabilitation plan.

Although strategies for skill and support development make up the core information on the rehabilitation plan, the underlying purpose for all of the planned objectives is to accomplish the overall rehabilitation goal (e.g., "I intend to live at Power Apartment through September"). The most important question being asked during the planning phase of rehabilitation is whether or not the objective indicated will result in successful goal achievement. The rehabilitation plan is designed to link the interventions with the assessment. The psychiatric

Table 1-7 A Rehabilitation Plan. *Overall Rehabilitation Goal for Joan:* **Joan wants to live in the Pine Valley Supervised Apartments for the next year**

Priority Skill/Resource Development Objective	Interventions	Person(s) Responsible	Starting Dates		Completion Dates
			Projected	Actual	
Joan asks if she can help 75% of the time when other residents request assistance	Skills programming	Provider: House counselor Monitor: Joan	Oct. 1	Oct. 1	Nov. 30
Joan writes a "task by timeline" list 4 weeks per month after residential chore assignment meetings	Direct skills teaching	Provider: House counselor Monitor: Staff	Nov. 15	Nov. 21	Jan. 2
The residential counselor issues supplementary food coupons four times per month at the beginning of the week before food shopping has been scheduled	Resource coordination	Provider: Department of Social Services Monitor: House counselor	Oct. 1	Oct. 10	Jan. 2

I participated in the development of this plan ___*Joan Lum*___

(client signature)

Note. Adapted from Anthony, W.A., Cohen, M.R., & Farkas, M.D., *Psychiatric Rehabilitation.* Copyright 1991 by Center for Psychiatric Rehabilitation, Boston University.

rehabilitation plan connects the assessed skill and support deficits with corresponding interventions. The interventions are designed to increase client's skill functioning and provide the exact support necessary to achieve the overall rehabilitation goal. The interventions prescribed on a plan must accurately reflect the opportunity to overcome specific deficits impeding a client's success. Table 1-7 illustrates a rehabilitation plan with its specified overall rehabilitation goal, the objectives that address the assessed deficits, and the planned interventions.

When one is conducting rehabilitation planning, it is important to note that not all interventions may already exist in a program. Rehabilitation planning is not a process of fitting the person's objectives into the set menu of program activities offered by an agency. If rehabilitation plans are to relate genuinely to rehabilitation goal achievement, they may require program administrators to develop additional rehabilitation interventions.

THE COMPONENTS OF A PSYCHIATRIC REHABILITATION PLAN

The psychiatric rehabilitation plan contains four components. They are high-priority skill and/or resource objectives, personnel responsibilities, timelines, and a monitoring plan.

Selecting High-Priority Skill and Resource Objectives

Selecting priority skill and resource objectives allows clients to participate in those interventions that are most critical to the accomplishment of their overall rehabilitation goal. A comprehensive assessment of strengths and deficits may describe an overwhelming number of skill and support deficits. Assigning priorities to the deficits allows the client and practitioner to disregard unessential skill and support deficits. Objectives are developed for only those deficits that most influence the client's success and satisfaction in a particular environment. These criteria for selecting high-priority objectives include urgency, client motivation, available support, and the client's present ability. Assigning priorities suggests which interventions will occur immediately and which will occur at a later date.

Organizing Responsibilities

Organizing responsibilities allows the client to understand who will be responsible for delivering each skill or support development intervention. An agreement is reached by the client, program personnel, and any significant others who plan to participate in the rehabilitation interventions about each of the identified responsibilities.

Projecting Timelines

Projecting timelines gives the client and practitioner an estimated schedule for achieving rehabilitation milestones. Timelines suggest the duration of a skill or support development intervention. Timelines provide the client with a sense of when an intervention will begin and how long each intervention will last.

Monitoring the Plan

Monitoring the plan involves at least one person's being responsible for determining the plan's progress and continued relevance over time. The monitor ensures that interventions begin and end according to the timelines. If problems arise in the timelines, the monitor ensures that revisions are discussed and the plan is altered. The monitor further ensures that periodic meetings are held to discuss the ongoing progress and outcomes of the interventions so that relevant revisions can be made in a timely fashion.

CONCLUSION

This chapter has presented an overview of the psychiatric rehabilitation philosophy and process. It has contrasted psychiatric assessment and traditional planning procedures with those of a psychiatric rehabilitation approach. An increase in clarity about what psychiatric rehabilitation is and is not will hopefully result in the development of more focused rehabilitation services for persons with severe psychiatric disabilities.

REFERENCES

Allen, R., & Velasco, F. (1980). An inpatient setting: The contribution of a rehabilitation approach. *Rehabilitation Counseling Bulletin, 23,* 108–117.

American Psychiatric Association. (1987). *Diagnostic and statistical manual of mental disorders* (3rd ed.—rev.). Washington, DC: Author.

Anthony, W. A. (1979). *The principles of psychiatric rehabilitation.* Baltimore: University Park Press.

Anthony, W. A. (1980). A rehabilitation model for rehabilitating the psychiatrically disabled. *Rehabilitation Counseling Bulletin, 24,* 6–21.

Anthony, W. A. (1982). Explaining "psychiatric rehabilitation" by an analogy to "physical rehabilitation." *Psychosocial Rehabilitation Journal, 5* (1), 61–65.

Anthony, W. A., Buell, G. J., Sharratt, S., & Althoff, M. E. (1972). Efficacy of psychiatric rehabilitation. *Psychological Bulletin, 78,* 447–456.

Anthony, W. A., Cohen, M. R., & Cohen, B. F. (1983) Philosophy, treatment process, and principles of the psychiatric rehabilitation approach. In L. L. Bachrach (Ed.), *Deinstitutionalization* (New Directions for Mental Health Services, No. 17, pp. 67–69). San Francisco: Jossey-Bass.

Anthony, W. A., Cohen, M. R., & Cohen, B. F. (1984). Psychiatric rehabilitation. In J. A. Talbott (Ed.), *The chronic mental client: Five years later* (pp. 137–157). Orlando, FL: Grune & Stratton.

Anthony, W. A., Cohen, M. R., & Farkas, M. D. (1982). A psychiatric rehabilitation treatment program: Can I recognize one if I see one? *Community Mental Health Journal, 18,* 83–96.

Anthony, W. A., Cohen, M. R., & Farkas, M. D. (1990). *Psychiatric rehabilitation.* Boston: Boston University, Center for Psychiatric Rehabilitation.

Anthony, W. A., Cohen, M. R., & Nemec, P. B. (1987). Assessment in psychiatric rehabilitation. In B. Bolton (Ed.), *Handbook of measurement and evaluation in rehabilitation* (pp. 299–312). Baltimore: Paul Brookes.

Anthony, W. A., Cohen, M. R., & Vitalo, R. L. (1978). The measurement of rehabilitation outcome. *Schizophrenia Bulletin, 4,* 365–383.

Anthony, W. A., & Farkas, M. D. (1982). A client outcome planning model for assessing psychiatric rehabilitation interventions. *Schizophrenia Bulletin, 8,* 13–38.

Anthony, W. A., & Jansen, M. A. (1984). Predicting the vocational capacity of the chronically mentally ill: Research and policy implications. *American Psychologist, 39,* 537–544.

Anthony, W. A., Kennard, W. A., O'Brien, W., & Forbess, R. (1986). Psychiatric rehabilitation: Past myths and current realities. *Community Mental Health Journal, 22,* 249–264.

Anthony, W. A., & Liberman, R. P. (1986). The practice of psychiatric rehabilitation: Historical, conceptual, and research base. *Schizophrenia Bulletin, 12,* 542–559.

Anthony, W. A., & Nemec, P. B. (1984). Psychiatric rehabilitation. In A. S. Bellack (Ed.), *Schizophrenia: Treatment, management, and rehabilitation* (pp. 375–413). Orlando, FL: Grune & Stratton.

Bachrach, L. L. (1982). Program planning for young adult chronic clients. In B. Pepper & H. Ryglewicz (Eds.), *The young adult chronic client* (New Directions for Mental Health Services, No. 14, p. 254). San Francisco: Jossey-Bass.

Ball, J., & Havassy, B. (1984). A survey of the problem and needs of homeless consumers of acute psychiatric services. *Hospital and Community Psychiatry, 35*(9), 917–921.

Beard, J. H., Propst, R. N., & Malamud, T. J. (1982). The Fountain House model of psychiatric rehabilitation. *Psychosocial Rehabilitation Journal, 5*(1), 47–53.

Berzinz, J. I., Bednar, R. L., & Severy, L. J. (1975). The problem of intersource consensus in measuring therapeutic outcomes: New data and multivariate perspectives. *Journal of Clinical Psychology, 84*(1), 10–19.

Blackman, S. (1982). Paraprofessional and client assessment criteria of client's recovery: Why the discrepancy? *Journal of Clinical Psychology, 37*(4), 903–907.

Carkhuff, R. R., & Anthony, W. A. (1979). *The skills of helping: An introduction to counseling skills.* Amherst, MA: Human Resource Development Press.

Cheadle, A. J., & Morgan, R. (1972). The measurement of work performance of psychiatric clients: A reappraisal. *British Journal of Psychiatry, 120,* 437–441.

Cnaan, R. A., Blankertz, L., Messinger, K. W., & Gardner, J. R. (1988). Psychosocial rehabilitation: Toward a definition. *Psychosocial Rehabilitation Journal, 11*(4), 61–77.

Cohen, B. F., & Anthony, W. A. (1984). Functional assessment in psychiatric rehabilitation. In A. S. Halpern & M. J. Fuhrer (Eds.), *Functional assessment in rehabilitation* (pp. 79–100). Baltimore: Paul Brookes.

Cohen, M. R. (1989). Integrating psychiatric rehabilitation into mental health systems. In M. D. Farkas & W. A. Anthony (Eds.), *Psychiatric rehabilitation programs: Putting theory into practice* (pp. 162–170, 188–191). Baltimore: Johns Hopkins University Press.

Cohen, M. R., Anthony, W. A., & Farkas, M. D. (1991). Tertiary prevention: Psychiatric rehabilitation. In C. Hudson & A. Cox (Eds.), *Dimensions of state mental health policy.* New York: Praeger.

Cohen, M. R., Farkas, M. D., & Cohen, B. F. (1986). *Psychiatric rehabilitation training technology: Functional assessment* (Trainer Package). Boston: Center for Psychiatric Rehabilitation.

Cohen, M. R., Farkas, M. D., Cohen, B. F., & Unger, K. V. (1992). *Psychiatric rehabilitation training technology: Setting an overall rehabilitation goal* (Trainer Package). Boston: Boston University, Center for Psychiatric Rehabilitation.

Cohen, M. R., Nemec, P. B., Farkas, M. D., & Forbess, R. (1989). *Psychiatric rehabilitation training technology; Case management* (Trainer Package). Boston: Boston University, Center for Psychiatric Rehabilitation.

Coulton, C. L., Holland, T. P., & Fitch, V. (1984). Person-environment congruence and psychiatric client outcome in community care homes. *Administration in Mental Health, 12,* 71–88.

Craig, T., Peer, S., & Ross, M. (1989). Psychiatric rehabilitation in a state hospital transitional residence. In M. Farkas & W. Anthony (Eds.), *Psychiatric rehabilitation programs: Putting theory into practice* (pp. 57–69). Baltimore: Johns Hopkins University Press.

Danley, K. S., Rogers, E. S., & Nevas, D. (1989). A vocational rehabilitation approach to psychiatric rehabilitation. In M. D. Farkas & W. A. Anthony (Eds.), *Psychiatric

Rehabilitation Programs: Putting Theory into Practice (pp. 83–95). Baltimore: Johns Hopkins University Press.

Dellario, D. J., Anthony, W. A., & Rogers, E. S. (1983). Client-practitioner agreement in the assessment of severely psychiatrically disabled persons' functional skills. *Rehabilitation Psychology, 28,* 243–248.

Dellario, D. J., Goldfield, E., Farkas, M. D., & Cohen, M. R. (1984). Functional assessment of psychiatrically disabled adults: Implications of research findings for functional skills training. In A. S. Halpern & M. J. Fuhrer (Eds.), *Functional assessment in rehabilitation* (pp. 239–252). Baltimore: Paul Brookes.

Dimsdale, J., Klerman, G., & Shershow, J. (1979). Conflict in treatment goals between clients and staff. *Social Psychiatry, 14,* 1–4.

Dion, G. L., & Anthony, W. A. (1987). Research in psychiatric rehabilitation: A review of experimental and quasi-experimental studies. *Rehabilitation Counseling Bulletin, 30,* 177–203.

Dion, G. L., & Cohen, M. R., Anthony, W. A., & Waternaux, C. S. (1988). Symptoms and functioning of clients with bipolar disorder six months after hospitalization. *Hospital and Community Psychiatry, 39,* 652–657.

Distefano, M. K., & Pryer, M. W. (1970). Vocational evaluation and successful placement of psychiatric clients in a vocational rehabilitation program. *American Journal of Occupational Therapy, 24,* 205–207.

Erickson, R. C., & Binder, L. M. (1986). Cognitive deficits among functionally psychotic clients: A rehabilitative perspective. *Journal of Clinical and Experimental Neuropsychology, 8,* 257–274.

Farkas, M. D., Anthony, W. A., & Cohen, M. R. (1989). Psychiatric rehabilitation: The approach and its programs. In M. D. Farkas & W. A. Anthony (Eds.), *Psychiatric rehabilitation programs: Putting theory into practice* (pp. 1–27). Baltimore: Johns Hopkins University Press.

Farkas, M. D., Cohen, M. R., & Nemec, P. B. (1988). Psychiatric rehabilitation programs: Putting concepts into practice. *Community Mental Health Journal, 24,* 7–21.

Frey, W. D. (1984). Functional assessment in the 80s: A conceptual enigma, a technical challenge. In A. S. Halpern & M. J. Fuhrer (Eds.), *Functional assessment in rehabilitation* (pp. 11–43). Baltimore: Paul Brookes.

Funk, R. (1987). Disability rights: From caste to class in the context of civil rights. In A. Gartern & T. Joe (Eds.), *Images of the disabled, disabling images* (pp. 7–30). New York: Praeger.

Gaebel, W., & Pietzcker, A. (1987). Prospective study of course of illness in schizophrenia: Part II: Prediction of outcome. *Schizophrenia Bulletin, 13,* 299–306.

Goering, P. N., & Stylianos, S. K. (1988). Exploring the helping relationship between the schizophrenic client and rehabilitation therapist. *American Journal of Orthopsychiatry, 58*(2), 271–280.

Goffman, E. (1961). *Asylums: Essays on the social situation of mental clients and other inmates.* Garden City, NY: Doubleday-Anchor.

Goin, M., Yamamoto, J., & Silverman, J. (1965). Therapy congruent with class linked expectations. *Archives of General Psychiatry, 133,* 455–470.

Griffiths, R. (1974). Rehabilitation of chronic psychotic clients. *Psychological Medicine, 4,* 316–325.

Griffiths, R. D. (1973). A standardized assessment of the work behavior of psychiatric clients. *British Journal of Psychiatry, 123,* 403–408.

Grob, S. (1983). Psychosocial rehabilitation centers: Old wine in a new bottle. In I. Barofsky & R. D. Budson (Eds.), *The chronic psychiatric client in the community: Principles of treatment* (pp. 265–280). Jamaica, NY: Spectrum Publications.

Hannon, R. (1975). *The effects of participation in goal-setting on goal acceptance and performance: A laboratory experiment.* Unpublished doctoral dissertation, University of Maryland, College Park.

Holroyd, J., & Goldenberg, I. (1978). The use of goal attainment scaling to evaluate a ward-treatment program for disturbed children. *Journal of Clinical Psychology, 34,* 732–739.

Hutchinson, P., Lord, J., Savage, H., & Schnarr, A. (1985). Synthesizing the interests of consumers, citizens and administrators in gathering client feedback. *Evaluation and Program, 2,* 263–267.

Keith, S. J., & Matthews, S. M. (1984). Research overview. In J. A. Talbott (Ed.), *The chronic mental client: Five years later* (pp. 7–13). Orlando, FL: Grune & Stratton.

Lamb, H. R. (1982). *Treating the long term mentally ill.* San Francisco: Jossey-Bass.

Lazare, A., Eisenthal, S., & Wasserman, L. (1975). The customer approach to patienthood: Attending to client requests in a walk-in clinic. Archives of General Psychiatry, 32, 553–558.

Leitner, L., & Drasgow, J. (1972). Battling recidivism. *Journal of Rehabilitation,* July/August, 29–31.

Leviton, G. (1973). Professional and client viewpoints on rehabilitation issues. *Rehabilitation Psychology, 20,* 1–80.

Liberman, R. P. (1982). Assessment of social skills. *Schizophrenia Bulletin, 8,* 62–83.

Locke, E. A., Shaw, K. N., Saari, L. M., & Latham, G. P. (1981). Goal setting and task performance: 1969–1980. *Psychological Bulletin, 90,* 125–152.

McGlashan, T. H. (1987). Recovery style from mental illness and long-term outcome. *The Journal of Nervous and Mental Disease, 175,* 681–685.

Merwin, M., & Ochberg, R. (1983). The long voyage: Policies for progress in mental health. *Health Affairs, 2*(4), 96–127.

Miles, P. G. (1967). A research-based approach to psychiatric rehabilitation. In L. M. Roberts (Ed.), *The role of vocational rehabilitation in community mental health.* Washington, DC: Rehabilitation Services Administration.

Mitchell, J. E., Pyle, R. L., & Hatsukami, D. (1983). A comparative analysis of psychiatric problems listed by clients and physicians. *Hospital and Community Psychiatry, 34*(9), 848–849.

Möller, H., von Zerssen, D., Werner-Eilert, K., & Wuschenr-Stockheim, M. (1982). Outcome in schizophrenic and similar paranoid psychoses. *Schizophrenic Bulletin, 8,* 99–108.

Parrish, J. (1988). Consumer movement: A personal perspective. *Community Support Network News, 5*(2), 1–3.

Paul, G. L., & Lentz, R. J. (1977). *Psychosocial treatment of chronic mental clients: Milieu versus social learning programs.* Cambridge, MA: Harvard University Press.

Pelletier, J. R., Rogers, E. S., & Thurer, S. (1985). The mental health needs of individuals with severe physical disability: A consumer advocate perspective. *Rehabilitation Literature, 46,* 186–193.

Ridgway, P. (1988). *The voice of consumers in mental health systems: A call for change.* Unpublished manuscript, Boston University, Center for Psychiatric Rehabilitation, Boston.

Ryan, W. (1976). *Blaming the victim.* New York: Vintage Books.

Schmieding, N. J. (1968). Institutionalization: A conceptual approach. *Perspectives in Psychiatric Care, 6,*(5), 205–211.

Segal, S., Everett-Dille, L., & Moyles, E. (1979). Congruent perceptions in the evaluation of community care facilities. *Journal of Community Psychology, 7,* 60–68.

Smith, D. L. (1976). Goal attainment scaling as an adjunct to counseling. *Journal of Counseling Psychology, 23,* 22–27.

Strauss, J. S. (1986). Discussion: What does rehabilitation accomplish? *Schizophrenia Bulletin, 12,* 720–723.

Strauss, J. S., & Carpenter, W. T. (1972). The prediction of outcome in schizophrenia: I. Characteristics of outcome. *Archives of General Psychiatry, 27,* 739–746.

Strauss, J. S., & Carpenter, W. T. (1974). The prediction of outcome in schizophrenia: II. Relationships between predictor and outcome variables. *Archives of General Psychiatry, 31,* 37–42.

Strauss, J. S., Carpenter, W. T., & Bartko, J. J. (1974). Part III. Speculation on the processes that underlie schizophrenic symptoms and signs. *Schizophrenia Bulletin, 11,* 61–69.

Stubbins, J. (1982). The clinical attitude in rehabilitation: A cross-cultural view. *World Rehabilitation Fund Monograph, 16.* New York: World Rehabilitation Fund.

Tichenor, D., Thomas, K., & Kravetz, S. (1975). Client counselor congruence in perceiving handicapping problems. *Rehabilitation Counseling Bulletin, 19,* 299–304.

Townes, B. D., Martin, D. C., Nelson, D., Prosser, R., Pepping, M., Maxwell, J., Peel, J., & Preston, M. (1985). Neurobehavioral approach to classification of psychiatric clients using a competency model. *Journal of Consulting and Clinical Psychology, 53,* 33–42.

Turner, J. E., & TenHoor, W. J. (1978). The NIMH Community Support Program: Pilot approach to a needed social reform. *Schizophrenia Bulletin, 4,* 319–348.

Ward, M. (1988). *The many factors of self-determination: Transition summary.* Washington, DC: National Information Center for Children and Youth with Handicaps.

Watts, F. N. (1978). A study of work behavior in a psychiatric rehabilitation unit. *British Journal of Social and Clinical Psychology, 17,* 85–92.

Willer, B., & Miller, G. (1978). On the relationship of client satisfaction to client characteristics and outcome of treatment. *Journal of Clinical Psychology, 34,* 157–160.

Wood, P. H. (1980). Appreciating the consequence of disease: The classification of impairments, disability, and handicaps. *The WHO Chronicle, 34,* 376–380.

Chapter 2

Functional Assessment in Psychiatric Disability

Jerome Yoman and Barry A. Edelstein

"The overall goal of psychiatric rehabilitation is to assure that the person with a psychiatric disability can perform those physical, emotional, social and intellectual skills needed to live, learn, and work in the community, with the least amount of support necessary from agents of the helping professions" (Anthony, 1979, p. 30). Rehabilitation comprises three overlapping processes: (a) assessment, (b) planning, and (c) skill training. These three processes may be required repeatedly over the lifetime of an individual. Assessment occurs at the symptomatic, functional, and resource levels (Anthony, Cohen, & Cohen, 1983). Assessment at the functional level will be the focus of this chapter.

The initial client assessment may employ interviews, inventories, information from significant others, and direct observation of behavior in analogue or in vivo situations. The data derived from these assessments can then be contrasted with the skills required by the environment in which the client hopes to live and the support provided by that environment. A rehabilitation plan can then be constructed in concert with the client and, when appropriate, significant other individuals (e.g., family members). The purpose of the plan is to lay out the necessary skill development steps that will enable the client to function in the desired environment.

While numerous instruments and scales exist for the conduct of assessment (see Wallace, 1986), we will focus on the more individualized assessment that enables the clinician to establish target behaviors and develop focused skill-training programs. This form of assessment has been termed "functional assessment." Two related definitions have been applied to the term "functional assessment." The first definition characterizes functional assessment as the assessment of adaptive or independent living skills (e.g., Wallace, 1986). The second definition describes functional assessment as assessment of the stimuli and consequences that control behavior (also called "functional analysis"; see Hawkins, 1986). The principal focus of this chapter will be functional assessment of adaptive skills; a brief discussion of functional analysis as it is applied to maladaptive behaviors that can impede the rehabilitation process will follow.

SCOPE AND CONTEXT OF FUNCTIONAL ASSESSMENT

Functional assessment involves assumptions about established conceptual frameworks for understanding the behavior of psychiatrically disabled clients, which are explicated below.

Behavioral and Psychosocial Models

The behavioral and psychosocial models have been instrumental in the development of effective rehabilitation programs for individuals with major mental disorders (Liberman et al., 1987). Consequently, functional assessment draws upon and integrates these two models.

Each model has strengths and limitations. The behavioral model (see Hawkins, 1986; Levis, 1982) offers a demonstrated effective change technology. Its methods are disconfirmable because of emphasis on observable results and minimum inference in measurement. This allows refinement over training sessions/trials and adaptability to individual cases. The behavioral model focuses on the specification of behaviors (targets) and aspects of the environment that are involved in the control of the behavior (antecedents and consequences). Such specification facilitates assessment and focused intervention. An emphasis on the functional relationship between a behavior and its environment makes the assessment process very prescriptive since interventions are directed at this functional relationship. That is, interventions typically address the environmental antecedents and consequences of a target behavior.

Potential weaknesses of the behavioral model arise from variability in its application by clinicians. Some applications employ a myopic level of analysis and an oversimplified, single-linear-cause approach to clinical problems (Kanfer, 1985). One must be careful to include the multiple determinants of a behavior in an analysis. An oversimplified ABC model of analysis may be associated with a narrow range of behavior change across situations (Kanfer, 1985). The model may also be applied using ambiguous or poorly justified criteria for selection of targets (see Evans, 1985; Kanfer, 1985). One must keep in mind that these shortcomings are a function of the clinician who is applying the model and not a function of the model per se.

Among the psychosocial model's assets are its encouragement of a flexible level of analysis and its emphasis on both client and environmental change. Indeed, the psychosocial model encourages assessors to consider a broad range of potential target behaviors, including the actions and reactions of collateral persons toward the client (Liberman et al., 1987), and anticipate the impact of change in a target behavior upon the community context into which the client will be placed. The potential weaknesses of this model are that it is heavily conceptual, may lead to the specification of targets in a broad manner that makes them difficult to measure, and lacks a well-delineated change technology.

A combined behavioral psychosocial model provides useful and comprehensive assessment, which is the cornerstone of effective intervention. Such assessment (a) suggests specific focused interventions (i.e., is prescriptive); (b) gauges the effectiveness of interventions, allowing for their accountability, refinement, and disconfirmation; and (c) uses a flexible level of analysis, examining potentially complex causal relationships of all relevant treatment and community-living environments to client-adaptive behavior (cf. Anthony & Liberman, 1986; Liberman et al., 1987). Moreover, behavioral psychosocial assessment strategies focus on specific targets in both client behavior and environmental events.

Adaptiveness

In consistency with a behavioral psychosocial model, functional assessment emphasizes the adaptiveness rather than the abnormality of behavior. This means that a behavior does *not* become important to functional assessment because it is statistically rare, violates a particular set of social norms, or causes client suffering or distress (see Davison & Neale, 1986, for a discussion of definitions of abnormality). Rather, behaviors are important to functional assessment if they encourage or allow an individual's successful adaptation to a living, working, or learning environment (cf. Hawkins, 1986).

Inherent in this perspective is a constructive focus on desired behavior instead of undesired behavior (see targeting guidelines below). However, equating desired behavior with *normal* behavior provides a poor basis for functional assessment because the normal/abnormal continuum is typically *not* defined relative to environmental context. For example, judgments by any given observer may not follow the same social norms (as a result of socioeconomic class, ethnic, or other differences) as those of people in the client's living or working environment. Moreover, one may violate a number of social norms or behave in a statistically rare fashion and still adapt successfully (even exceptionally) to one's environment. Similarly, clients, particularly those who are chronically mentally ill, may express no distress, and may in fact show signs of being comfortable with marginal functioning and what others might deem a poor quality of life.

On the other hand, much behavior that is adaptive in a particular environment may also qualify as "normal" by common definitions. The following are examples of this: (a) norm conformity that encourages approach by others and prevents stigma, generalized avoidance by others, or legal sanctions; (b) statistically common functioning that enhances the client's quality of life; and (c) behaviors associated with long-term well-being as well as short-term comfort. In functional assessment, however, successful client adaptation to environments is key; normality is incidental.

Functional assessment is concerned with the adaptiveness of behavior and the concept of behavioral competence. Competence is the success of behavior in producing valued environmental impacts (cf. Argyle, 1972; Gilbert, 1978; Edelstein, Sims, & Scott, 1979; McFall, 1982). Functional assessment involves assessing valued environmental impacts of clients' behavior as well as identifying and assessing the behavior that produces those impacts. Client outcome goals (see below) are the central long-term valued impacts of interest in functional assessment. The behaviors essential in client outcome goals are the critical behaviors assessed in functional assessment.

Rehabilitation Goals

Anthony, Cohen, and Kennard (1990) and Pallak (1990) have argued convincingly for a client outcome orientation in services for the mentally ill, with rehabilitation outcome being the basis for functional assessment. Practically speaking, one begins with the ultimate rehabilitation outcome expected for a client and works backward in the development of functional assessment and appropriate intervention procedures.

Rosen and Proctor (1981) present a typology of treatment goals that may greatly facilitate an outcome orientation. This typology is anchored upon *ultimate outcomes,* which are "sufficient conditions for treatment to be terminated and considered a success" (p. 419). An important caveat to consider with seriously and persistently mentally ill individuals is that assessment and intervention may continue indefinitely, albeit with different forms and frequencies over time. One may find that many terminations of therapeutic relationships involve transferring a case to another professional in a different setting. Thus outcomes are less "ultimate" with this population than with less disabled populations.

Once delineated, client outcome goals serve as focal points for functional assessment. Specifying these ultimate outcomes highlights (a) gaps between skills required in outcome environments and skills present in the client's current repertoire, and (b) assets and deficits in the client's current performance of behaviors instrumental to outcome goals. This allows targeting of crucial client behaviors. Outcome goals also identify specific environments to which trained skills must be transferred and maintained. Finally, outcome goals provide the ultimate criterion for judging the success of treatment. Evaluation research in psychiatric rehabilitation has emphasized three types of outcome. The first of these is deinstitutionalization. This outcome has been operationalized as readmission rate (e.g., Banzett, Liberman, Moore, & Marshall, 1984; Falloon, Boyd, & McGill, 1984; Linn, Klett, & Caffey, 1980; Wallace & Liberman, 1985), community retention (Banzett et al., 1984; Falloon et al., 1984), time spent in rehospitalization (Falloon et al., 1984), and group discharge rates (Banzett et al., 1984; Brown et al., 1989; Hall, Baker, & Hutchinson, 1977). Experience has taught us that deinstitutionalization alone is an inadequate representation of successful outcome (Anthony et al., 1990; Brown, 1982; Lerman, 1982; Pepper & Ryglewicz, 1982; Test, 1981; Wing, 1987). Other types of outcome are receiving increasing attention. For example, one might focus on quality of life, which might include number and quality of interpersonal relationships (Falloon et al., 1984; Halford, Hayes, & Varghese, 1990; Liberman, Lillie, et al., 1984) with family, friends, coworkers, and other peers. Other outcome measures might be a client's maintenance of a household (Falloon et al., 1984); adequate food, clothing, and shelter; and work or study success (Banzett et al., 1984; Falloon et al., 1984). Improvement or maintenance of health status (particularly in conditions affected by diet, exercise, and hygiene) may be another quality of life outcome. Resources consumed is another potential outcome variable. Cost per unit of effectiveness (see Brown et al., 1989; Falloon et al., 1984) is one way of quantifying this outcome. For example, one might compute the ratio of staff costs (hours spent $\times$ hourly salary) of a client's rehabilitation to number of days retained in a targeted placement.

While these standard treatment outcomes have been developed for groups of clients, they also constitute critical criteria of success for individual clients. These and other outcomes can be negotiated with individual clients, client advocates, and significant others. The resulting client outcome goals can specify the desired goals of the current treatment contract. For example, client goals could include a placement goal specifying the restrictiveness and structure of the client's proposed living, working, and learning environment. Client outcome goals could also delineate the quality of life envisioned for the client, specifying environmental opportunities and expectations for relationships, self-care, and work or study.

Note that such goals do not specify exactly what clients will *do,* but the *results* they will obtain from the environment. Thus, a client outcome goal does not state that a client will learn to initiate conversations, but that he or she will establish at least one friendship (as evident in individualized observable indicators involving responses of the other persons to the client). Similarly, a client outcome goal does not state that a client will meet behavioral placement criteria for a halfway house, but that he or she will actually be placed there.

Once client outcome goals are identified, there are many ways to quantify and assess their attainment. One might use indicators such as number of days retained in a community placement or time spent in peer social contacts (see

Halford et al., 1990). Falloon and colleagues (1984) and Liberman, Lillie, et al. (1984) employed outcome measures of the quality of family interactions (e.g., expressed emotion, communication, problem-solving success). One might also measure the outcome of perceived social support with an instrument such as the Provision of Social Relations scale (Turner, Frankel, & Levin, 1983). Simple indexes of work productivity and promotion and educational advancement might be developed for individual working and learning environments.

Consideration of goal feasibility is ideally part of treatment contract negotiation. The optimum objective is the least restrictive placement and highest level of functioning thought possible for the client by the end of the current treatment contract. Resources consumed (e.g., fees for outside agency services, staff time) can be specified in the description of interventions for each outcome goal. The availability of such resources to the client is critical to the feasibility analysis of those goals. Obviously, it can be pointless and counterproductive to state goals for which funding or expertise will not be available. Client history is also a factor in the feasibility analysis of goals. Review of premorbid functioning, highest level of previous functioning, placement history, history of maintaining improved functioning, and past response to similar treatment can greatly assist the clinician in setting feasible goals. Contrasting skills required for success in future environments with the client's current adaptive skills repertoire is critical for realistic goal setting.

Some examples may clarify the idea of client outcome goals:

1 A hospitalized client has never lived independently. The onset of his schizophrenia was at age 19, and his premorbid functioning was poor. He has remained continuously hospitalized, with the exception of several brief elopements. He does not maintain minimal hygiene independently, follow ward fire safety rules, or converse with anyone he has known for less than approximately 6 months. These problems prevent discharge and remain refractory after interventions available in the hospital and other milieus accessible to the client have been exhausted. If all attempts to prepare the client for discharge to a less restrictive environment have failed, a client outcome goal may be improved quality of life within the hospital (Anthony & Liberman, 1986). This might include resolution of dermatologic and gum disease through improved assisted hygiene (as determined by physician after observation for accepted diagnostic criteria), more frequent positive family and peer interactions (as confirmed by ratings by family members, peers, and client), and increased quality of participation in treatment and ward activities (measured by participation ratings by staff and number of times peers smile at or compliment the client during his active participation).

2 A hospitalized individual has a history of brief employment at unskilled jobs 10 years ago, prior to the onset of his schizophrenia. Impulsive spending and social isolation led to rehospitalizations after previous stays (approximately 1 year) in boarding homes. The client might have outcome goals of placement at a boarding home and day treatment program, which provide opportunities and encouragement for continued improvement of deficits in money management and initiating social interaction. The outcome goal may further specify that an acceptable day treatment program offer occupational therapy and a variety of structured and informal peer interaction activities. The client's attempts to initiate social interaction will result in at least one 5-minute conversation daily. Another client goal might be maintenance of adequate financial resources to consistently meet his needs for food, clothing, shelter, treatment participation, and socialization.

3   Five years ago, a community-residing client held a job as a bookkeeper for a small business. Since then she has been unemployed and hospitalized at least 6 months out of every year. She is married and has two adolescent children. When not hospitalized, she has been treated in a day treatment center. Her outcome goals follow: The client's husband and children will express satisfaction with her maintenance of her agreed-upon share of parenting and housekeeping duties within her family home. The house will appear clean at weekly social worker visits (according to a specific checklist). The client and her husband will indicate marital satisfaction by scores of 110 or greater on the Dyadic Adjustment Scale (Spanier, 1976). In addition, she will have completed training for, and begun, supported employment in a clerical setting. She will not report nervousness on the job and will be obtaining "satisfactory" performance ratings by her supervisor.

Client outcome goals provide the organizing focus for other rehabilitation goals. Functional assessment is most directly and immediately concerned with behaviors that lead to the ultimate outcomes of intervention, and thus with instrumental goals involving those behaviors. *Instrumental goals* are "those effects of intervention that are assumed (whether on the basis of theoretical formulations, empirical evidence, or practice wisdom) to lead necessarily to other outcomes without further intervention" (Rosen & Proctor, 1981, p. 419). Daily bathing and delivery of compliments for peer accomplishments or attributes might be instrumental goals for a particular client.

We will see below that complex relationships may exist among instrumental behaviors and goals such that one goal may be instrumental in the attainment of another. For example, clients' learning the skill of recognizing a family problem situation (one instrumental goal) may be instrumental in their regularly discussing such problems with their family (another instrumental goal).

The final type of rehabilitation goal suggested by Rosen and Proctor (1981) is the intermediate (process) goal. *Intermediate goals* are those "presumed to contribute to a facilitative climate for continued intervention" (p. 420). Establishment of therapist approval as a social reinforcer for client behavior and client self-disclosure of events relevant to treatment is an example of an intermediate goal. While such goals are important to changing adaptive behavior, space limitations preclude our consideration of them in the context of functional assessment. Kanfer and Schefft (1988) have offered an excellent treatment of such process issues.

Impairments, Disabilities, and Handicaps

The perspectives of adaptiveness, competence, and client outcome goals provide helpful insights into Anthony and Liberman's (1986) conceptual model for rehabilitation. The description here eliminates a problematic aspect of Anthony and Liberman's model: hierarchical causation. They present impairments as causing disabilities, and impairments and disabilities as causing handicaps. This reifies concepts that would be more productively employed as alternate levels of analysis for psychiatric clients' behavior. Also, hierarchical causation seems to overemphasize the biological diathesis as a "first cause," neglecting the role of stressors, iatrogenic responses to impairments, and maladaptive contingencies in the environment. For example, such a model may lead one to overlook the direct influence of impoverished environments, such as institutions, in creating some handicaps. Eliminating the idea of hierarchical causation reconciles Anthony and Liberman's tripartite model with their subsequent discussion of the role of stressors. It also makes the model consistent with (a) research findings of no correlation between impairments and disabilities, which Anthony and Liberman cite, and (b) Falloon's (1987) argument against equating severity of disability with severity of handicap.

Anthony and Liberman's model describes three partially overlapping levels of analysis for the behavior of the psychiatrically disabled: impairments, disabilities, and handicaps. These three levels of analysis also constitute three levels of relevance to individual client outcome goals, and thus, three levels of relative usefulness to functional assessment.

The first level of analysis for psychiatric client behavior Anthony and Liberman (1986) present is impairments. *Impairments* include "any loss or abnormality of psychological, physiological, or anatomical structure or function" resulting from lesions or abnormalities in the central nervous system (p. 545). The positive (e.g., delusions) and negative (e.g., anhedonia) symptoms of schizophrenia are impairments. As described by Anthony and Liberman (1986), the impairment level of analysis encompasses covert and pervasive physiological (i.e., neurological) and cognitive (i.e., neuropsychological and emotional) pathology as its contents (cf. Cone, 1978). These contents are viewed primarily in the context of the individual client.

Impairments may have indirect and diffuse impacts on outcome, often through the learning process in rehabilitation. Although the bulk of assessment literature for the major mental disorders has focused on impairments (see Neale & Oltmanns, 1981, for a representative review), impairments are not central to functional assessment. They comprise a client behavioral repertoire other than adaptive skills, conceived at a level that excludes the natural environments in which the client must function. Anthony and colleagues (1990) assert that client skills and environmental supports (which determine disabilities and handicaps) relate more strongly to outcomes than do impairments.

Although not addressed by functional assessment, reduction of, or compensation for, impairments through pharmacotherapy (see Liberman et al., 1987) and/ or self-control interventions (see Falloon, 1987) may in many cases become intermediate or instrumental goals of rehabilitation (cf. Anthony & Liberman, 1986; Bellack, 1986; Hogarty, 1989; Liberman, Lillie, et al., 1984; Liberman, Falloon, & Wallace, 1984). Thus, it is important that functional assessment and adaptive skill intervention be integrated and coordinated with assessment and intervention for impairments (Anthony & Liberman, 1986; Liberman et al., 1987). However, the latter will not be a focus of this chapter.

Anthony and Liberman's (1986) second level of analysis for psychiatric client behavior is disabilities. *Disabilities* are "any restriction or lack . . . of ability to perform an activity in the manner or within the range considered normal for a human being" (p. 545). For example, a score below the normative range on a role-play test of social skills would indicate disabilities. The content (cf. Cone, 1978) of this level of analysis is clients' overt motoric repertoire. This content is examined in the context of the "normal" range of human activities.

Disabilities are potentially relevant to adaptive skills, but they are defined relative to a vague standard of normality rather than the particular requirements of the client's living, working, and learning environment. This also leaves their relationship to client outcome goals in question. Functional analysis of disabilities (as they are defined by Anthony & Liberman) would lead the clinician to ask questions such as (a) Who is the audience considering the behavior normal or abnormal? and (b) What consequences or implications, if any, do their judgments have for the successful adaptation of the client to the environment (or, more specifically, to the accomplishment of client outcome goals)? This would allow the clinician to determine which disabilities actually handicap the individual in his or her living, working, or learning environment.

The third and final level of analysis for psychiatric client behavior presented by Anthony and Liberman (1986) is handicaps. *Handicaps* are any "disadvantage for a given individual . . . that limits or prevents the fulfillment of a role that is normal (depending on age, sex, social, and cultural factors) for that individual" (p. 545). Unemployment and homelessness are examples of handicaps. This level of analysis incorporates both client motoric behavior and environmental events as its contents. Each of these contents is viewed in the context of the other.

Thus it becomes apparent that, in Anthony and Liberman's (1986) model, the handicap represents the level of analysis most compatible with functional assessment. While still tied to a concept of "normality," handicaps are defined in terms of (a) what is normal for that individual, which may allow delineation of local social and cultural expectations directly relevant to successful adaptation for a particular client and (b) fulfillment of a role, which seems closely related to successful adaptation to one's environment. The "disadvantage" for an individual that constitutes a handicap can be viewed in terms of gaps between (a) the client's repertoire and skills required in environments specified in client outcome goals, (b) instrumental behaviors for client outcome goals and client's current performance, or (c) environmental demands and supports. Thus, some handicaps may be caused not by disabilities but by exceptional or unrealistic demands by the environment (e.g., impoverished or high-crime neighborhoods where boarding homes are located) or a lack of environmental supports (Falloon, 1987). Analyzing client functioning at this broader level allows for more comprehensive assessment, which arguably leads to more effective intervention.

A Conceptual Model for Functional Assessment

The desired result of the foregoing conceptual discussion is a viable model to guide functional assessment. In general terms, we established that the emphasis is upon adaptive rather than normal behavior. Valued impacts in the client's living, working, and learning environments, specified in client outcome goals, define such adaptive (or competent) behavior. Handicaps represent the level of analysis for functional assessment and delineate its scope. Handicaps are conceived as gaps between the client's current performance and the demands of environments to which the client must adapt. This level of analysis allows assessment of complex causal networks that connect environment and behavior. Both client behavior (primarily motoric) and environmental events are possible targets for intervention. Thus, a conceptual model for functional assessment facilitates the practical task of selecting targets (cf. Evans, 1985; Kanfer, 1985).

SELECTING TARGETS FOR ASSESSMENT

A helpful beginning for any discussion of target selection is a definition of "target" and some related terms. As used here, the word "target" can be a verb or noun (see Hawkins, 1986). As a noun, "target" means an entity designated as the focus of intervention (i.e., target behavior or target event—see below). The verb "target" means to designate a specified entity as the focus of intervention (e.g., to target use of the public bus to get to and from the day treatment center). A "target behavior" is an action of the client designated as the focus of treatment (e.g., making a weekly meal plan including sufficient servings of the major food groups). A "target environment" is the current or future living, working, or learning environment (cf. Anthony & Liberman, 1986) in which target behaviors must be performed for accomplishment of client outcome goals (e.g., boarding home, sheltered workshop, family home, grocery store). Finally, a "target event" is an occurrence in the target environment that must be changed to prompt, reinforce, or punish a target behavior and/or accomplish one or more client outcome goals (e.g., a van driver providing praise for careful grocery shopping rather than pressuring and nagging the client to finish shopping quickly, a staff member taking a few moments to chat pleasantly when a client makes a desired statement to start a conversation, a boarding home operator promptly depositing a client's benefit check in the bank).

Targeting Guidelines

Six general targeting principles and specific guidelines that follow from them are described below. The reader is forewarned that these guidelines sometimes conflict. For example, desirable targets are not always feasible; and significant and pervasive target impacts are not always measurable. Target selection is a complex clinical decision-making process (see Evans, 1985, and Kanfer, 1985, for a discussion of such decision making). The overriding principle in use in the guidelines below is maximization of objectively confirmed client outcome goal attainment.

1   Focus on the function, not the form or appearance, of target behaviors. The function of target behaviors is revealed in their relationship to events in the environment. For example, naturally occurring environmental events may punish or reinforce the target behavior. The ideal here is to target client behavior changes that fit (will be maintained by) the future environment (Kanfer, 1985; cf. behavioral trapping, Baer & Wolf, 1970). Overlooking the functions of skills in target environments may be partly responsible for the widely reported difficulties (see Hogarty, 1989; Liberman et al., 1984; Liberman, Massel, Mosk, & Wong, 1985) with maintenance of adaptive skill training. Conversely, choosing functional treatment objectives may enhance maintenance and other forms of generalization (Banzett et al., 1984). Addressing the similar issue of educational transitions, Hoier and Cone (Hoier & Cone, 1987; Hoier, McConnell, & Pallay, 1987) suggest enhancing transfer of change by tailoring students' repertoires to the environments into which they will be placed.

Although helpful, training behavior that is naturally reinforced in the environment is not foolproof. Such behavior may not be adaptive in the broader sense of the word. For example, a workshop supervisor may consistently reinforce passive subjugation of some clients wants and needs by reinforcing high productivity and calling those who never express their wishes "good workers." If a therapist preparing a client for such a setting teaches passive productivity at all costs, the client may encounter a high rate of reinforcement from the supervisor. However, the resultant stress for the client after placement may well lead to ultimate failure at the workshop.

The notion of competent or effective performance provides a more constructive, longer term targeting framework (see Hawkins, 1986) than merely targeting what the environment reinforces. The reader will recall that the critical impacts defining competent client performance in psychiatric rehabilitation involve client outcome goal accomplishment. Similarly, the critical function of target behaviors is accomplishing outcome goals (cf. Kazdin, 1985). Therefore, if placement in a boarding home is an outcome goal, then the "access behavior" (Hawkins, 1986) of scheduled toileting and fluid intake to resolve functional incontinence may become a target. Attainment of the instrumental goal of continence may then allow admittance to the home, and thus accomplish the client outcome goal.

Targeting behaviors and events functionally related to client outcome goals permits flexibility in the choice of target behaviors since a number of behaviors or events may lead to the same outcomes. For example, when maintaining an increased level of peer interaction is a client's goal, several skills besides the particular conversation initiation skill described in a training manual may success-fully start conversations without making others uncomfortable (cf. Hawkins, 1986). Similarly, a number of staff responses (verbal and nonverbal, obvious and subtle events) besides the commonly suggested statement "good job" may reinforce desired conversation initiation.

The above discussion implies that a connection between targets and outcome can be ensured neither automatically nor intuitively. Teaching the intuitively selected skills contained in a treatment "package" does not guarantee the desired impact on outcome (Bellack, 1986). For example, the sheltered workshop supervi-sor described above may respond to the very direct and assertive requests taught in social skill training as "inappropriate supervisee behavior." He may resist or criticize such requests, creating stress that threatens work success. On the other hand, successful clients in the workshop may have learned to get their wishes met by stating them as problems they would like the supervisor's assistance in solving.

Several means are available for identifying behaviors potentially instrumental in client outcome goals. Program evaluation may reveal skills and skill levels that generally predict positive outcome. For instance, prerelease social skills may influence relapse rates (Linn et al., 1980). Alternatively, treatment record review may reveal improvements in skill or performance levels that preceded periods of success for the client. A methodology called template matching (Hoier & Cone, 1987; Hoier et al., 1987), which will be discussed later, enables one to identify instrumental skills for specific future environments and clients. Regard-less of the method of identifying targets, validation of the target-outcome relation-ship is vital (Rosen & Proctor, 1981; Halford et al., 1990). This requires concurrent measurement of target behaviors and client outcome goal attainment (see Kazdin, 1985). That is, one must measure the *impact* of behavior change as distinguished from behavior change itself. One such measure is ratings of target behavior impact by critical judges (e.g., boarding home operators, employers, and others who control important contingencies in target environments) (cf. Hawkins, 1986). However, such "social validation" (see Hansen, St. Lawrence, & Christoff, 1985) may identify "normal" targets that are not necessarily adaptive for the client. It is more important to establish the "functional validity" (Hawkins, 1986) of target behaviors for each client. Evidence for functional validity comes from direct measurement of client outcome goal attainment (i.e., the critical *function* or impact of target behaviors) both during treatment and at follow-up.

It is apparent in some of the examples above that what is adaptive and instrumental in client outcome goals is relative to community context. Thus, a focus on function leads logically to our second principle of targeting.

2   Target the client's behavioral repertoire, and demand characteristics and contingencies of current and future living, working, and learning environments (cf. Anthony & Liberman, 1986; Hawkins, 1986; Halford et al., 1990; Hoier et al., 1987). Functional assessment ideally takes place at the interface between client adaptive behavior and the target environments specified in client outcome goals. Indeed, client outcome goals, adaptiveness, and handicaps and the behavioral and psychosocial models are all defined in terms of the relationships between behavior and the environment.

Functional assessment, therefore, assesses the contingencies in target environments. "Contingencies" specify the conditions under which behavior is reinforced or punished, including the frequency and timing of such consequences. Ideally, one would have clients practice skills in target environments (e.g., during structured trial visits), then target either client behaviors or environmental events to attain the client outcome goal. Observation of the client in simulations of the target environments (e.g., role-play) and observation of other successful clients in the target environments are more feasible alternative assessment procedures. For example, a client preparing for a volunteer job involving contact with the public may have difficulty selecting matching clothes. Observation of interaction between the client and the boarding home operator may reveal two problems. The client has marginal skills at matching clothes, and the operator spends much more time attending to the client when the client arrives for breakfast in mismatched clothes. The target behavior might be the client's clothes-matching repertoire. The target event might be attention from the home operator. The aim might be to make more attention available for desired clothes matching.

Besides being sequelae of impairments or early learning history, deficits may often be created by more recent disuse, reinforcement of a sick role, or loss of motivation (Liberman et al., 1985). As in the above example, these phenomena are likely to be caused by problems with environmental antecedents and consequences for adaptive and maladaptive behavior in past or current environments. Such problems may reemerge in a future environment, setting the stage for repeated skill atrophy. Thus, assessment of the environmental reaction to target behavior change becomes important (Kanfer, 1985). One can then target environmental event changes that will maintain or improve the client's performance of target behaviors (cf. behavioral trapping, Baer & Wolf, 1970).

These ideas may be particularly useful in facilitating environmental transitions of the psychiatrically disabled. Targeting to enhance transfer to and maintenance in specific future environments, instead of generalization to all possible environments (cf. Liberman et al., 1985), may result in more efficient, realistic, and effective assessment and treatment. Such targeting entails preference for particular target behaviors that are likely to transfer and maintain, and emphasis on specific target events in the current and future environments that will facilitate transfer and maintenance. For example, an inpatient client's outcome goal specifies discharge to a group home where much effort is expended toward clients' participation in meal preparation, and all client transportation needs are served by the group home van. Cooking skills might be preferred as a timely target over use of public transportation. Such targeting will allow the client to capture reinforcers readily available for cooking behaviors in existing contingencies in the target environment (cf. Baer & Wolf, 1970). Group home staff responses to residents might be observed to determine the rate at which events that generally work as reinforcers for the target client occur. Observation may also identify the range of types and rates of prompts used by group home staff during meal preparation. Types and rates of such prompts used by hospital staff in teaching the client cooking skills might also be assessed. Events (prompts and reinforcers) might then be targeted to make them similar in the current and future environments to facilitate the client's transition (cf. Hoier et al., 1987).

Assessment of target environments is also the first step in tailoring prosthetic environments for client deficits that remain following training. In such cases the emphasis is on altering target events to prompt, maintain, and otherwise compensate for the client's current deficient repertoire. For example, a client has attention or memory impairments that allow her to complete individual housekeeping tasks, but not to recall when she is expected to complete them or when she most recently completed each of several such tasks. When placed at a group home, she will be required to meet novel expectations for maintaining her personal living area in accordance with her outcome goal. In such circumstances, it would be important to assess (either through direct observation or interview) what prompts (target events) are in the group home staff's repertoire to help the client compensate for deficits and impairments. The range of staff's performance expectations (which may include subtle antecedents and consequences) for group home residents represents another set of potential target events that might be similarly assessed.

The mental health professional has a critical ethical responsibility in tailoring client's behavior to environments. This is to advocate effectively for creation and maintenance of environments that not only enable accomplishment of client outcome goals, but (a) provide opportunities for continued client progress toward a higher level of functioning and placement in an even less restrictive setting, and (b) preserve clients' dignity and civil rights. Teaching clients to adjust to and accept stagnant or repressive environments is an unethical use of professional skills.

3 Individualize target selection. Consistencies and similarities exist in targets across clients, but every client's environment and repertoire, and the behavioral principles involved in their interaction, are unique (see Hawkins, 1986). Therefore, it is necessary to create an individualized model of adaptive behavior for each client and environment (cf. Evans, 1985). As demonstrated above, client outcome goals provide the foundation for individualization by pointing to target events and instrumental target behaviors of interest for the client.

In addition, it is important to consider the client's material and behavioral resources for changing chosen targets (Evans, 1985; Hawkins, 1986; Kanfer, 1985). This is similar to the evaluation of client outcome goal feasibility described above, but that evaluation does not replace this one. Though a client outcome goal may have been judged feasible, only certain targets may be feasible routes to accomplishing the goal. For instance, if establishment of a peer friendship (which might be defined as a relationship of at least 2 months' duration where a peer reciprocates and otherwise reinforces the client's social approach) is the client outcome goal, client participation in day treatment center outings may be a feasible target. However, independent client initiation of social activities may not be a feasible target because of either financial resources or a greatly impoverished social skills repertoire.

It is also wise to choose targets whose change the client values and will facilitate (Kanfer, 1985; Hawkins, 1986). Involving the client in client outcome goal setting and target selection may encourage this (see Kanfer & Schefft, 1988). In the case of a client whose goal is part-time employment, for example, the client's values and vocational interests may suggest which target skills to teach. If the client talks proudly about her past ability to repair mechanical devices and has a significant other she admires for her mechanical skills, then such skills might be preferred over clerical skills as targets of vocational training.

4 Select targets for which change and the impact of change can be readily monitored (Kanfer, 1985) and objectively measured. Limiting inference in measurement, and in hypothesizing connections between targets and impacts (e.g., client outcome goals), will guide this effort. For example, direct observation of the targets and impacts of interest is the preferred measurement method (see Hawkins, 1986). Specifying targets and impacts in behavioral terms will facilitate observation and other forms of measurement. Therefore, one might target work attendance and output rather than motivation that is inferred from such variables. Targeting behaviors instrumental in client outcome goals, or behaviors that directly impact such instrumental behaviors, will limit inference in the hypothesized connections between targets and client outcome goals (cf. Hawkins, 1986).

An illustration may clarify this targeting principle. "Appropriate social behavior" is a poorly specified target behavior. A client outcome goal of "increased peer acceptance" is also poorly specified. Targeting "will compliment (make a positive value statement about behavior or qualities) two peers each week" with a client outcome goal of "will be spontaneously invited by peers to join two informal (not staff-led) dyadic or small group social activities (e.g., card game, discussion) each week" is a better specified target behavior and impact, respectively. The latter would facilitate measurement and would tend to discourage misleading inference.

5 Remain mindful that effective targeting may often be indirect (Evans, 1985; Goldiamond, 1984; Hawkins, 1986; cf. Rosen & Proctor, 1981). Although simple causal models are preferable in targeting, more complex models involving indirect targeting are often necessary. Indirect targets are not directly or immediately instrumental in client outcome goals, but they are somehow linked to instrumental behaviors. For instance, learning to read a bus schedule would usually not be sufficient to accomplish a client outcome goal related to securing a volunteer job. However, schedule reading might be a necessary prerequisite to other behaviors that would establish independent mobility and allow the client to interview for volunteer positions to accomplish the client outcome goal. One might target prerequisite behaviors because they are amenable to change via available treatment methods (Evans, 1985; Kanfer, 1985; Kazdin, 1985), whereas behaviors instrumental in client outcome goals are currently not.

Indirect targeting might also occur because of preference for acceleration of desired behaviors over deceleration of undesired behaviors (Goldiamond, 1974; Hawkins, 1986). For example, if a client's inappropriate touching is maintained by attention, one might target a desired behavior (e.g., appropriate conversational behavior) that will obtain the same reinforcement (Hawkins, 1986). Such targeting can reduce the use of punishment, maintain a constructional approach (Goldiamond, 1974), and prevent attendant threats to rehabilitation success (Hawkins, 1986).

Several authors recommend targeting "keystone" behaviors, whose change will have the maximum generalization of therapeutic effects on other behaviors and events across situations and over time (Evans, 1985; Hawkins, 1986; Kanfer, 1985; Kazdin, 1985). Such targeting may often be indirect. For example, one might target problem-solving skills, since they are hypothesized to have broad general impacts upon client competence. Yet since such skills are cognitive/verbal behaviors, it is through their relationship with motoric behaviors that they indirectly contribute to client outcome goal accomplishment.

Other behaviors not directly or immediately instrumental in client outcome goals may be targeted to promote motivation, prevent or counter resistance, or facilitate the working alliance among the therapist, client, and staff or significant others involved in the client's treatment. Such targeting may help therapists influence other targets more closely and directly linked to client outcome goals (Evans, 1985; Kanfer, 1985). Targets related to therapeutic process are beyond the scope of this chapter, but the reader is referred to Kanfer and Schefft (1988) for a thorough discussion of these important variables.

Irrespective of the hypothesized relationship among targets or between targets and impact, once a target is selected, the impact of a change in it merits assessment. One might ask such questions as (a) What new relationships among behaviors in the client's repertoire does the change create? (b) What old relationships does it destroy? and (c) How will nontarget client behaviors react to environmental changes aimed at the target? (Evans, 1985; Kanfer, 1985; Kazdin, 1985). Assessment data can confirm or disconfirm hypotheses about relationships among behaviors (Halford et al., 1990; Rosen & Proctor, 1981). Although it is helpful to measure all direct and indirect targets, the highest priority, and the most frequent and intensive focus of assessment, should be upon behaviors instrumental to outcome, and upon outcome itself.

6 Drive the target selection process with working hypotheses. Kanfer (1985) describes target selection as an iterative process informed by ongoing data collection. The hypotheses around which this effort is organized should be made explicit. Many hypotheses will involve the relationships among targets, and between targets and client outcome goals. For example, one might hypothesize that both improved hygiene (target) and improved nonverbal social skills (target) are necessary for establishing a friendship (outcome goal). Once stated, hypotheses are at all times subject to modification based on data on target change, environmental reaction, and client outcome (cf. Kanfer, 1985).

Template Matching as a Method of Target Selection

The template-matching approach of Hoier and Cone (1987) readily accommodates the targeting guidelines described above. Template matching may identify skills important in local communities and placements by examining the performance of "stars" (of various functioning levels) who remain in those settings with a good quality of life (cf. Gilbert's, 1978, use of exemplars to define competence). This approach presents a methodology for collecting empirical confirmation of the instrumentality of target behaviors in client outcome goals. It also greatly facilitates functional assessment by allowing adaptation and selective application of skill-training technology based on the functioning level of the client (cf. Liberman et al., 1985) and the requirements of the idiosyncratic environments in which the client lives, works, and receives treatment (cf. Anthony et al.'s, 1990, emphasis on a range of service alternatives). Furthermore, template matching allows the clinician to become familiar with the contingencies of the target environments, so that clients can be trained to adaptively contact these contingencies (e.g., during structured trial visits), encouraging transfer and maintenance of skill training. Finally, through template matching, a clinician may identify environmental changes important in maintaining client therapeutic changes or compensating for refractory deficits.

Template Matching: An Illustration

An example integrating the above targeting principles will describe template matching to the reader. Consider the case of a 30-year-old female client, Sandy, who enrolled in college at age 21 after working for 3 years as an operator for a local phone company. Near the end of her senior year in college, she experienced a manic episode that led her to drop out of school. She had been a B student until that time. She was hospitalized for approximately a year after the onset of her disability, during which time she had several severe manic and depressive episodes. She was discharged to her current group home and subsequently made three unsuccessful attempts at independent living in an apartment while being employed part-time and attending college part-time. She is currently deemed ready for discharge from day treatment and her group home. Social isolation and difficulties in money management created the precipitating stress for manic episodes during the first two independent-living attempts; and for a depressive episode during the third.

1 Set client's outcome goals (cf. Hoier et al., 1987). The client outcome goals for this client might include the following: (a) Accept placement in a supported apartment with weekly visits by a caseworker. (b) Complete one college course per semester until bachelor's degree is earned. (c) Establish one friendship with another client at a similar level of functioning who reciprocates social initiations and contacts client weekly. (d) Receive supportive contact (as rated by client) from family member once per week. (e) Maintain adequate diet, wardrobe, and social activities described above while remaining within a weekly budget. (f) Obtain 20-hour-per-week job, involving contact with the public and coworkers, paying at least $5 per hour.

2 Identify tentative targets (cf. Hawkins, 1986; Goldfried & D'Zurilla's, 1969, "situational analysis"). Once client outcome goals have been set, behaviors instrumental for attaining those goals can be tentatively identified. Significant others (e.g., family, prospective care givers) sensitive to norms and behaviors critical in the target environments specified in the outcome goals may suggest such targets (cf. McFall, 1982). The assessor may identify behaviors predicted to elicit social reinforcement and support (and possibly sustained therapeutic effort) (cf. Baer & Wolf, 1970; Banzett et al., 1984; Hoier & Cone, 1987). For example, family members might be interviewed to identify client behaviors that would reinforce the family's initiation of supportive contacts. Family interactions during meetings with the assessor may also reveal potential targets. Behaviors descriptive of the exemplary performer in the target environments might be solicited from several sources (Hoier & Cone, 1987). The student counseling center or other mental health professionals might be contacted to discuss behaviors associated with scholastic success in specific cases they have known at the client's functioning level. The supported apartment agency might be contacted regarding behaviors preferred in clients with whom they work (Hoier & Cone, 1987) or to arrange observation of their work with a favorite client.

The following is a list (by no means exhaustive) of tentative target behaviors for Sandy: (a) Vacuum apartment weekly. (b) Be home for at least 95% of appointments with supported-apartment caseworker. (c) Listen without cutting off others when they telephone or visit. (d) Express appreciation of family contacts and favors. (e) Establish and use a 2-hour study period weekly. (f) Attend review sessions before all college exams.

Contacts that gleaned the above target behaviors also provide indirect indexes of expectations and contingencies in Sandy's target environments. This may reveal potential target events such as (a) increased complimenting of desired performance by Sandy's father; (b) discussion of Sandy's favorite topics by supported-apartment caseworker on his first visit to establish him as a source of social reinforcers.

3   Combine suggested targets from all relevant judges to form a template or behavior profile (Hoier & Cone, 1987). Efforts to identify tentative targets may generate a list too long to address realistically in treatment, and/or a list that includes obviously superfluous items. Such lists might be reduced by having judges rank items and indicate which are critical. Those items generated or highly ranked by the most judges would be addressed first. For example, listening skills might be important in nearly all of Sandy's client outcome goals, whereas vacuuming her apartment may be of less consequence.

4   Identify "star" clients of target client's general functional level and measure their performance of tentative targets. Stars are clients who are doing well (attaining outcome goals similar to the client's) in the target environments. (With the rare exception of situations where a similarly impaired sibling lives at home, stars will not be available for the family home environment.) Measurement of star performance allows identification of (a) differences between performance of star and target clients and (b) differences in demand characteristics and contingencies for target behaviors between the target client's current and future environments (cf. Hoier et al., 1987). These discrepancies point to target behaviors and target events, respectively (cf. Hoier & Cone, 1987).

For Sandy, her therapist may survey other professionals for data on study scheduling and attendance of review sessions by anonymous college-attending stars (with their permission and due caution to protect confidentiality). Similar data may be requested on appointment keeping by successful clients of the supported-apartment program.

5   Elicit change in targets. This is where intervention fits into the assessment sequence. Assessment of both target change and client outcome goal progress should continue throughout treatment.

6   Collect program evaluation (or experimental) evidence for validity of targets selected on the basis of outcome data. Ongoing assessment can confirm target change, client outcome goal progress, and a relationship between the two. For Sandy, if listening skills improve to a targeted level and supportive family contacts occur regularly on a weekly basis, then assessment data are consistent with the hypothesized target–client outcome goal relationship. If Sandy schedules and uses weekly study time but fails a course, then the hypothesized relationship between scheduled study time and academic advancement is brought into question. Star behavior might then be reexamined for further specification of competent target behavior, or for alternate target behaviors that may bring about client outcome goal attainment.

Template matching, like all targeting, is an iterative process that assessors may refine and shorten as they gain experience with clients at various functioning levels and in various target environments. Once prospective target behaviors have been identified, one can proceed with their actual assessment.

BEHAVIORAL IMPEDIMENTS TO THE REHABILITATION PROCESS

A client's maladaptive behaviors can potentially compromise an otherwise sound rehabilitation program. Maladaptive client behaviors can impede the learning process and preclude movement of the client to a more desirable setting. The same problem-solving skills taught to clients, coupled with a sound functional analysis, are frequently the best combination of approaches to client behaviors that impede rehabilitation progress. Since we do not have the space to cover adequately the intricacies of functional (behavioral) analysis, the interested reader is referred to Cormier and Cormier (1991), Groden (1989), Haynes and O'Brien (1990), Kanfer and Grimm (1977), and Kanfer and Saslow (1965) for detailed discussions.

"Functional analysis" is a term employed by behaviorally oriented clinicians to refer to the analysis of variables that influence or exert control over a particular behavior or class of behaviors (operant). One of the goals of the analysis is to determine the function of the behavior in question and how the environment maintains it. The functional analysis model most often seen is referred to as the ABC model. "A" refers to the environmental antecedents of a target behavior that reliably precede the behavior. These are also termed "discriminative stimuli." The more immediate antecedents of a behavior might be an activity in which the individual is engaging, some aspect of the activity (e.g., interactions with a particular staff member), cognitions (private/covert events) pertaining to the interaction, affective responses to the interaction, and so forth. Virtually any stimulus, covert or overt, may serve as an antecedent to a target behavior. Thorough interviewing and observation of the client's behavior in the context of the therapeutic environment are typically required to reveal antecedent stimuli that reliably precede and set the occasion for the target behavior. When such antecedents are not relatively apparent, one can begin to look for patterns in the target behavior. For example, one can ask about the conditions under which the behavior is most likely to occur, the times of day it is most likely to occur (e.g., early morning, noon, late afternoon), the activities during which it occurs (e.g., mealtime, staff shift changes), and the individuals (particular staff members or other clients) in whose presence the behavior occurs.

"B" refers to the target behavior, which is the behavior of interest. It is essential that the behavior be defined in very concrete terms that will enable multiple observers to note reliably whether the behavior has occurred at any particular point in time. Operational definitions are often helpful.

"C" refers to the environmental consequences of the behavior that influence the occurrence of the behavior. These consequences are either reinforcers or punishers that strengthen or weaken a behavior, respectively. It is sometimes easiest to determine the consequences that maintain the behavior by determining the function that the behavior is serving for the individual. For example, a client may engage in maladaptive behaviors to gain the attention of the staff or to avoid an undesirable activity.

Prior to conducting a functional analysis, it is frequently helpful to ask staff or family members to keep a record of the maladaptive behaviors in question. A simple record can be constructed whereby staff members record the time and location of the occurrence of the behavior, noting what happened prior to emission of the target behavior and what happened following the behavior.

The foregoing oversimplifies the functional analysis in several ways, the most important of which is the characterization of the ABCs as a simple linear model. In practice, each target behavior has multiple determinants (antecedents and consequences). Moreover, any one of the three terms of a contingency (antecedents, behaviors, and consequences) can serve multiple roles. For example, a behavior can also be an antecedent for another behavior. A consequence can also serve as an antecedent for another behavior.

Perhaps an example will allow the reader to assemble all of this information into a meaningful whole. Let's pretend that you are a psychologist at an institution that provides services for clients with the diagnosis of schizophrenia. The client of interest has been discussed at a recent interdisciplinary team meeting, and the staff agreed that something must be done about his outbursts. Not only do the outbursts disrupt the general activities of the unit, but they also preclude the client from participating in several skills-training programs. Your task is to define "outbursts" and determine the conditions under which the outbursts occur so that an intervention program can be developed. You spend considerable time talking with staff members who have observed the outbursts and arrive at an operational definition that characterizes the outbursts, including the intensity and duration of the outbursts. You then ask staff to begin recording each occurrence of the outbursts, noting what preceded and followed the behavior. In the meantime you question staff about when the outbursts began and learn that they began approximately 1 week ago. Your first question is what is different in the client's environment now when compared with 1 week ago? Were his medications changed? Has his diet changed? Has the daily routine of activities changed? Have any clients left the unit, or have any new ones joined the unit? Has there been a change in staff? Did the outbursts begin at about the time discharge began to be discussed?

Over a period of 3 days you learn, first, that the outbursts occur most often when the client is not involved in an activity or when he states he is tired or bored with an activity. Second, when the client engages in the outbursts, staff members rush to his side and attempt to calm him down by talking with him.

Third, although the outbursts were first noticed approximately 1 month ago, they increased in frequency during a period when several student nurses began working on the unit. Moreover, the frequency of outbursts increased on the days that the student nurses were not working on the unit. During the time that the student nurses are on the unit, they each spend considerable time with the client each day. You carefully analyze the data you have obtained over the past 3 days and conclude the following. The client has become quite accustomed to having considerable attention from the student nurses in addition to what he typically receives from the regular staff. When the nurses are absent, he loses a source of considerable reinforcement, leaving him with less attention from nurses and other staff members. He has learned that to obtain additional attention, he merely has to engage in one of his outbursts. These have occurred most often when nursing staff are attending to other clients. Our discussions with staff members and examination of the data obtained from the 3 days of observation reveal that one of the antecedents for the outbursts appears to be the client's observation of a staff member caring for another resident. For the next 3 days the nursing staff continue their recording of outbursts and also maintain a running count of each time they care for another resident in view of the client of interest. Three days of these data confirm that the outbursts occur almost exclusively when nursing staff are caring for other clients. While the antecedents and consequences of the outbursts are relatively clear, continued assessment and analysis is recommended.

The foregoing is a simple example of how staff members can inadvertently increase the frequency of a maladaptive behavior that was initially strengthened by other staff members (student nurses). Once this information is available, the design of an intervention is typically quite straightforward. The implementation, however, is not always so simple.

While this example may not be representative of the problems encountered by the reader, the approach to analysis and the principles that have been illustrated can be applied to many client problem behaviors.

SUMMARY

It was our goal to offer a conceptual and practical description of functional assessment that would enable the reader to have an understanding of the conceptual underpinnings of this approach to assessment and gain practical knowledge that would be sufficient for carrying out a functional assessment and identifying behavioral impediments. We have offered an integrated model of functional assessment that captures the strengths of behavioral and psychosocial models. This was followed by an in-depth discussion of the identification of client outcome goals, which we believe is the most critical element of functional assessment. By concentrating on client outcome goals, we have emphasized the effectiveness of client behaviors and skills in achieving goals, while downplaying what the client does to attain the goals. Consequently, we encourage clinicians to begin with outcome goals and move backward to the skills that are necessary to accomplish those goals.

Anthony and Liberman's (1986) foci of rehabilitation (impairments, disabilities, and handicaps) are discussed as representing three levels of analysis. We suggest that the handicap represents the level of analysis most compatible with a functional approach to assessment. Such a focus emphasizes adaptive rather than normal behavior since we are more interested in how a client adapts to unique living, working, and learning environments than we are with how "normal" the client's behaviors might appear.

Six guidelines for selecting targets for assessment and intervention are discussed in detail: (a) focus on the function, not the form or appearance, of target behaviors; (b) target the client's behavioral repertoire and demand characteristics and contingencies of current and future living, working, and learning environments; (c) individualize target selection; (d) select targets for which change and the impact of change can be readily monitored and objectively measured; (e) remain mindful that effective targeting may often be indirect; and (f) drive the target selection process with working hypotheses. The template-matching method of target selection is advocated as a method of matching the ultimate performance of clients with the demands and support of the environments in which they will function.

Finally, the analysis of behavioral impediments to the rehabilitation process is discussed. Functional analysis is defined and briefly discussed as an approach to identifying the variables in a client's environment that are controlling or influencing maladaptive behaviors that interfere with the functional assessment and rehabilitation process.

REFERENCES

Anthony, W. A. (1979). *Principles of psychiatric rehabilitation.* Baltimore: University Park Press.

Anthony, W. A., Cohen, M., & Cohen, B. (1983). The philosophy treatment process and principles of the psychiatric rehabilitation approach. *New Directions in Mental Health, 17,* 213–252.

Anthony, W. A., Cohen, M., & Kennard, W. (1990). Understanding the current facts and principles of mental health systems planning. *American Psychologist, 45,* 1249–1252.

Anthony, W. A., & Liberman, R. P. (1986). The practice of psychiatric rehabilitation: Historical, conceptual, and research base. *Schizophrenia Bulletin, 12,* 542–559.

Argyle, M. (1972). *The psychology of interpersonal behavior.* Middlesex, England: Penguin Books.

Baer, D. M., & Wolf, M. M. (1970). The entry into natural communities of reinforcement. In R. Ulrich, T. Stachnik, & J. Mabry (Eds.), *Control of human behavior* (Vol. II; pp. 319–324). Glenville, IL: Scott, Foresman.

Banzett, L. K., Liberman, R. P., Moore, J. W., & Marshall, B. D. (1984). Long-term follow-up of the effects of behavior therapy. *Hospital and Community Psychiatry, 35,* 277–279.

Bellack, A. S. (1986). Schizophrenia: Behavior therapy's forgotten child. *Behavior Therapy, 17,* 199–214.

Brown, E. D., Simpson, J. C., Spoltore, J. D., Noel, N. E., Lockwood, G. F., & Dean, L. D. (1989, November). *From chronic inpatient to community resident. III, Early results from a psychosocial rehabilitation program based in the hospital and the community.* Poster presented at the meeting of the Association for Advancement of Behavior Therapy, Washington, DC.

Brown, P. (1982). Approaches to evaluating the outcome of deinstitutionalization: A reply to Christenfeld. *Journal of Community Psychology, 10,* 176–281.

Cone, J. D. (1978). The behavioral assessment grid (BAG): A conceptual framework and a taxonomy. *Behavior Therapy, 9,* 882–888.

Cormier, W. H., & Cormier, S. L. (1991). *Interviewing strategies for helpers* (2nd ed.). Monterey, CA: Brooks/Cole.

Davison, G. E., & Neale, J. M. (1986). *Abnormal psychology: An experimental clinical approach.* New York: John Wiley.

Edelstein, B. A., Sims, C., & Scott, O. (1979, November). *A functional analysis of social competence.* Paper presented at meeting of the Association for Advancement of Behavior Therapy, San Francisco.

Evans, I. M. (1985). Building systems models as a strategy for target behavior selection in clinical assessment. *Behavioral Assessment, 7,* 21–32.

Falloon, I. R. H. (1987). Cognitive and behavioural interventions in the self control of schizophrenia. In J. S. Strauss, W. Boker, & H. D. Brenner (Eds.), *Psychosocial treatment of schizophrenia* (pp. 180–190). Toronto: Hans Huber.

Falloon, I. R. H., Boyd, J. L., & McGill, C. W. (1984). *Family care of schizophrenia: A problem-solving approach to the treatment of mental illness.* New York: Guilford Press.

Gilbert, T. F. (1978). *Human competence.* New York: McGraw-Hill.

Goldfried, M. R., & D'Zurilla, T. J. (1969). A behavioral-analytic model for assessing competence. In C. D. Spielberger (Ed.), *Current topics in clinical and community psychology* (Vol. I; pp. 151–196). New York: Academic Press.

Goldiamond, I. (1974). Toward a constructional approach to social problems: Ethical and constitutional issues raised by applied behavioral analysis. *Behaviorism, 2,* 1–85.

Goldiamond, I. (1984). Training parent trainers and ethicists in nonlinear analysis of behavior. In R. J. Kangel & R. A. Polster (Eds.), *Parent training: Foundations of research and practice* (pp. 504–546). New York: Guilford Press.

Groden, G. (1989). A guide for conducting a comprehensive behavioral analysis of a target behavior. *Journal of Behavior Therapy and Experimental Psychiatry, 20,* 163–169.

Halford, W. K., Hayes, R. L., & Varghese, F. N. (1990, November). *Do social skills matter? The relationship between social skill, social functioning, and quality of life.* Paper presented at the annual convention of the Association for Advancement of Behavior Therapy, San Francisco.

Hall, J. N., Baker, R., & Hutchinson, K. A. (1977). A controlled evaluation of token economy procedures with chronic schizophrenic patients. *Behaviour Research and Therapy, 15,* 261–283.

Hansen, D. J., St. Lawrence, J. S., & Christoff, K. A. (1985). Effects of interpersonal problem-solving training with chronic aftercare patients on problem-solving component skills and effectiveness of solutions. *Journal of Consulting and Clinical Psychology, 53,* 167–174.

Hawkins, R. P. (1986). Selection of target behaviors. In R. O. Nelson & S. C. Hayes (Eds.), *Conceptual foundations of behavioral assessment* (pp. 331–385). New York: Guilford Press.

Haynes, S. N., & O'Brien, W. H. (1990). Functional analysis in behavior therapy. *Clinical Psychology Review, 10,* 649–668.

Hogarty, G. E. (1989). Meta-analysis of the effects of practice with the chronically mentally ill: A critique and reappraisal of the literature. *Social Work, 34,* 363–373.

Hoier, T. S., & Cone, J. D. (1987). Social skills in children: Identifying intervention targets using template matching procedures. *Behavior Modification, 11,* 137–163.

Hoier, T. S., McConnell, S., & Pallay, A. G. (1987). Observational assessment for planning and evaluating educational transitions: An initial analysis of template matching. *Behavioral Assessment, 9,* 5–19.

Kanfer, F. H. (1985). Target selection for clinical change programs. *Behavioral Assessment, 7,* 7–20.

Kanfer, F. H., & Saslow, G. (1965). Behavioral analysis: An alternative to diagnostic classification. *Archives of General Psychiatry, 12,* 529–538.

Kanfer, F. H., & Grimm, L. G. (1977). Behavioral analysis: Selecting target behaviors in the interview. *Behavioral Modification, 1,* 7–28.

Kanfer, F. H., & Schefft, B. K. (1988). *Guiding the process of therapeutic change.* Champaign, IL: Research Press.

Kazdin, A. E. (1985). Selection of target behaviors: The relationship of the treatment focus to clinical dysfunction. *Behavioral Assessment, 7,* 33–47.

Lerman, P. (1982). *Deinstitutionalization and the welfare state.* New Brunswick, NJ: Rutgers University Press.

Levis, D. J. (1982). Experimental and theoretical foundations of behavior modification. In A. S. Bellack, M. Hersen, & A. E. Kazdin (Eds.), *International handbook of behavior modification and therapy* (pp. 333–56). New York: Plenum Press.

Liberman, R. P., Falloon, I. R. H., & Wallace, C. J. (1984). Drug-psychosocial interventions in the treatment of schizophrenia. In M. Mirabi (Ed.), *The chronically mentally ill: Research and services* (pp. 175–210). New York: SP Medical & Scientific Books.

Liberman, R. P., Jacobs, H. E., Boone, S. E., Foy, D. W., Donahoe, C. P., Falloon, I. R. H., Blackwell, G., & Wallace, C. J. (1987). Skills training for the community adaptation of schizophrenics. In J. S. Strauss, W. Boker, & H. D. Brenner (Eds.), *Psychosocial treatment of schizophrenia* (pp. 94–109). Toronto: Hans Huber.

Liberman, R. P., Lillie, F. J., Falloon, I. R. H., Harpin, E. J., Hutchinson, W., & Stoute, B. (1984). Social skills training for relapsing schizophrenics: An experimental analysis. *Behavior Modification, 8,* 155–179.

Liberman, R. P., Massel, H. K., Mosk, M. D., & Wong, S. E. (1985). Social skills training for chronic mental patients. *Hospital and Community Psychiatry, 36,* 396–403.

Linn, M. W., Klett, J., & Caffey, F. M. (1980). Foster home characteristics and psychiatric client outcome. *Archives of General Psychiatry, 37,* 129–132.

McFall, R. M. (1982). A review and reformulation of the concept of social skills. *Behavioral Assessment, 4,* 1–33.

Neale, J. M., & Oltmanns, T. F. (1981). Assessment of schizophrenia. In D. H. Barlow (Ed.), *Behavioral assessment of adult disorders* (pp. 87–128). New York: Guilford Press.

Pallak, M. S. (1990). Community-based care for the mentally ill: Client outcome orientation in research, program planning, and service delivery. *American Psychologist, 45,* 1237.

Pepper, B., & Ryglewicz, H. (1982). Testimony for the neglected: The mentally ill in thepost-deinstitutionalized age. *American Journal of Orthopsychiatry, 52,* 388–392.

Rosen, A., & Proctor, E. K. (1981). Distinctions between treatment outcomes and their implications for treatment evaluation. *Journal of Consulting and Clinical Psychology, 49,* 418–425.

Spanier, G. B. (1976). Measuring dyadic adjustment: New scales for assessing the quality of marriage and similar dyads. *Journal of Marriage and the Family, 38,* 15–28.

Test, M. A. (1981). Effective community treatment of the chronically mentally ill: What is necessary? *Journal of Social Issues, 37,* 71–86.

Turner, R. J., Frankel, B. G., & Levin, D. M. (1983). Social support: Conceptualization, measurement, and implications for mental health. *Research in Community Mental Health, 3,* 67–111.

Wallace, C. J. (1986). Functional assessment in rehabilitation. *Schizophrenia Bulletin, 12,* 604–630.

Wallace, C. J., & Liberman, R. P. (1985). Social skills training for schizophrenics: A controlled clinical trial. *Psychiatry Research, 15,* 239–247.

Wing, J. K. (1987). Psychosocial factors affecting the long-term course of schizophrenia. In J. S. Strauss, W. Boker, & H. D. Brenner (Eds.), *Psychosocial treatment of schizophrenia* (pp. 13–29). Toronto: Hans Huber.

Chapter 3

The Standardized Assessment of Cognitive and Behavioral Components of Social Skills

Jeffrey R. Bedell and Shelley S. Lennox

A fundamental component of psychiatric rehabilitation is the assessment of the skills needed by an individual to function effectively. Clearly, the concept of social skill is fundamental to both assessment (see Chapters 1 and 2) and treatment (see Chapters 5, 6, 8, and 11) in psychiatric rehabilitation. In particular, two types of skill, cognitive and behavioral, have currently become the focus of social skill research and program development. Yet there is little objective information on the constituents of effective cognitive and behavioral skills and, therefore, on what skills meaningfully differentiate psychiatrically disabled and normal populations. Consequently, there is no consensus regarding what social skill phenomena to assess and train.

The current chapter was intended to achieve three primary objectives: (a) to provide the reader with a basic understanding of a conceptual definition of social skills and major deficiencies in their assessment, (b) to describe a standardized assessment instrument that attempts to remediate these deficiencies, and (c) to present preliminary data on results of a study comparing the cognitive and behavioral social skill functioning of individuals with schizophrenia and normal individuals. It is hoped that this information will assist practitioners and researchers in the development and evaluation of sophisticated and useful social skillas-sessments.

THE SOCIAL SKILLS CONSTRUCT: WHAT IS IT?

As a prerequisite to any discussion of the assessment of social skills, the construct must be defined. Unfortunately, although substantial progress has been made in defining the construct of social skills, no consensus about a definition yet exists. It has variously been defined in terms of its topography (i.e., the descriptive features of communication, comprising verbal, nonverbal, and paralinguistic elements) and/or function (i.e., the outcome(s) of social interactions, including short-term goal attainment and long-term maintenance of relationships), with social perception and information-processing skills now included in a number of conceptual models (see Bellack, Morrison, & Mueser, 1989, for discussion; Liberman, 1982). Social perception and information-processing skills include those cognitive abilities that enable one to (a) recognize the existence of a problem, (b) generate and evaluate alternative solutions, (c) select the most effective solution, (d) evaluate and implement the solution selected, and (e) evaluate the cost-benefits of the solution (McFall, 1982; Spivak, Platt, & Shure, 1976).

A comprehensive definition of social skills, consolidating the various concepts presented in the literature, states that they entail the abilities to (a) accurately perceive information derived from an interpersonal context, (b) transform that information into a viable behavioral program, and (c) execute that program through verbal and nonverbal behaviors that maximize the likelihood of goal attainment and the maintenance of good relations with others. This definition implies that social skills comprise two sets of abilities, cognitive (social perception and information-processing skills that define, organize, and guide social skills) and behavioral (verbal and nonverbal behaviors used to implement the decision derived from the cognitive processes), which predict certain consequences (e.g., short-term goal attainment, good interpersonal relations). Those who emphasize the importance of cognitive factors and view skills in this sphere as essential to effective behavioral performance espouse the problem-solving model of social skills (e.g., Bedell, Archer, & Marlowe, 1980; Bedell & Michael, 1985; Liberman et al., 1986; McFall, 1982; Trower, Bryant, & Argyle, 1978; Wallace, 1982). Assessment and training programs based upon this model are particularly applicable to individuals with schizophrenia, whose cognitive deficits probably contribute substantially to defective social performance.

Although a number of training programs based upon one of several similar problem-solving models have been developed, the focus of assessment has been on the behavioral component of social skills, especially nonverbal and paralinguistic elements (e.g., eye gaze, voice volume). Relatively little emphasis has been placed on evaluation of cognitive variables. With the exception of several problem-solving inventories (D'Zurilla & Nezu, 1990; Heppner & Petersen, 1982) and a videotaped assessment developed by Donahoe and colleagues (1990), the authors are aware of no other instruments designed to provide a comprehensive evaluation of the relevant cognitive skills. Moreover, the assessment developed by Donahoe and colleagues (1990), based upon the problem-solving model of Wallace (1982), is the only one that has been used to investigate these skills in schizophrenics (see Sullivan, Marder, Liberman, Donahue, & Mintz, 1990, as well). If, in fact, cognitive problem-solving skills, which are presumed deficient in schizophrenia, are a prerequisite of effective behavioral performance, then much greater effort must be expended on their assessment. It is incumbent upon the social skills researcher/trainer to be able to identify specific cognitive deficits and target them for intervention. As previously indicated, problem-solving ability comprises several skills, not all of which may be deficient in any one individual.

SOCIAL SKILL ASSESSMENT: COGNITIVE COMPONENT

To help redress this deficiency in the social skill assessment armamentarium, we developed an instrument designed to evaluate both the cognitive and the behavioral aspects of social skills. To evaluate cognitive skills we used a problem-solving model developed by Bedell and Michael (1985). This model of problem solving is a refinement that operationalized and expanded on the work of D'Zurilla and Goldfried (1971), who proposed that effective problem solving consists of a sequence of stages. The original stages proposed by D'Zurilla and Goldfried include (a) problem orientation, which they define as a generalized response set that the individual brings to particular problems, (b) problem definition and formulation, the objective of which is to obtain factual information about the problem, clarify its nature, and establish goals, (c) alternatives generation, which consists of generating a number of potentially effective solutions, (d) decision making, which involves selection of the best alternative, and (e) implementation and verification, which involves the behavioral execution of the decision, and its evaluation in terms of the degree to which it achieves the established goals.

In the D'Zurilla and Goldfried model, the problem orientation component, unlike the other four, "does not include the specific skills or abilities that are required to solve a particular problem successfully" (D'Zurilla, 1988, p. 89). It is, rather, a general style by which one approaches problems. Bedell and Michael (1985) transformed the problem orientation stage into a skill-directed task analogous to the others (e.g., problem definition, alternative generation). In their model, problem orientation is replaced by problem recognition, which consists of several cognitive skills that are required for successful resolution of particular problems.

Problem recognition is defined as the ability to identify both (a) the relevant elements of the problematic situation, including who is involved, what is transpiring, and when and where it is occurring, and (b) personal "cues" that suggest the existence of a problem. These personal or self-awareness cues are certain types of thoughts, feelings, and behaviors. Thinking cues focus on awareness of unfulfilled wants. Feeling cues consist of emotions that are strong, long lasting, or inappropriate to the situation. Behavioral cues are those that are unusual for or uncharacteristic of the person, socially inappropriate, or illegal.

As indicated, the remainder of the model essentially operationalizes the four remaining stages (i.e., problem definition, alternatives generation, decision, implementation and verification) into component skills. *Problem definition* is operationalized as the ability to (a) identify the wants of the people involved in the problem situation, and (b) establish a goal consistent with the wants of the people involved in the problem situation. *Alternatives generation* is operationalized as the ability to generate a number of potential solutions, then evaluate them in terms of their congruence with the goal established in the previous stage. To be considered appropriate, alternatives must be (a) related to the problem, (b) within the person's power and ability, (c) legal, and (d) socially acceptable. *Decision* is defined as the ability to select an alternative that is likely to fulfill the goal identified in the problem definition stage. Finally, *problem implementation and verification* requires the abilities to execute the decision behaviorally and verify that it, in fact, has fulfilled the goal.

The assessment described in the current chapter evaluates schizophrenic adults on the abilities required in the first four stages of the model described above, that is, problem recognition through decision. These are the cognitive components of the problem-solving model that assess the mental activities that are precursors to behavioral output.

SOCIAL SKILL ASSESSMENT: BEHAVIORAL COMPONENT

As stated previously, the behavioral component of social skills (i.e., the behaviors emitted in a social interaction) has generally been the focus of assessment. Behavior has been evaluated in one of several ways, in terms of either its overall skill quality (global measurement) or the specific verbal and nonverbal components it comprises (molecular measurement). Although global ratings can distinguish among criterion groups (Bellack, Morrison, Mueser, Wade, & Sayers, 1990; Donahoe et al., 1990; Conger, Moisan-Thomas, & Conger, 1989; Conger & Conger, 1982; Bellack, 1979), they don't provide specific information about the criteria upon which they are based (Conger et al., 1989; Bellack, 1979) and are readily biased (Nelson, Hayes, Felton, & Jarrett, 1985). As such, they are subjective measures and cannot serve as targets of rehabilitation interventions. Ratings of discrete behaviors that can be operationalized (molecular measures) resolve these problems, but are associated with several other disadvantages. For example, as Conger and colleagues (1989) and Bellack (1979) indicate, we do not know all the relevant behaviors that make up social skills. As a result, the literature reflects substantial variability in the specific behavioral variables assessed.

Kupke and his colleagues (Kupke, Hobbs, & Cheney, 1979; Kupke, Calhaun, & Hobbs, 1979) attribute the problem in molecular measurement to the fact that relatively simple, easy to count behaviors have frequently been selected for assessment. Instead of the relatively simple overt behaviors typically evaluated in the literature (e.g., talk time, number of silences), they suggest that more complex conversational skills (e.g., personal attention statements, those that direct the conversation back to the other) be assessed. Their study demonstrated the value of such assessment, with findings revealing a significant relationship between such conversational skills and ratings of interpersonal attraction among college students.

Although much progress has been made in the social skills assessment arena since the publication of Kupke and colleagues' (1979) findings, relatively little emphasis has been placed on the assessment of these conversational skills in schizophrenic adults. Millbrook, Farrell, and Curran (1986) did attempt to assess such skills in "psychiatric" patients, though they had to drop one measure from analysis because of low interrater reliability, and another measure exhibited such low frequency of occurrence that analysis was not meaningful.

The assessment instrument to be described below was developed not only to evaluate the cognitive component of problem-solving skills but also to evaluate a set of these relatively more complex and relevant communication skills.

METHOD

Subjects

The subjects were 20 individuals, 10 with a diagnosis of schizophrenia (five male, five female), and 10 nonpsychiatric controls (three male, seven female), all of whom were randomly selected from a larger pool of similar individuals evaluated with the social skills assessment under discussion. The psychiatric sample consisted of patients with schizophrenia who were recommended for social skills training as part of their rehabilitation program at the Sound View Throgs Neck Community Mental Health Center, Albert Einstein College of Medicine. Their mean age was 39.0 years. The nonpsychiatric sample consisted of counseling staff who were employed at a nearby adult psychiatric residential facility. The mean age of the counselors was 37.6 years.

THE STANDARDIZED INSTRUMENT

The instrument we developed is an analogue assessment of social skills in which the stimulus material is presented to subjects on videotape. This mode of presentation was selected to maximize control over stimulus input to subjects, and thus increase the likelihood of standardized administration. The videotaped format was also economical in terms of resources, rendering the instrument more practical for clinical application, for which it was developed.

The assessment was divided into three components. The first component measured the cognitive aspect of problem solving. The second component measured subjects' behavioral output in the form of communication skills, and the third assessed assertiveness in conflict situations. As the assertion data have not yet been analyzed, that component will not be described in this chapter.

The instrument is administered by an interviewer who presents the videotape, stopping it at designated times to ask the subject to respond to the video material. The evaluation proceeds according to instructions provided in the "Interviewer's Guide." Administration time generally ranges from 50 to 60 minutes.

The Cognitive Component

The cognitive component focused on problem-solving skills. It comprises three vignettes, each of which depicts an interaction of two individuals, one of whom is experiencing either anger, anxiety, or sadness in response to a social situation. For example, the first interaction is between a man and a woman, the latter of whom is obviously angry and reprimands the man for arriving too late for them to be able to attend a movie they planned to see together. The second and third scenes, respectively, depict a person experiencing social anxiety in response to being invited to a social activity and an individual expressing regret for not speaking out in a general equivalency diploma (GED) class. Each vignette is approximately 1 minute in duration. A narrator, also on videotape, introduces each scene, providing sufficient contextual information to orient the viewer to the situation depicted.

After each of the three vignettes is presented, the interviewer stops the videotape and asks the following series of questions, designed to assess cognitive skills.

Problem Recognition The first six questions (indicated below) assess different aspects of problem recognition. We wanted not only to assess whether or not the subjects could recognize the existence of a problem, but also to determine if subjects were cognizant of the information that would logically be the basis of that judgment. Therefore, we first asked the subjects to describe factually the situation they had observed (question 1). Next, we evaluated the subjects' ability to recognize the thoughts, feelings, and behaviors of the main character (questions 2, 3, and 4). Then, subjects were asked if they recognized the existence of a problem in the stimulus situation (question 5). Finally, they were asked to describe what information was used to enable them to recognize the existence of a problem (question 6).

1 Give an objective description of the situation you just watched.
2 Name one behavior you observed in the tape.

3 Tell me one thought (NAME OF PERSON IN VIGNETTE) might have had.

4 What was (NAME) feeling?

5 Does the scene you watched suggest that (NAME) has a problem that needs to be solved?

6 What about the scene makes you think that (NAME) has a problem?

Problem Definition   Once it was determined that a problem existed, the primary cognitive element of the next step in the process (problem definition) was to state a goal that defined the problem in such a way that it could be solved. This was asked in question 7.

7 Given that (NAME) has a problem because (INSERT SUBJECT'S RESPONSE TO QUESTION 6), what is a goal that (NAME) could have? In other words, state the problem in such a way that it could be more easily solved.

Alternatives Generation and Decision   Questions 8 and 9 evaluate abilities to think of alternative solutions and select an appropriate solution.

8 (NAME's) having recognized a problem and defined a goal, what is the next thing (NAME) should do?

9 (NAME's) having generated alternatives, what is the next step (NAME) should take in seeing this problem through?

The Behavioral Component: Communication Skills

Three communication skills are assessed, which include the abilities to (a) empathize (i.e., to communicate understanding of what another person wants and/or feels), (b) paraphrase (i.e., to repeat, in one's own words, the content of another's message), and (c) ask an open-ended question (i.e., a question that cannot be answered yes or no and that keeps the conversation going). These particular skills were selected on the basis of findings demonstrating their relevance to interpersonal effectiveness (e.g., Kupke et al., 1979; Melnick, 1973; Kagan, 1975). They all assess active listening skills as they require the individual to both attend to another's statement and generate a response directly relevant to it. The listening aspect of these communication skills was not directly evaluated, only the behavioral output. These communication skills are particularly appropriate to assess in persons with schizophrenia given well-known deficits in these skills for this population. Deficits in these skills are probably apparent in the broader population of chronic psychiatric patients found in rehabilitation programs.

For this component of the assessment, the stimulus material is a female actor (i.e., the speaker) on videotape who conveys information to the subject (i.e., viewer). The information presented consists of one or more statements in response to which the subject is instructed to communicate in a specified way. Depending upon which of the three communication skills is being assessed, the subject is asked to respond to the actor by talking to her and (a) "repeating, in your own words, what she said to you" (paraphrase), (b) "asking an open question that cannot be answered yes or no and will keep the conversation going" (ask an open question), or (c) "making a statement that shows you understand the emotions or feelings she is having" (empathize). A videotaped narrator provides instructions to the subject prior to, and after, each stimulus statement the actor makes. Each skill is assessed twice, and the stimulus statements to which the subject responds are the following:

Subject instructed to paraphrase:
   "I have so many things to study for my test tomorrow, I could stay up all night and not get finished."
   "We have a trip planned for this weekend and now my boss says that I might have to work. I wonder if I should cancel my plans now or wait until the weekend."

Subject instructed to ask an open question in response to:
   "Hi, I just got back from my vacation in Jersey."
   "You know that new restaurant down on the square? I went over there the other day and ate lunch."

Subject instructed to empathize in response to:
   "Man, I went down to the store last night and, when I left, it was dark and the parking lot was empty and I had to walk to the car alone. I didn't know if I was going to make it to my car without being mugged. Boy, I'm never going to do that again."
   "You know, this is the third overdue bill I've gotten for my electric. I've already paid this stupid bill. You'd think those idiots would get this straightened out and stop bothering me. I'm going to write a nasty letter to the public service commission. That will show them!"

Procedure

The interviewer introduced each of the cognitive and behavioral tasks to the subject, who was seated in front of the video monitor. The videotape with the stimulus situations was played, and the narrator on the tape introduced the first problem scene, following which the scene was presented to the subject. After the subject viewed the scene, the videotape was turned off and the interviewer asked the relevant problem-solving questions. These questions, which were listed earlier under "The Standardized Instrument," were specified in the "Interviewer's Guide." The same procedure was followed for scenes 2 and 3.
   Following the scenes used to assess cognitive skills, the interviewer oriented subjects to the behavioral assessment task. As indicated in "The Standardized

Instrument" section, the videotaped narrator provided a context for the stimulus statements, also informing subjects of the skill they would be asked to demonstrate in response to the stimulus statement. Following each statement, the interviewer stopped the tape and repeated the narrator's instructions to the subject. The subject's response was videotaped.

Scoring

Cognitive Component   The first six questions (see "The Standardized Instrument" section of this chapter) evaluated the ability to (a) describe the problem situation (question #1); (b) identify a thought (#2), feeling (#3), and behavior (#4) of the main character in the scene observed; (c) recognize the existence of a problem (#5); and (d) state the information used to recognize the problem (#6).

As indicated previously, a thorough description of each of the problem situations contained the following four bits of information, each associated with a point value: (1) who was involved, with 1 point awarded for the correct identification of each of the two actors; (2) what they were doing, with 3 points given for the accurate description of what happened between the actors (1 point for mention of each of the three relevant components describing "what" was going on); (3) when the situation occurred (1 point); and (4) where it occurred (1 point). Scores could range from 0 to 7.

The response to each of questions 2, 3, and 4, which required the identification of a thought, feeling, and behavior respectively (e.g., "Tell me one thought (name of person in vignette) might have had"), of the main character, was scored 1 or 0 (e.g., zero for naming a feeling when asked to identify a thought).

Recognition of the existence of a problem (question 5) was awarded 1 point. Saying there was no problem was scored zero. In addition, if the subject was unable to recognize the existence of a problem (question 5), subsequent questions were not scored. The assumption was that a deficit in the basic skill of problem recognition precluded evaluation of subsequent problem-solving stages.

The subject was next asked what information he or she used to recognize the existence of the problem (question 6). A correct response was defined as one that could be classified as a thought, feeling, or behavior of the individual with the problem in the vignette. Subjects could respond to each of the three vignettes differently, thus producing various combinations of thought, feeling, and behavior explanations for their decisions. The unit of analysis for this variable was the number of subjects (either schizophrenic or normal) using each classification (i.e., thought, feeling, or behavior).

The ability to define the problem (question 7) was awarded 1 point. A problem was considered to be defined if the goal or problem statement reasonably followed from the vignette.

The alternative solutions provided by the subject were counted and classified as (a) appropriate or (b) inappropriate, thus yielding two scores for question 8. An appropriate alternative was defined as one that (a) reasonably assisted in the accomplishment of the goal specified by the subject in the problem definition step (i.e., question 7), (b) was within the person's power and ability, and (c) was legal and socially acceptable.

Finally, question 9, designed to evaluate the subject's ability to select one or more solutions to the problem, was scored on a scale ranging from 0 to 2, with 0 given for selecting an inappropriate solution, 1 for selecting a combination of inappropriate and appropriate solutions, and 2 if one or more appropriate solutions only were selected. A solution was deemed appropriate if it either (a) was one of the appropriate alternatives provided in response to question 8 (alternatives generation) or (b) would have been rated as appropriate had it been generated as an alternative.

Subject scores for each question (except #6) were aggregated across the three vignettes to increase the reliability of assessment. In other words, the final score for each question was the sum of the three scores. If one of the three responses was missing, it was calculated as the mean of the other two, then added to their sum to yield a final score. If two responses were missing, the subject's score was not computed for that question.

Behavioral Component   The range of scores for each of the two "paraphrase" items was 0–3, with one point awarded for each of the three bits of information contained in the stimulus statements. For example, for the response to the first vignette, one point was given for statements communicating the following information: (a) so much to study, (b) stay up all night, and (c) never finish it. Any other statements were not given credit. For the open question, scores ranged from 0 to 2, with (a) 0 given for a closed-ended question that could be answered "yes" or "no", (b) 1 point awarded for a closed-ended question that could be answered with one word *other than* "yes" or "no," and (c) 2 points given for an open-ended question, that is, one that required more than a one-word response and that would keep the conversation going.

Each response to the "empathy" stimulus earned a score of 0 or 1, with 0 given if either no feeling or the wrong feeling was identified. One point was given for an empathic response that correctly identified the actor's feeling (vignette 1—fear; vignette 2—anger).

The scores of the responses to the two vignettes evaluating each of the three behavioral skills were aggregated to increase reliability. Any missing responses resulted in exclusion of the subject's data for that item.

RESULTS

Interrater reliability for the two independent raters who evaluated the 785 scorable responses of the 20 subjects (some responses were missing because of technical difficulties during data collection) was determined with the kappa statistic (as the range of numerical values was small before responses were aggregated, we treated them as categorical data for the determination of reliability). Four kappas were obtained, .67, .75, .77, and .86, indicating a satisfactorily high level of reliability. Responses on which raters initially disagreed were discussed and rerated. The two raters agreed on all but six (99.24%) of the ratings after this procedure. The final determination of scores for these items was made by a third rater, who chose between the scores given by the primary reviewers.

With the exception of the data generated from question 6 (i.e., "What about the scene makes you think that (Name) has a problem?"), which consisted of frequencies, the variables were analyzed with t-tests for independent means. One-tailed tests were used, as our hypothesis was that the controls would perform better than the schizophrenic group in these cognitive and behavioral skills.

Problem Recognition   The first variables to be analyzed measured the subjects' ability to describe objectively the situation that they observed. The t-tests applied to each of these variables (who, what, when, and where) revealed no significant group differences. In other words, normals were no better than schizophrenics in, identifying the relevant components of an interaction, that is, who was involved, what happened, and where and when it occurred.

The ability to identify thoughts, feelings, and behaviors of the actors in the vignettes was evaluated next. There were no significant group differences observed in the ability to identify a behavior, or make reasonable inferences about what the main character was thinking and feeling. Interestingly, when asked to identify a thought or a feeling, both schizophrenic patients and normals tended to make errors about 25% of the time. That is, when they were asked to identify a feeling, about 25% of the responses were either thoughts or behaviors, and when they were asked to identify a thought, about 25% of the responses were either behaviors or feelings. However, when asked to identify a behavior, patients and normals alike mistakenly indicated either a thought or a feeling on 58% of the trials.

Although there was no difference in the ability to describe the situation, or to identify thoughts, feelings, and behaviors, group comparisons revealed that normals were better able to recognize the existence of a problem ($t = 2.22$, $df = 18$, $p < .025$), than were the schizophrenic subjects.

The type of information (thought, feeling, or behavior) used by the subject to determine the existence of the problem was analyzed next. The frequency with which schizophrenics and normals identified a thought, feeling, or behavior as the basis of recognition was evaluated with three Fisher's exact probability tests. These analyses revealed no group differences in the use of thoughts and feelings, but did indicate that groups identified behaviors with different frequencies ($p < .05$). Specifically, the normals used behavioral cues significantly more often than did the schizophrenics.

Problem Definition   When asked to formulate a reasonable goal to resolve the problem, the normals were better able to define the problem than were the schizophrenic subjects ($t = 6.44$, $df = 18$, $p < .0005$).

Alternative Generation and Decision   The next analyses indicated that there were no significant differences in the ability to generate appropriate alternatives ($t = -.17$, $df = 15$, n.s.). Schizophrenics, however, generated significantly more inappropriate alternatives ($t = -2.03$, $df = 15$, $p < .05$). Too many missing data (due to technical problems) precluded analysis of the ability to make a decision.

Behavioral Assessment of Communication Skills   Analyses conducted on the behavioral skills revealed that normals demonstrated more ability to paraphrase ($t = 1.73$, $df = 18$, $p < .025$), showed more skill in asking open questions ($t = 2.51$, $df = 18$, $p < .025$), and more accurately reflected back the speaker's feelings ($t = 1.83$, $df = 17$, $p < .05$) than the schizophrenic subjects. In sum, normals performed better on all three of the behavioral skills assessed.

DISCUSSION

This research provides information on the viability of a new measure of cognitive as well as behavioral social skills that can be used with severely psychiatrically handicapped and normal individuals. The instrument, replete with an "Interviewer's Guide" and a format to ensure standard administration and scoring, has thus far demonstrated adequate psychometric properties, with further evaluation in progress. Specifically, it has revealed good interrater reliability and the ability to distinguish groups with known differences in social skill. Moreover, with regard to the latter, the assessment has begun to accumulate evidence on (a) those social skills that meaningfully differentiate normal from chronic psychiatric populations, and (b) the value of interpersonal problem-solving training for the psychiatrically disabled.

The specific cognitive skills assessed, following from Bedell and Michael's (1985) adaptation of D'Zurilla and Goldfried's (1971) model, include those of (a) *problem recognition,* comprising (1) awareness of intrapersonal, interpersonal, and situational factors associated with social interaction; (2) recognition of the existence of a problem in an interpersonal situation; and (3) ability to identify information relevant to determination of the presence of an interpersonal problem; (b) *problem definition,* the ability to formulate a goal; and (c) *alternatives generation,* the ability to generate appropriate solutions and the likelihood of developing inappropriate ones. The behavioral skills assessed were relatively complex communication skills, requiring subjects to paraphrase statements, ask open-ended questions, and reflect the feelings of another person.

Table 3-1   A Comparison of Cognitive and Behavioral Skills of Normal and Schizophrenic Subjects

Cognitive Variables

Problem Recognition
1. Awareness of intrapersonal, interpersonal, and situational factors
   a. Describe situation (who, what, when, where) .... NS
   b. Identify a thought, feeling, and behavior .... NS

2. Factor used to determine existence of a problem
   a. Thought .... NS
   b. Feeling .... NS
   c. Behavior .... N > SZ

3. Ability to recognize the existence of a problem.................. N > SZ

Problem Definition
4. Ability to formulate a goal................................. N > SZ

Alternatives Generation
5. Ability to generate appropriate alternatives.................... NS

6. Likelihood of generating inappropriate alternatives .... N < SZ

Behavioral Variables
7. Ability to paraphrase .... N > SZ

8. Ability to ask an open question .... N > SZ

9. Ability to be empathic .... N > SZ

Abbreviations: NS = no significant difference; N = normal subjects; SZ = schizophrenic subjects.

The pattern of performance on these variables was very interesting when normal and schizophrenic subjects were compared. As can be seen in Table 3-1, there were no significant differences between these groups in awareness of intrapersonal, interpersonal, and situational factors associated with a social interaction. However, schizophrenics were less likely to use this information to recognize the existence of a problem. Moreover, when they did recognize its existence, they were less likely than normals to base their decision on behavioral (vs. affective or cognitive) information. Although the reliability of this finding needs to be further demonstrated, it suggests that utilization of more directly observable, and therefore more objective, behavioral information may result in more socially skilled behavior.

Having recognized the existence of a problem, the normals and schizophrenics were equally well able to think of appropriate solutions to the problem, but the schizophrenics were more likely to think of inappropriate solutions. This apparent inability to distinguish between potentially effective and ineffective alternatives suggests a deficit in the ability to anticipate consequences.

Performance on the behavioral tasks revealed that the normal controls were better able to (a) restate in their own words what had been said by another, (b) ask a question that would tend to keep the conversation going, and (c) accurately reflect the feelings expressed by another. Thus, the normals were superior to the schizophrenics in all three communication skills assessed.

It was expected that the normal subjects would outperform the schizophrenic patients on many of these skills. When the definition of social skills provided at the beginning of this chapter is used the results of the present investigation indicate that schizophrenic patients were equal to normal subjects in the ability to "perceive information derived from an interpersonal context." That is, schizophrenic patients were equally as able as normals to extract complex and sophisticated factual information from observations of a social situation. They were able to understand the nature of the social interaction and, to the same extent as controls, describe the wishes, wants, desires, expectations, feelings, and actions of the actors. This finding suggests that, for schizophrenics, skill deficits in social perception may not be as great as typically believed. "Receiving skills" may not be the social skills that differentiate this population from nonpsychiatric controls. This hypothesis must be stated tentatively, however, as Donahoe and associates (1990) did find that schizophrenics were deficient in these skills as well as all other problem-solving skills evaluated.

Though present findings revealed equal ability of groups to perceive information from the environment, they clearly demonstrated that schizophrenics were less able to make use of, that is, "process," this information to (a) recognize a problem's existence, (b) define an appropriate goal, and (c) differentiate between potentially appropriate and inappropriate solutions. In other words, according to the definition of social skills presented earlier, they were deficient in the ability to "transform the information perceived into a viable behavioral program." With regard to alternative generation, Spivack and colleagues (1976) similarly found that schizophrenics generated more inappropriate solutions than normals. In contrast to our observations, though, their schizophrenic sample also generated fewer appropriate solutions. This discrepancy may require additional research to determine if it is due to methodological or real sample differences.

Finally, the normals were clearly superior when it came to "sending" information, performing significantly better on all three communication behaviors assessed. Specifically, the controls were better able to follow directions and communicate with a paraphrase, an open question, and an empathy statement (each of which was defined along with the request for its use). It is not known how subjects would have spontaneously responded to the stimulus statements, that is, if they were asked to respond as they would normally, without the narrator's directive. This could be a topic of future research.

Another interesting observation of the present investigation was that both normals and schizophrenics were able to identify thoughts and feelings with greater accuracy than behaviors. This finding is somewhat counterintuitive since behaviors are directly observable, whereas thoughts and feelings must be inferred from behavioral and situational cues. Identifying the latter would seem to be a more difficult task. In any case, the degree of proficiency in identifying thoughts, feelings, and behaviors (75%, 75%, and 42% accuracy, respectively) indicates that individuals do not have as clear an understanding of these basic human characteristics as one might predict. This relative deficiency must certainly contribute to social skill deficits whenever accurate phenomenological labeling is required. Several contemporary models of treatment (e.g., cognitive restructuring) focus their interventions on the interactions and relationships among thoughts, feelings, and behaviors, and thus promote understanding of these concepts. The present findings suggest that these types of treatment address a skill deficit common to the majority of individuals.

In summary, the present findings suggest that individuals with schizophrenia are as capable as normals in perceiving interpersonal information. They are equally able to identify the relevant elements of an interpersonal interaction (i.e., who is involved, what's happening, and where and when it is occurring) and to make inferences about others' thoughts and feelings, and identify behaviors that others exhibit. However, they appear to be relatively deficient in abilities required to make use of this information to resolve problems effectively. They have, according to our definition of social skills, difficulty "transforming information perceived from the interpersonal situation into viable behavioral programs" and "executing these programs." Thus, the idea that social skills training should stress the teaching of skills that help the patient to define, organize, and guide behavior seems highly appropriate. The authors present in Chapter 5 a model of skills training that stresses these factors. Certainly, the assessment of social skills using methods such as those described in this chapter will enable rehabilitation programs to better focus training efforts on skills most in need of remediation.

It should be stated that the current study is primarily a presentation of objective and standard methods of social skill assessment. Although the application of these standard methods has raised some interesting and provocative questions, there are limitations to the research findings presented. The primary case in point is that, although these findings are based on a relatively large number of observations, the sample size underlying these observations is relatively small. Therefore, at present, it is impossible to tell which of our null findings actually reflect no group differences or insufficient power to detect their existence. The investigation is proceeding, and the results of further research will help clarify this issue.

REFERENCES

Bedell, J. R., Archer, R. P., & Marlowe, H. A., Jr. (1980). A description and evaluation of a problem-solving skills training program. In D. Upper & S. M. Ross (Eds.), *Behavioral group therapy: An annual review.* Champaign, IL: Research Press.

Bedell, J. R., & Michael, D. D. (1985). Teaching problem solving skills to chronic psychiatric patients. In D. Upper & S. M. Ross (Eds.), *Handbook of behavioral group therapy*. New York: Plenum Press.

Bellack, A. S. (1979). A critical appraisal of strategies for assessing social skills. *Behavioral Assessment, 1,* 157–176.

Bellack, A. S., Morrison, R. L., & Mueser, K. T. (1989). Social problem solving in schizophrenia. *Schizophrenia Bulletin, 15,* 101–116.

Bellack, A. S., Morrison, R. L., Mueser, K. T., Wade, J. A., & Sayers, S. L. (1990). Role-play for assessing social competence of psychiatric patients. *Psychological Assessment, 2,* 248–255.

Conger, J. C., & Conger, A. J. (1982). Components of heterosocial competence. In J. C. Curran & P. M. Monti (Eds.), *Social skills training: A practical handbook for assessment and treatment* (pp. 314–347). New York: Guilford.

Conger, J. C., Moisan-Thomas, P. C., & Conger, A. J. (1989). Cross-situational generalizability of social competence: A multilevel analysis. *Behavioral Assessment, 11,* 411–431.

Donahoe, C. P., Carter, M. J., Bloem, W. D., Hirsch, G. L., Laasi, N., & Wallace, C. J. (1990). Assessment of interpersonal problem solving skills. *Psychiatry, 53,* 329–339.

D'Zurilla, T. J. (1988). Problem solving therapies. In K. S. Dobson (Ed.), *Handbook of cognitive behavioral therapies* (pp. 85–135). New York: Guilford.

D'Zurilla, T. J., & Goldfried, M. R. (1971). Problem solving and behavior modification. *Journal of Abnormal Psychology, 78,* 107–126.

D'Zurilla, T. J., & Nezu, A. M. (1990). Development and preliminary evaluation of the social problem solving inventory. *Psychological Assessment, 2,* 156–163.

Heppner, P. P., & Petersen, C. H. (1982). The development and implications of a personal problem solving inventory. *Journal of Counseling Psychology, 29,* 66–75.

Kagan, N. (1975). Influencing human interaction: Eleven years with IPR. *Canadian Counsellor, 9,* 75–97.

Kupke, T. E., Calhaun, K. S., & Hobbs, S. A. (1979). Selection of heterosocial skills. II, Experimental validity. *Behavior Therapy, 10,* 336–346.

Kupke, T. E., Hobbs, S. A., & Cheney, T. H. (1979). Selection of heterosocial skills. *Behavior Therapy, 10,* 327–335.

Liberman, R. P. (1982). Assessment of social skills. *Schizophrenia Bulletin, 8,* 62–83.

Liberman, R. P., Mueser, K. T., Wallace, C. J., Jacobs, H. E., Eckman, T., & Massel, H. K. (1986). Training skills in the psychiatrically disabled: Learning coping and competence. *Schizophrenia Bulletin, 12,* 631–647.

McFall, R. M. (1982). A review and reformulation of the concept of social skills. *Behavioral Assessment, 4,* 1–33.

Melnick, J. (1973). A comparison of replication techniques in the modification of minimal dating behavior. *Journal of Abnormal Psychology, 81,* 51–59.

Millbrook, J. M., Farrell, A. D., & Curran, J. P. (1986). Behavioral components of social skills: A look at subject and confederate behaviors. *Behavioral Assessment, 8,* 203–220.

Nelson, R. O., Hayes, S. C., Felton, J. L., & Jarrett, R. B. (1985). A comparison of data produced by different behavioral assessment techniques with implications for models of social skills inadequacy. *Behavior Research and Therapy, 23,* 1–11.

Spivack, G., Platt, J. J., & Shure, M. B. (1976). *The problem solving approach to adjustment.* San Francisco: Jossey-Bass.

Sullivan, G., Marder, S. R., Liberman, R. P., Donahue, C. P., & Mintz, J. (1990). Social skills and relapse history in outpatient schizophrenics. *Psychiatry, 53,* 340–345.

Trower, P., Bryant, B., & Argyle, M. (1978). *Social skills and mental health.* Pittsburg:University of Pittsburg Press.

Wallace, C. J. (1982). The social skills training project of the mental health clinical research center for the study of schizophrenia. In J. P. Curran & P. M. Monti (Eds.), *Social skills training: A practical handbook for assessment & treatment* (pp. 57–89). New York: Guilford Press.

Chapter 4

What Do Patients Say About Program Planning? Perspectives From the Patient-Authored Literature

Leona L. Bachrach

Persons who have been patients in the mental health service system sometimes write about their experiences as service recipients. They are perforce experts in the field of mental health program planning, and their products are often frank, articulate, and exceedingly sensitive. Although these writings contain important clues and information from which mental health program planners might take direction, surprisingly little note has been taken of the patient-authored literature in the development of program initiatives for mentally ill individuals.

In this article I examine the patient-authored literature and seek to establish points of agreement between patient-authors and professionals who design and plan mental health programs. Are the pet planning concepts that professionals espouse reinforced or contradicted in patients' writings? And what, if anything, that is important to patient-authors have professionals tended to overlook?

To answer these questions I employ three basic concepts that have assumed increasing popularity in professional program-planning circles in recent years:

This chapter is based on a lecture presented at the 40th Institute on Hospital and Community Psychiatry, New Orleans, October 24, 1988.

the notion that treatment resistance among patients ("difficult patienthood") has more than one source; the notion that the disabilities accompanying severe mental illness are complex and multivariate; and the idea that service planning for mentally ill persons should, ideally, be tailored to the needs of each patient.

These three concepts are perhaps more accurately described as "conceptual fields," for each is intricately intertwined with other principles and concepts. Together they generate the framework for the present analysis, which reviews patient-authored writings retrieved through a Medline search of periodical literature for the past decade. Occasional earlier writings by patients that seem especially relevant to the subject of inquiry have also been examined, as have patient-authored writings from a variety of miscellaneous sources—the so-called fugitive literature, consisting of letters, newspaper clippings, agency publications, conference proceedings, and other unindexed statements.

It is important to note at the outset what this article is not. It does not purport to present a comprehensive review of patient-authored literature. The focus here is specifically on program-planning issues as they are discussed in that literature. Nor is this article concerned with the politics of the patient rights movement or with advocacy for mental patients, important as those matters are. Instead, my aim in this article is to take a small step toward bridging the gap between the perspectives of patient-authors and professional program designers. To say this differently, this article represents an effort to assess what outsiders looking in may learn from insiders speaking out about issues in mental health program planning and service delivery.

On the assumption that patients' own words are superior to paraphrases, direct quotations are liberally interspersed throughout this review. Serendipitously, this carries a distinct aesthetic reward, for patients' writings are often poetic and lyrical, as the late Jack Weinberg (1978) noted when he wrote about "the words of the emotionally ill . . . the poetry of the anguished mentality."

By way of example, a patient at the Rhode Island Institute of Mental Health (1984) who signs his name as Tom writes:

Getting out of here
And into something
Like work
Or something payable
Like caddying
I've had some good days
And some rainy ones
Sometimes it would
Break your heart
To see the rain
When it comes
But to be able
To hang around and hope

Helps a lot
But to sit
And be incarcerated
Almost drives you
To be tapioca

Another patient at the same hospital who signs his name as Robert writes:

Fill my mind with knowledge
Fill my body with definition
Fill my life with total well being
Fill my pockets with money
Fill my head with normal thoughts
Fill my nerves with relaxation
Fill myself with the old me

PLANNING CONCEPTS

Mental health program planning today—at least on paper if not in actual fact—is generally influenced by the convergence of three interrelated conceptual developments: first, emerging ideas about what makes a patient treatment resistant, noncompliant, or "difficult"; second, our understanding of the concept of disability as it affects mentally ill individuals; and, third, our promotion of individualized treatment planning for the members of the patient population.

Difficult Patienthood

The words "difficult patient," which are frequently used to indicate treatment resistance or lack of cooperation (Bachrach, Talbott, & Meyerson, 1987), are inherently stigmatizing. They are also in some ways inherently contradictory, since "all patients who have been designated as having a psychiatric condition are expected to be problems to themselves as well as to their respective environments, which includes the psychiatrist who comes into contact with them" (Chrzanowski, 1980). For these reasons, recent literature has discussed difficult patienthood from both patient and extra-patient sources.

Three interrelated kinds of precipitants are typically discussed (Bachrach, et al., 1987). First, difficult patienthood may be attributed to patients themselves: to certain behaviors, characteristics, or attributes that distinguish some patients from other "nondifficult" patients. Neill (1979) reports that difficult patients tend generally to be more demanding, more puzzling, less likely to evoke empathy, more dangerous to themselves and others, more attention seeking and manipulative, more likely to polarize staff, more technically difficult as psychiatric cases, and more likely to misuse medication than nondifficult patients.

Second, difficult patienthood may be attributed to the clinician who works with the patient: to the clinician's biases or expectations or to the so-called rules that clinicians often superimpose on the clinical interaction. Examples might include stipulations that the illness be treatable and preferably curable, that the patient be fully cooperative, and that the patient regard the condition as something that must be changed (Jeffery, 1979). When a patient breaks these or similar rules, the clinician may well perceive that individual as a difficult patient.

It is, however, exceedingly difficult in practice to separate the first and second sources of difficult patienthood. There is increasing consensus in the literature that the distinguishing personal characteristics, attributes, and behaviors of so-called difficult patients are troublesome only contextually: that they may be necessary, but are not sufficient, for the definition of difficult patienthood (Bachrach, et al., 1987). A particular patient's behaviors or attributes are thus difficult only when they are perceived to be so by clinicians, administrators, or service planners.

Third, difficult patienthood may be attributed to the service system itself, or more precisely, to deficits within that system. When the service system lacks sufficient will or resources to provide continuity of care and comprehensive care, it tends to build a protective shield around itself. Harris and Bergman (1986–1987) have introduced the concept of the "narcissistically vulnerable system" to describe the defensive postures assumed by service structures that "are primarily concerned with maintaining an often fragile sense of self-esteem." It is not uncommon for the service system to identify patients whom it will not or cannot serve, or whom it will not or cannot treat, as difficult patients and thereby absolve itself of the obligation to care for these individuals.

These three sources of difficult patienthood are highly interactive and, according to the literature, rarely operate independently (Bachrach, et al., 1987). Conceptually, the most critical point concerning them is that it takes more than just a patient to make a difficult patient. It takes a context as well—a context that consists of both clinician variables and system variables.

Patients' Views

These sources of difficult patienthood are fully acknowledged in the patient-authored literature, often with great insight. As for the first source of difficult patienthood, patients frankly admit in their writing that they at times exhibit behaviors or characteristics that are sufficiently removed from the mainstream to be troublesome to clinicians, service systems, relatives, and society at large. Indeed, far from denying this, this literature frequently implies—and sometimes explicitly states—that such behaviors and characteristics should be considered predictable manifestations of severe and invasive illness.

Moreover, patient-authors appear to have an unusual talent for demonstrating the intrinsic interdependence between the first and second sources of difficult patienthood. They frequently observe that patients' troublesome behaviors, attributes, and characteristics must be understood as the flip side of clinicians' attitudes and expectations. Thus, one former patient, Sharp (1988), implores clinicians to recognize and acknowledge their own role in promoting difficult patienthood: "If you don't like someone, get them a doctor who does like them. Don't just get stonefaced and argumentative, but have the strength to let go. Be more responsive."

Indeed, Sharp (1988), who in her writings often addresses clinicians directly in the second person, is not above mixing a bit of irony and humor with her eloquence:

> Doctors, pills are pills, however you slice them, and you have all the control, but only the patient knows if he wants to take one a second time, whether it helps or hurts. You're not veterinarians, so your patients can speak and you will get your best clues by listening to them, and by believing them you will get the truth.

Similarly, patient-authors are often direct and persuasive in offering illustrations of the relationship between difficult patienthood and system inadequacy. They frequently report personal histories filled with searches for appropriate and responsive programs—programs that are, most often, simply not to be found. Or, if the programs can be found, the barriers to using them are perceived as multiple, subtle, and generally insuperable.

The message here is clear. Patient-authors tell us in no uncertain terms that if patients are to become more compliant and less burdensome to the system of care, the system must do its part to welcome them and respond to their needs. Indeed, concern with system deficits has led one well-known patient-author, Allen (1974), to formulate a patients' bill of rights. Allen, who in the late 1970s served as one of the commissioners on President Carter's Commission on Mental Health, delivers a strong and persuasive message that is oft repeated in the patient-authored literature: that comprehensive services, full access to care, and individualized treatments delivered with regard for patients' personhood and dignity must be made available to mentally ill individuals.

In this connection Brundage (1983) writes:

> The effectiveness in reaching and working with patients rests largely upon the ability of the caregiver to perceive and comprehend how particular patients are experiencing their illnesses. . . . Meticulous honesty and fairness on the part of the caregiver is important. Sometimes patients . . . get even more confused in the face of ambiguity and deception. . . . Tact and understanding of the patients' distress will go a long way toward increasing self-esteem and feelings of self-worth.

SOURCES OF DISABILITY

A second conceptual field that strongly influences contemporary program planning for mentally ill individuals involves the notion of disability. There is a growing awareness today that disability typically derives from more than one source. Although some portion is directly attributable to the illness, other contributing sources are the manner in which the individual patient responds to the illness, and the manner in which the system of care and society respond to the circumstances of the patient. These ideas are central in the writings of several British investigators, including Wing and Morris (1981) and Shepherd (1984), who discuss three essential varieties of disability.

Primary Disability

The primary disabilities are those that are associated with illness per se and consist of psychiatric impairments or dysfunctions that may otherwise be described as symptoms of illness. Thus, for example, individuals diagnosed with chronic schizophrenia might exhibit such primary disabilities as lethargy, odd and unacceptable behavior, a lack of awareness of their handicaps, and disturbances in social relationships. It is typically the appearance of these symptoms of illness or primary disabilities that leads to diagnosis, and, for many individuals, although not for all, to treatment in the system of care.

Many patient-authors discuss their primary disabilities openly. Leete (1987), a former patient who is currently program director for education, advocacy, and support at Consumer-Centered Services of Colorado in Denver, describes her hallucinations, suspiciousness, and disorganization in vivid language: "Sometimes I pace endlessly to relieve the anxiety. I may become frozen in a certain position just because it feels right. . . . [I] curl up, rock back and forth, pace, or become rigid, at times knowing how bizarre this appears." And McKay (1986), a schizophrenic woman who lives in a shelter for homeless women in Washington, D.C., writes: "I have been a homeless woman for five years. Sometimes I am sharply aware of my surroundings; sometimes I am like a plastic doll, my staring eyes open but unseeing, or I am like a zombie, moving but unfeeling." A former English teacher, McKay has authored two moving and most instructive articles for the *Washington Post.*

In fact, the importance of accepting one's primary disabilities—one's acknowledgment of illness per se—emerges as a common theme in much of the patient-authored literature. Leete (1987) articulates this idea precisely with the words, "It was not until I had come to accept my illness that I could seriously devise ways of overcoming it."

In this connection some, though certainly not all, patient-authors—perhaps because they are willing and able to acknowledge their primary disabilities—do not summarily dismiss the need for pharmacotherapies. The literature frequently acknowledges that medications, appropriately prescribed and reviewed, are essential to progress. Leete (1987) writes:

> Despite the embarrassment of troublesome side effects, I now use medication as an adjunct to my other coping mechanisms. However, for many years before I came to

realize the role medication could play in the management of my illness, I was caught in a vicious circle. When I was off the medication I couldn't remember how much better I had felt on it, and when I was taking the medication I felt so good that I was convinced I did not need it. Fortunately, through many years of trial and error, I have now learned what medication works best for me and when to take it to minimize side effects.

Similarly, Harris (1988) notes: "I now must take daily medication. I didn't realize until the last time I went off of it how important the medicine is. Without it, I can't function. It's the difference between being insane and sane."

Secondary Disability

In addition to the illness itself, Wing and Morris (1981) and Shepherd (1984) have written about secondary disabilities that build upon the primary ones. These disabilities stem not from the illness per se, but rather from the *experience* of illness. Wing has referred to secondary disabilities as "adverse personal reactions," and Shepherd notes that "a major psychiatric episode is a frightening and disturbing experience and its effects may persist long after the primary symptoms have disappeared." Secondary disabilities, then, represent individual patients' idiosyncratic responses to their illness.

Once again, patient-authors concur. The notion of secondary disability is clearly expressed in an anonymous article appearing in the *American Journal of Psychiatry:* "Even if medication can free the schizophrenic patient from some of his torment, the scars of emotional confusion remain, felt perhaps more deeply by a greater sensitivity and vulnerability" (Recovering Patient, 1986).

Robinson (1983), another former patient, offers this description of her secondary disabilities:

I was pretty terrified at how far I [had] deteriorated into psychosis. . . . The world of a psychotic is definitely not a pretty one. I remember well the feverish, sleepless nights I spent getting carried away to some magical realm by my own thoughts. My thinking process seemed to me a miracle that could conquer anyone else's. Yet those same thinking processes could overwhelm me into crying oceans of tears over some nostalgic trivia; worse, I could be seized by episodic spasms of sheer unknowable terrors.

The patient-authored literature in fact contains recurrent references to personal reactions of anger, as exemplified in an article by McGrath (1984).

I sound angry—I guess I am—at the illness for invading my life and making me feel so unsure of myself . . . at the medical researchers who now only want to pick and probe into brains or wherever so they can program measurements into their computers while ignoring me, the person . . . at all the literature which shrouds schizophrenia in negativity, making any experience connected with it crazy and unacceptable . . . at the pharmaceutical industry for being satisfied that their pills keep me "functional" when all the while I feel drugged and unreal to myself. And I'm angry at me for believing and trusting too much in all this information and becoming nothing more than a patient, a victim of some intangible illness. It's no wonder to me anymore why I feel I've lost my self, why my existence seems a waning reflection.

The McGrath article (1984) also captures the essence of fear: "My illness is a journey of fear, often paralyzing, mostly painful. If only someone could put a bandaid on the wound . . . but where? Sometimes I feel I can't stand it any longer."

Feelings of extreme isolation are also commonly expressed. A patient writing anonymously in the *New York Times* (Anonymous, 1986) asks, "Can I ever forget that I am schizophrenic? I am isolated and I am alone. I am never real. I play-act my life, touching and feeling only shadows." And Beeman (1988) writes:

So you end up alone. I think the depression is caused by your isolation, and by the emotional biochemical changes that mental illness causes. It's something you have to experience. . . . It's a painful, yearning kind of thing. It's torture. You yearn to be part of society, but you're locked into your own private prison and you can't get out. It's a terrible thing.

Both Wing and Morris (1981) and Shepherd (1984) have noted that the secondary disabilities may present as much of a problem for successful engagement and treatment as do the primary symptoms of the illness. From the patients' perspective, the critical point regarding these secondary disabilities is that they generally persist, even after the primary symptoms have disappeared.

Tertiary Disability

Finally, Wing and Morris (1981) and Shepherd (1984) have discussed tertiary disabilities or "social disablements" that are external to the patient. These disabilities come neither from the illness per se nor from personal responses to illness but rather from societal reactions to mental illness.

Leete (1987) provides a particularly succinct and moving description of tertiary disabilities:

Sadly, in addition to handicaps imposed by our illnesses, the mentally disabled must constantly deal with barriers erected by society as well. Of these, there is none more devastating, discrediting and disabling to an individual recovering from mental illness than stigma. We are denied jobs, unwanted in our communities. We are seen as unattractive, lazy, stupid, unpredictable, and dangerous.

Some sources of tertiary disability are quite obvious—for example, inadequate housing markets, stigma, poverty, unemployment, and the general absence of a niche in society. Yet, serious as these are, we are at least able to name them and so, potentially, to consider means for eradicating them. It is the more subtle sources of tertiary disability—the ones for which we have no names—that most worry many professionals who are involved in mental health program planning.

For example, bureaucratic decisions in federal and state agencies to separate mental health, drug abuse, and alcoholism services may promote unrecognized tertiary disabilities (Bachrach, 1987). Because patients often have multiple problems, they may require services offered in all three classes of agencies. Far from encouraging comprehensiveness and continuity of care, categorical separation results in severe service fragmentation. It may at times even provide extraordinary gatekeeping powers to agencies serving the mentally ill by legitimizing their exclusion of certain kinds of patients. This increases patients' vulnerability to falling through the cracks in the absence of a central authority to determine where they "really" belong.

Patient-authors are generally strong and direct in voicing their concern over tertiary disabilities, both the obvious ones and the more subtle ones. In fact, the literature contains so many excellent examples of their distress over tertiary disabilities that one could probably devote an entire literature review to this subject alone. Rogers (1986), the chairperson of the National Mental Health Consumers' Association, captures the general sense of that literature in testimony presented before a Senate subcommittee:

> Over the years, I have found that there is very little understanding in the community of the problem of mental illness, and a lot of fear. There's a great deal of stigma, a negative attitude on the part of the public and, unfortunately, in many communities on the part of public officials. There's a feeling that we must sweep this illness under the rug; we must lock the people away; we must not deal with it.

Relationships Among Disabilities

In many of the examples cited here it is difficult to sort out primary, secondary, and tertiary disabilities precisely. Indeed, the patient-authored literature makes a major contribution in its eloquent reinforcement of the important point that these are separable only in theory and that they are inextricably interwoven in patients' daily lives. The result of this complexity is a milieu filled with pain and despair. The previously cited anonymous author in the *American Journal of Psychiatry* writes:

> During times when I am able to recognize ... [a] need for closeness, yet remain afraid of it, pushing people away while perceiving them as rejecting me, I struggle with incredible pain. It seems that a great chasm spans between myself and that which I want so much and which I try so hard to get. Even as I write these words

I am overcome by what seems the impossibility of closing the gap; I must struggle
every day not to lose sight of the fact that I am learning and although I feel stagnant
at times and overrun by fears both from within and without, it is indeed possible
that one day I will achieve that which I seek. (Recovering Patient, 1986)

The same writer is moved to question the unqualified value of treatment:

With the struggles back and forth it almost seems questionable at times whether all
this is really worth it. There are days when I wonder if it might not be more humane
to leave the schizophrenic patient to his own world of unreality, not to make him
go through the pain it takes to become a part of humanity.

DISABILITY AND DIFFICULT PATIENTHOOD

Not only do patient-authors document the inextricable link among the various
sources of disability; they go far beyond this to establish that there is also
an inescapable relationship between this conceptual field and that of difficult
patienthood. Patient-authors thus encourage professionals to ask a basic, but
perhaps uncomfortable, question: Are patients burdensome to clinicians and to
service systems—that is, are they difficult patients—because of their illnesses:
their primary disabilities? Or might other circumstances account for their lack
of cooperation or compliance?

The answer is, of course, a complex one. Certainly, some portion of difficult
patienthood resides in illness-related primary symptoms. Yet it seems likely that
other major precipitants of patients' apparent intractability are related to the fact
that professionals often expect mentally ill people to behave in ways that compli-
cate their clinical course and exacerbate their disabilities. Clinicians' expectations
and service system deficits often conspire to increase patients' secondary and
tertiary disabilities and to cause immeasurable pain to them, a point once again
underscored simply and forcefully by Leete (1987): "I have come to believe that
mental health patients are not treatment-resistant, as is so often stated, but instead
only system-resistant."

Thus, it is not enough to offer patients pharmacotherapies that might reduce
their symptoms: that respond exclusively to their primary disabilities. Those
disabilities most assuredly must be treated, but they are only part of the picture.

Similarly, it is not enough to provide patients with therapies and rehabilitative
interventions that might reverse their secondary disabilities: that might help them
respond more appropriately to their illnesses. These kinds of interventions are
certainly important; but, once again, they are only part of a larger picture.

The patient-authored literature leaves little doubt, in sum, that mental health
service systems wishing to respond to the needs of mentally ill individuals must
also be sensitive to the societal dimensions of illness. It strongly and definitely

supports the notion that service systems must try, as best they can, to mitigate conditions like service fragmentation, urban gentrification, limited housing markets, stigma, inadequate health and welfare resources, and even more subtle circumstances that we have not yet named that profoundly affect what we offer to people who are mentally ill.

INDIVIDUALIZED TREATMENT PLANNING

A third conceptual area influencing mental health program planning today is our growing understanding of the need for individualized treatments. The fact that those patients who need the most comprehensive and sophisticated care are often given the least individualized treatment has become a source of great concern to many planners, and it is probably accurate to predict that the future success of mental health programs will depend upon our ability to implement the concepts associated with individualized treatment (Bachrach, 1989).

Once again, statements in the patient-authored literature support this notion, often with great poignancy. McKay (1987), for example, writes of the need that homeless mentally ill women have for individualized interventions:

> In my view, the big mistake people make in trying to help the homeless is that they expect, or hope, that one single solution will solve the problems of all of us. Generally we, the homeless, are viewed as strands on the same gray mop. . . . My view from the park bench, from the narrow cot in crowded shelters, from the shuffling lines at feeding stations is that we are not all alike by any means and that, in fact, the solution for one of us can spell disaster for another.

SOME NEGLECTED POINTS

The foregoing observations reveal that, generally speaking, there is considerable concordance between the expressed service needs of patient-authors and the notions that, at least in theory, increasingly inform professional planning efforts. This should be gratifying to program planners who have apparently not, from the point of view of patient-authors, gone off into orbits that are removed from their expressed concerns.

That is the good news. At the same time, however, the patient-authored literature reveals a number of relevant notions and ideas that are at best rarely given credence by professional program planners. Among these are the importance of hope to patients, their need for validation and encouragement, and their wish to be more fully involved in program-planning efforts.

A patient at the Rhode Island Institute of Mental Health (1984) who signs her name as Hilda expresses the need for hope in a short poem:

> I've got room for friends
> I've got room for sunshine

I've got room for laughter
I've got room for fortune
I've got room for tomorrow

And the futility of having no hope is poetically documented in narrative form by Leete (1987):

> We are met by profound silence by all when we ask if we will ever be all right. Imagine our feelings of worthlessness as we are continually bounced from hospital to hospital, transferred from doctor to doctor, switched from one medication to another, and thrown into one living situation after another, making any kind of coordinated or consistent treatment impossible and only convincing us further that our situation is hopeless. The only uniform messages we get from others are that we are incapable of functioning successfully, that we cannot be independent, that we will never get well.

Thus, patient-authored writings strongly emphasize that where there is no hope there can be no improvement: that where there is no hope the patient is doomed to desolation. And although I have in the course of my professional lifetime reviewed many professionally authored articles on mental health program planning, I remember very few that deal with the idea of hope in any way, shape, or form.

This is true also for discussions of the role of professionals in instilling hope. The patient-authored literature is strong in stating that, in order for hope to flourish, patients must be given a chance by their care givers. They must be engaged through encouragement and support from professionals who validate their ability to change—a sentiment simply but very forcefully expressed by Peterson (1978), a former patient who is a member of the Fountain House program in New York City: "For me, rehabilitation is not having something done to me."

Still another theme related to hope that is prominent in the patient-authored literature, but once again largely ignored in the professional literature, is the notion that hope is often an outgrowth of a special relationship between patient and therapist. Leighton (1988), a former patient who is currently the director of the Family and Individual Reliance Project for the Mental Health Association of Texas, writes of a particular psychologist:

> She was more human than any of the other doctors I had seen and treated me more humanely. There was a rapport and an equality between us. . . . With the other doctors I had seen, I felt inferior in their presence. Of course, my ego was badly damaged by the illness. But their superior attitudes hurt me even more. This psychologist treated me like one human being helping another. For the first time, strength in me was recognized and fostered. Early in her treatment of me, she let me know I had responsibility over my own illness and wellness. She insisted that I try, something never suggested previously. Her expectations of me and the hard work she demanded on my part are the major reasons I recovered.

Time and time again the patient-authored literature reinforces the reciprocity between establishing a special and productive therapeutic relationship, the emergence of a feeling of acceptance, the birth of hope, and the beginnings of improved functioning. Lovejoy (1984) explains that, when these came together for her, she was able to change her life "through the help of others rather than being a passive victim, and to replace self-pity and helplessness with courage and honesty."

The lesson here for professionals is evident. Since patients' needs and characteristics differ widely, they may possibly have a better prognosis in some other program, in some other place, or with some other clinician. Professional planners must be prepared to acknowledge this circumstance and grant flexibility in program development (Bachrach, 1989).

Patient-authors also stress in their writings—and, once again, this emphasis is generally absent from the professional literature—a strong desire to be more fully involved in their own program planning. The failure to consult patients in matters that affect their own welfare is widely perceived among patient-authors as demoralizing and dehumanizing. A patient at the Rhode Island Institute of Mental Health (1984) who signs his name as Gavin describes the hopelessness that results from his inability to control the direction of his life:

> My whole life has been
> Wrapped up in the way
> Doctors, nurses, mental attendants
> Make a discussion over
> How to live my life in the hospital
> I've been in institutions so long
> I can't make a decision
> On my own

For some patient-authors the need for personal involvement in the planning process is expressed as a desire for more mutual help and peer-support groups. Chamberlin's (1978) *On Our Own* has become a classic reference for the development of patient self-help groups. Field (1988) reports on his attendance at a conference organized for former patients: "It's hard to describe how good it feels to be surrounded by hundreds of people who know what you're talking about. It was travelling one thousand miles only to find yourself at home."

ANALYSIS AND DISCUSSION

It is important to acknowledge that, although this analysis of patient-authored literature documents some general emphases and perhaps provides tentative direction for program planners, it also contains some serious methodological difficulties. Because the material examined can generate profound personal reactions and can lead to highly subjective conclusions, I have resisted referring to this work as a bona fide content analysis, and I have not presented my findings in a quantitative format. This, of course, makes it difficult to replicate the findings reported here and to verify their validity.

A cautionary word about the generalizability of these findings is also in order. The literature reviewed for this analysis reflects only the views of those patients or former patients who write, and there is obviously a possibility that they do not represent the majority of mentally ill individuals. On the other hand, these writings most assuredly do reflect the thinking of *some* current and former patients; and if we are attempting to listen to what patients have to say, we might just as well start with those who, by virtue of their writing, have indicated a willingness and an ability to share their thoughts.

Accordingly, the observations made here should perhaps be understood more as hypothesis-generating statements than as definitive findings. Nonetheless, there is a strong indication that attending to the patient-authored literature, which is obviously a just and humane exercise, is also a sensible thing for professionals to do, for they stand to learn much from the experience.

For example, McKay (1986) writes of her stay in a psychiatric ward: "Drugs every few hours. Forced recreation. Scolding if you lie down too much. Nothing to do but smoke. Boredom. Everyone half-stupefied under medication. The smell of hospital everywhere."

By contrast, life on the streets, though hardly desirable, offers some meager rewards:

> There is something to *do* outside [the hospital]. Something to look at. The homeless can go to their favorite corner to beg. . . . Once or twice, if they're lucky begging, they can go for a cup of coffee. They can hope that the next day will be different. They can make plans for themselves. . . . Inside an institution, there is nothing to do for yourself, for your future. (McKay, 1986)

Statements like these suggest that homelessness for mentally ill persons more often reflects service system deficits than it does an individual's abstract "choice" to live on the streets. Indeed, an anonymous report by a patient living in Oklahoma addresses the matter of choice directly:

> Someone who has been on the streets and is homeless and jobless and who has a disability, who doesn't have a car or food or a friend, and doesn't know what to do to change their situation, is in pain. Most people would probably agree that if given a choice they would trade that level of emotional pain for some good old-fashioned physical hurt anytime. But there is no choice. If you talk to someone who has been there, they will tell you they were alone and afraid. So afraid that help doesn't look like help, but like more torture. (Anonymous, 1988, reference unpaginated)

The patient-authored literature also reveals that the mental health service system may be different things at different times to different patients; or even to the same patient at different times, a fact that service planners frequently overlook. Leighton (1988) writes: "I'm one of the fortunate ones. I learned the hard way that what happens in the mental health system is not always good for your mental health. But sometimes it is. And for me, that's made all the difference." Those in the professional community who are inclined—and often with good reason—to view the service system as a massive monolith impervious to change may take heart from these words and be motivated to assume greater flexibility in their program planning as they respond to this variability.

Perhaps most importantly, however, the patient-authored literature can provide the professional planner with a heightened sense of the profoundness of patients' secondary disabilities—the vastness of their shattered hopes and terrible frustrations. Armed with this knowledge, mental health professionals may wish to call into question the very language that they employ.

For example, Leighton (1988) writes of the effect of a diagnosis:

> Being called "chronic," as I was, was killing. . . . It made me feel so helpless and hopeless. It made me want to give up. That's why as a mental health consumer advocate, I try to help change the terminology from "chronic" to "long-term."

Many professionals, I among them, see some positive value in using the word "chronic" and in not substituting other terminology that will probably turn out to be just as stigmatizing. They fear, moreover, that playing fast and loose with language might even have negative consequences by costing patients some of their entitlements and benefits (Bachrach, 1988). Nonetheless, Leighton's words carry an undeniable emotional force that may move professionals to understand that their "neutral" academic approach is really very charged for patients. From such understanding comes the possibility of change.

CONCLUDING COMMENTS

We have seen that the substantive value of patient-authored literature is considerable. The patient-authored literature is replete with perspectives that are relevant to mental health program planning, and these may be advantageously exploited by the professional community.

Beyond these substantive contributions, however, lie other important, albeit less tangible, benefits. Patient-authored writings generate a heightened awareness of the complexities surrounding relevant and sensitive program planning. Services for mentally ill persons must consist of much more than prefabricated program elements selected from a menu of offerings: They must be constructed with appreciation of the needs and hopes of the individuals who are to be served.

For me personally the experience of reviewing the patient-authored literature has been an introduction to humility; and in that vein I conclude with a moving quotation from an article by a former patient, Bockes (1985):

I still have a long road ahead of me. There is much that I don't understand about schizophrenia, but I realize I am not alone in my lack of knowledge about the illness. Slowly I am learning to accept the limitations of my illness, and I feel that I am beginning to make more constructive choices than I have in the past. Life puts various limitations on each person, but within those limitations there is always the freedom to make certain choices—an insight that I find relieving as well as revealing.

The professional community stands to learn a great deal from this and other extraordinary statements that make up the literature of patient-authors.

REFERENCES

Allen, P. (1974). A consumer's view of California's mental health care system. *Psychiatric Quarterly, 48,* 1–13.

Anonymous (1986). I feel I am trapped inside my head, banging against its walls, trying desperately to escape. *New York Times,* March 18.

Anonymous (1988, Summer). Someone who has been there. *Newsletter of New Beginnings,* Elgin, OK, unpaginated.

Bachrach, L. L. (1987). The chronic mental patient with substance abuse problems. In *Leona Bachrach speaks* (New Directions for Mental Health Services, No. 35, pp. 29–41). San Francisco, CA: Jossey-Bass.

Bachrach, L. L. (1988). Defining chronic mental illness: A concept paper. *Hospital and Community Psychiatry, 398,* 383–388.

Bachrach, L. L. (1989). The legacy of model programs. *Hospital and Community Psychiatry, 40,* 234–235.

Bachrach, L. L., Talbott, J. A., & Meyerson, A. T. (1987). The chronic psychiatric patient as a "difficult" patient: A conceptual analysis. In A. T. Meyerson (Ed.), *Barriers to treating the chronic mentally ill* (New Directions for Mental Health Services, No. 33, pp. 35–50). San Francisco, CA: Jossey-Bass.

Beeman, R. (1988, October 2). You're sort of trapped in this inner world in seeds of crisis. Special Report of the *Mesa-Tempe-Chandler* (Arizona) *Tribune,* September 28-October 2, 1988, p. 4.

Bockes, Z. (1985). First person account: "Freedom" means knowing you have a choice. *Schizophrenia Bulletin, 11,* 487–489.

Brundage, B. E. (1983). First person account: What I wanted to know but was afraid to ask. *Schizophrenia Bulletin, 8,* 583–585.

Chamberlin, J. (1978). *On our own: Patient-controlled alternatives to the mental health system.* New York: E. P. Dutton.

Chrzanowski, G. (1980). Problem patients or troublemakers? Dynamic and therapeutic considerations. *American Journal of Psychotherapy, 34,* 26–38.

Field, T. (1988, September/October). Salt Lake City Conference Peak Experience for Consumers. *Spotlight* (Newsletter published by Washington Advocates for the Mentally Ill, Seattle), *11,* unpaginated.

Harris, M., & Bergman, H. C. (1986–87). The narcissistically vulnerable system: A case study of the public mental hospital. *Psychiatry Quarterly, 58,* 202–212.

Harris, N. (1988). A personal history from a case management program client. *Psychosocial Rehabilitation Journal, 11,* 58–62.

Jeffery, R. (1979). Normal rubbish: Deviant patients in casualty departments. *Sociology of Health and Illness, 1,* 90–107.

Leete, E. (1987, October). *Overcoming mental illness: A survivor's perspective.* Paper presented at the Institute of Hospital and Community Psychiatry, Boston.

Leighton, D. C. (1988). Being mentally ill in America: One female's experience. In L. L. Bachrach & C. C. Nadelson (Eds.), *Treating chronically mentally ill women* (pp. 63–73). Washington, DC: American Psychiatric Press.

Lovejoy, M. (1984). Recovery from schizophrenia: A personal odyssey. *Hospital and Community Psychiatry,* 1984, 809–812.

McGrath, M. E. (1984). First person account: Where did I go? *Schizophrenia Bulletin,* 638–640.

McKay, P. (1986, February 16). My home is a lonely bed in a dreary D. C. shelter. *Washington Post,* pp. C1, C3.

McKay, P. (1987, December 29). We bag ladies aren't all alike. *Washington Post,* pp. C1, C2.

Neill, J. R. (1979). The difficult patient: Identification and response. *Journal of Clinical Psychiatry, 40,* 209–212.

Peterson, R. (1978). What are the needs of chronic mental patients? In J. A. Talbott (Ed.), *The chronic mental patient: Problems, solutions and recommendations for a Public Policy* (pp. 39–49). Washington, DC: American Psychiatric Association.

Recovering Patient. (1986). "Can we talk?" The schizophrenic patient in psychotherapy. *American Journal of Psychiatry, 143,* 68–70.

Rhode Island Institute of Mental Health. (1984). *Mindscapes.* Cranston, RI: Author.

Robinson, B. P. (1983, April 3). When I finally realized I was insane. *Washington Post,* pp. D1, D2.

Rogers, J. A. (1986, November 20). Testimony presented at Hearings on Schizophrenia, United States Senate Subcommittee on Labor, Health and Human Services Education, Washington, DC.

Sharp, M. L. (1988, April 14). *Life without Stelazine.* Paper presented at San Francisco General Hospital Psychiatric Grand Rounds, San Francisco.

Shepherd, G. (1984). *Institutional care and rehabilitation.* London: Longman.

Weinberg, J. (1978). The chronic patient: The stranger in our midst. *Hospital and Community Psychiatry, 29,* 25–28.

Wing, J. K., & Morris, B. (1981). Clinical basis of rehabilitation. In J. K. Wing & B. Morris (Eds.), *Handbook of psychiatric rehabilitation practice* (pp. 3–16). Oxford, England: Oxford University Press.

Part Two

Social and Vocational
Skills Development

Chapter 5

Social Skills Training

Jeffrey R. Bedell

Social skills training enjoys a popularity unrivaled in psychiatric rehabilitation. It is used by practitioners in many fields, in diverse settings, with individuals who have a wide range of psychological disorders. For example, practitioners in the fields of education, mental retardation, psychiatric rehabilitation, and mental health advocate the use of social skills training. Within these different fields of practice, social skills training has been demonstrated effective in a wide range of settings, including inpatient and outpatient mental health, day hospital, rehabilitation programs, schools, correction facilities, and vocational settings. And in these settings, social skills training has been applied to a wide range of disorders, including marital distress, school problems, vocational decision making, anxiety disorders, drug abuse disorders, depression, and schizophrenia. In fact, there have been over 100 published evaluations of social skills training. Most of the empirical studies demonstrate the effectiveness of this approach.

HISTORICAL BACKGROUND

Social skills training has not always enjoyed widespread acceptance. The value of teaching social skills began to emerge in the 1960s, as educational and psychological practices moved beyond theories that considered human behavior to be determined by lockstep developmental patterns of stable, unchanging personality traits. As long as this orientation dominated treatment, it was assumed that behavior was relatively immalleable and was determined by developmental, biological, and intrapsychic processes that were primarily beyond the control of the individual. However, as practitioners began to understand the role of learning in the development and maintenance of pathological behavior, the concept of skills training began to gain credibility.

The development of concepts of psychiatric rehabilitation (see Chapter 2) was also important in the evolution of social skills training techniques. In the field of psychiatric rehabilitation, it was recognized that many disorders such as mental retardation and schizophrenia can rarely be cured. Nonetheless, individuals with these disorders can learn skills that will enable them to live a full and complete life, despite the presence of the handicapping condition. Psychiatric rehabilitation focuses not on personality restructuring, as did the older models of treatment, but rather on the development of functional behaviors and the teaching of skills.

With these shifts in orientation, the social and environmental aspects of many mental disorders, including severe disabilities such as major depression and schizophrenia, began to be the focus of social skills training. For example, early researchers such as Libet and Lewinsohn (1973) discovered that the social skills of depressed persons were critical to the development and maintenance of this syndrome. They showed that individuals with depressive patterns of behavior were deficient in the social and interpersonal skills needed to elicit positive reinforcement from the environment. In fact, it was shown that the environment of depressed people often reinforced dysfunctional behavior. As this example suggests, the modification of social skills to increase reinforcement from the environment and to break dysfunctional patterns of interaction made it possible to alter the course of major depressive disorder. More broadly, Zigler and Phillips (1961) were among the first to explain how social skill deficits are a significant factor in a wide range of psychiatric disorders. Their work suggested that the debilitating effects of many psychological disorders could be reversed by teaching social skills to overcome skill deficits.

APPLICATIONS WITH THE SEVERELY DISABLED

In addition to the large number of research studies reported in the literature, six comprehensive critical reviews of research on social skills training with severely and persistently mentally ill patients have been conducted. The authors of these reviews concluded that strong evidence was present to support the effectiveness of this paradigm of treatment (Brady, 1984; Hersen & Bellack, 1976; Ladd & Mize, 1983; Morrison & Bellack, 1984; Robertson, Richardson, & Youngson, 1984; Wallace et al., 1980).

Most recently, Benton and Schroeder (1990) reported the results of a metaanalysis of 27 well-designed studies evaluating the effectiveness of social skills training with severely disturbed patients. Using this sophisticated statistical technique, they reported that research on social skills training reliably showed that (a) there was significant improvement in assertiveness, anxiety, and other specific behaviors, (b) the social skills learned in therapy generalized to natural settings, (c) the degree of superiority of social functioning of subjects given social skills training compared to other treatments increased over long periods of time, (d) social skills training resulted in superior hospital discharge rates, (e) social skills training resulted in lower rates of relapse compared to other treatments, and finally, (f) the superior effects associated with social skills training were the same with schizophrenic samples and samples composed of a heterogeneous mixture of severely mentally ill patients.

THREE ILLUSTRATIVE STUDIES

Although the research on social skills training is impressive, evaluations of treatment techniques are sometimes criticized for producing "statistically significant" but not "clinically significant" findings. These criticisms often cite the selection of "high functioning" subjects, the use of exceptionally well-trained or highly motivated staff, and the employment of clinically insignificant measures of outcome. Some of the many studies of social skills training are subject to these criticisms. Many studies, however, do demonstrate "clinically significant" results. To illustrate briefly the clinical significance of recent social skills training research, three studies have been selected to exhibit the potential effectiveness of this treatment technique with severely disabled patients.

The first illustrative study was conducted by Wallace and Liberman (1985). This is an extremely well-designed evaluation of carefully diagnosed schizophrenic patients living with families high in expressed emotions (Leff & Vaughn, 1980). Thus, these subjects were at risk of relapse. Subjects received a standardized 9-week program of intensive communication and problem-solving skill training emphasizing improvement in "receiving skills" (attending and accurately perceiving problem situations and cues), "processing skills" (interpreting interpersonal cues, generating alternatives for action, considering alternatives, choosing a reasonable response), and "sending skills" (effective use of language to make requests and respond to requests of others). Among the many clinically meaningful treatment outcome measures, the researchers reported rehospitalization rates. Results indicated that this program of social skills training reduced rehospitalization rates of the schizophrenic patients by nearly half compared to the other active program of treatment.

The following year, Hogarty and colleagues (1986) reported the results of a very similar study that also used schizophrenic subjects living with high expressed emotion families. Although the social skills training program was in many ways similar to that employed by Wallace and Liberman (1985), Hogerty and colleagues' treatment also emphasized (a) establishment of a low-stress environment, (b) flexibility of skill training, (c) development of social perception, and (d) provision of social support and empathy from staff. Also, the Hogerty and colleagues program provided continuous treatment for 2 years. Despite the differences in treatment methods, and although Hogerty et al. conducted their study completely independently of the Wallace and Liberman research, they also found that social skills training reduced the rehospitalization rates of schizophrenic patients by nearly 50% over an active control treatment.

The third illustrative study was conducted by Bedell and Ward (1989). It demonstrated that clinically significant results can be obtained from a comprehensive program of inpatient treatment based primarily on social skills training. The subjects were severely disturbed patients who were being treated in a community-based short-term inpatient unit. The experimental subjects were 102 patients admitted to the Intensive Residential Treatment (IRT) program in lieu of being sent to the state hospital. The comparison group consisted of 42 patients treated at the state hospital. All subjects in both groups met criteria for admission to IRT. The sample was primarily schizophrenic, with an average of 16.2 months of previous hospitalization and a history of extensive use of outpatient services when not in the hospital. The IRT program provided 14 hours of psychosocial treatment each day focused on cognitive-behavioral training of self-understanding, communication skills, and problem-solving skills. The state hospital where the control subjects were treated provided medical, custodial, and activities-oriented care. Compared to matched patients who received the state hospital treatment, the subjects in the social skills program showed a dramatic reduction in length of hospitalization (32 vs. 150 days), significantly reduced rehospitalization rate in three of five follow-up periods during the 30 months after discharge, and substantial reductions in the treatment costs for an episode of hospitalization ($4,130 vs. $13,282). It should be noted that at present-day hospital costs, these amounts would be 10 times greater in many states.

Other excellent studies have been reported, but space does not permit their presentation. In fact, each year the methodology of research on social skills training improves and confidence in results increases. As illustrated by the three studies highlighted above, there can be little question that social skills training is an effective treatment approach that can have a major impact on significant aspects of major mental disorders. On the basis of published research, it is reasonable to conclude that social skills training, in conjunction with appropriate psychopharmacology, is the treatment of choice for individuals with severe and persistent mental disorders. This suggestion has been well documented elsewhere (Liberman & Bedell, 1989).

CONTEMPORARY SOCIAL SKILLS TRAINING

Since social skills training has been demonstrated to be effective, it might appear that therapeutic methods have reached their terminal development. On the contrary, social skills training continues to evolve and become more effective as more sophisticated models and procedures are devised. This evolution of methods is a direct result of the empirical base that underlies social skills training and provides feedback on procedures as the results of experimental evaluations are made available. Recent developments of social skills training have paralleled those in the field of behavior therapy. As behavior therapy has become more "cognitive" as a result of the influence of social learning theory (Bandura, 1969), cognitive therapy (Beck, 1976; Ellis & Grieger, 1978), and cognitive-behavioral therapy (Meichenbaum, 1977), social skills training has also become more cognitive. For example, behavioral experts in social skills training like Liberman Mueser, Wallace, Jacobs, and Massel (1986) discussed the central role of cognitive "social schema" in their model of social competence. More recently, Bellack, Morrison, and Mueser (1989) reviewed the role of cognitive factors in social problem-solving skills and criticized as outdated the "motor skills model" that was popular in the past. Bellack, Morrison, and Mueser (1989) have taken the position that a strictly operant behavioral model is inadequate as a conceptual basis for understanding interpersonal behavior. The role of cognitive and affective aspects of social skills and social competence appears to be the current focus of development in social skills training.

A COGNITIVE MODEL OF SOCIAL SKILLS TRAINING

In spite of this shift in conceptualization, in actual practice many social skills programs do not yet incorporate the full array of concepts and procedures developed in social learning theory, cognitive therapy, and cognitive-behavioral therapy. It is my goal in the remainder of this chapter to present a cohesive model of social skills training based on social learning theory and cognitive-behavioral models of human learning. This chapter is heavily influenced by social learning theory (Bandura, 1969) and the determination that the cognitive representations that guide and direct behavior are formed from verbal instruction and the observation of models. A primary goal of the present chapter is to present clinically valid methods for teaching both the cognitive and the behavioral aspects of social skills. I will attempt to provide clear and consistent terminology and operational definitions of concepts. The program described in this chapter emphasizes the teaching of "skill concepts" that define, organize, and guide social behaviors.

Social skills training may be seen as having four interrelated, but clearly distinguishable, components: (a) instruction, (b) supervised practice, (c) feedback, and (d) independent practice. It must be emphasized that while these four components are considered to be separate and sequential steps in the training process, they usually are intermingled in actual practice and may not always be used in this sequence. For example, feedback is provided not only after the instruction and supervised practice phases are completed, but also during these phases of training as well. Similarly, it may be desirable to repeat the instruction, supervised practice, and feedback phases of training a number of times before proceeding to the independent practice phase. It is also possible that the patient who is involved in group social skills training will be engaged in both supervised practice and independent practice at the same time. Nonetheless, the sequence of (a) instruction, (b) supervised practice, (c) feedback, and (d) independent practice is a useful way to organize social skills training.

Later in this chapter, after a general description of these four components of training has been provided, a detailed practical example of the application of this training model will be presented.

Skill Training Component 1: Instruction

The most unique element of the training approach described in this chapter is the clear delineation of the instruction component. While other social skills training models described in the literature have included instructional components (e.g., Bellack, Turner, Hersen, & Luber, 1984; Liberman, DeRise, & Mueser, 1989), the full potential of this aspect of training does not seem to be fully appreciated or utilized. In the current model, the role of the instruction component of training is greatly emphasized, and is, in fact, the foundation for the other three skill-training components (i.e., supervised practice, feedback, and independent practice). The instructional phase of training focuses on the systematic teaching of many of the cognitive aspects of social skills. These cognitive elements are referred to as "skill concepts" that serve to define, organize, and guide (DOG) an individual's behavior. The acronym DOG is suggested to help the reader focus on these three cognitive factors of training.

Instruction may be provided to the patient by the use of both verbal description and behavioral modeling. For clarity of presentation and to emphasize the similarities and differences between verbal instruction and behavioral modeling, these two methods of instruction will be presented separately. In practice, the therapist uses verbal instruction and behavioral modeling concurrently.

Instruction using verbal descriptions of skill concepts. For each social skill being taught, we use verbal instruction to *define, organize,* and *guide* performance. First, the behavior being taught is *defined* by provision of an operational definition of the skill and its major components. For instance, when teaching patients how to make an empathic statement, we define it as "a statement that expresses our understanding of another's wants and/or feelings." This definition clarifies the fact that the empathic statement describes the wants or feelings of *another person* and not those of the speaker. Learning the meaning of concepts such as "want" and "feeling" is also part of this skill-training program, and these terms would also be taught to the patient. Following is a description of the skills taught and the sequence of instruction used in the program, part of which is presented in detail later in this chapter:

Module 1. Cognitive, affective, and behavior components of personality: definitions and interrelationships

Module 2. The five basic feelings—fear, love, anger, sadness, and happiness

Module 3. The empathic statement: showing another person you understand the person's wants and feelings

Module 4. The simple request: making a request when there is no conflict

Module 5. The emphatic request: making a request when there is a conflict

Module 6. The emphatic request with feedback: asking someone to change an undesired behavior

Module 7. Deciding what type of request to make: review and practice

Module 8. How to respond to a request from another person: grant, refuse, and compromise

Module 9. Introduction to the concepts of assertive, passive, and aggressive communication

Module 10. Nonverbal aspects of assertive, passive, and aggressive behavior

Module 11. Consequences of assertive, passive, and aggressive behavior

To make our *definition* of an empathic statement clearer, we delineate three different types of empathic statements that can be made. They are (a) a statement that reflects the wants of another person, (b) a statement that reflects the feeling(s) that another person is experiencing, and (c) a statement that reflects both the wants and feelings of another person.

We also attempt to *define* the skill being taught by differentiating it from other behaviors with which it might be confused. Referring to the training regarding the empathic statement, we differentiate among an empathic statement, sympathetic statement, and emphatic statement. Most importantly, defining these three statements stresses that a sympathetic statement and an empathic statement differ in terms of whether the want(s) and/or feeling(s) of the sender or the receiver of the message are being described. Thus, the concept of stating another's wants and feelings and not one's own is clarified.

Information that will help *organize* thinking and behavior associated with a social skill is also provided. In the example of the empathic statement, the skilled individual must be able to organize the vast array of information available in the environment and attend to those aspects that will help him or her to understand the wants and feelings of the other person. To help organize the patient's thinking so that he or she may deduce useful information that may indicate what the other is thinking or feeling, five recommendations are made. Each recommendation focuses on one way for an individual to acquire information about another's wants and/or feelings. The patient is instructed to (a) listen to the verbal information the other person provides about want(s) and feeling(s), (b) observe the behavioral cues provided by the other person, (c) be aware of situational cues, (d) imagine what you would want or feel if you were the other person, and (e) remember the other person's feelings and wants in prior similar situations.

Information that individuals can learn to keep in mind to *guide* performance is also provided in the instructional phase of training. Again, with the example of the empathic statement, patients are given a guide by which to pattern their statement. Patients are taught that an empathic statement is often started with an introductory phrase such as "It seems like . . . ," "I know you . . . ," and "It sounds like. . . ." This type of "guiding phrase" is used to help the patient in beginning to communicate an empathic statement. After this guiding phrase is verbalized, the empathic statement is completed by the patient's indicating the want or feeling that is attributed to the other person. The use of a guiding phrase seems to be helpful in getting the empathic statement started. It is the first step in the composition of an empathic statement such as "It seems like you want to get home in a hurry," "I know you are upset about losing your wallet," and "It sounds like you are angry and want to get even with your brother."

The verbal instruction component of social skill training may also provide guidelines regarding when a particular social behavior is appropriate. An empathic statement, for example, is said to be appropriate when individuals (a) want to show they are actively listening, (b) make a request, and (c) refuse a request from another.

In addition to defining, organizing, and guiding thinking and behavior, it is often useful in the instruction phase to describe the possible *consequences* of using the skill being taught. Regarding the empathic statement, we suggest to patients that its use promotes the development and maintenance of close positive relationships with friends, family, and acquaintances.

Instruction Using Behavioral Modeling   In addition to verbal instruction, modeling is used to define, organize, and guide behavior. In the current program, the therapist modeling a behavior is providing the patient with an example of the behavior that has been described using verbal instruction. Because of the complex nature of social behavior, a verbal description of each element of the skill being taught may be inordinately complicated. For this reason, the main elements are described (defined) verbally, and modeling is a beneficial supplement to the verbal description of the behavior being taught. The saying that a picture is worth a thousand words is applicable here. However, it is important that the verbal instruction and the modeling be two sides of the same coin. Since the overall goal of both the verbal instruction and the modeling is to develop a clear cognitive map that defines, organizes, and guides behavior, the modeled behavior should illustrate the same defining, organizing, and guiding concepts that were presented to the patient verbally. When teaching the empathic statement, for example, the therapist defines the behavior by modeling examples of the empathic, sympathetic, and emphatic statements. The distinguishing characteristics of these three types of statements, as explained earlier in the verbal description phase, are highlighted through modeling. The role model will demonstrate the three kinds of empathic statements presented earlier and will use the "guiding phrases" that had been presented to the patient.

Some aspects of social skills training are purely cognitive, such as deciding the want or feeling the other person is experiencing. This cognitive function cannot be role-played. In this case, the thinking process used by the model is verbalized in order to demonstrate it (Meichenbaum, 1977).

Using a combination of verbal descriptions of skill concepts and behavioral modeling to illustrate these thoughts helps to establish the linkages between the cognitive and behavioral aspects of skilled functioning and demonstrates how the cognitive and behavioral elements fit together to augment each other. For example, when a model demonstrates that he or she first recalls from memory the definition of an empathic statement (a statement that expresses the wants and feelings of another person) and then makes a statement that matches this definition, the cognitive and behavioral components of the skill are closely linked.

Skill-Training Component 2: Supervised Practice

In the instructional component of training, the patient is provided information by the therapist that defines the behavior(s) being taught and helps the patient understand ways to organize information and direct behavior. In the supervised-practice component of training, the trainee has an opportunity to behave in such a way as to *match* the skill concepts that were presented in the instruction phase. That is, having received instruction regarding new ways of thinking and acting, the patient attempts to think and act in the ways described.

Supervised Practice: Cognitive Aspects Most skilled social behavior requires some cognitive activity prior to performance. The "thinking" component of skilled behavior enables the individual to (a) define the appropriate behavior for the situation (i.e., Should I make an empathic or sympathetic statement?), (b) organize behavior (i.e., What information do I need in order to make an empathic statement?), and (c) sequence behavior (i.e., What should be done or said first, second, third, etc?). A proficient, socially skilled person, when making a response, may not need to review mentally a well-articulated process involving all of these factors. This is because, for the skilled individual, the behavior is well learned, is routine, and has become "automatic" (Beck, 1976). For the individual learning a new skill, however, the thoughts that define, organize, and guide behavior must be systematically elicited and practiced. In order for these cognitive activities to be supervised by the therapist, the thinking elements of social performance are brought to mind by the patient and verbalized. For example, a patient engaging in supervised practice of an empathic statement in response to a role-play vignette might engage in the following sequence of thoughts and verbalize them to the therapist (and other therapy group members):

> In this situation, first I have to decide what I want to do. I want to show Bill that I am hearing what he is saying to me and am "tuned in" to him. In order to do that, I will make an empathic statement. That means I express my understanding of *his* wants or feelings. I don't want to be sympathetic and express *my* feelings. How am I going to figure out how he feels? I can tell by his behavior that he is fearful (he is talking very fast and said something that sounded like he expected something bad was going to happen). Also, my prior knowledge of Bill reminds me that he felt afraid the last time he had a meeting like this with his boss. To be empathic I'll comment on his feeling of fear. I'll say, "Bob, it sounds like you are really scared of what will happen when you speak to your boss tomorrow."

Supervised Practice: Behavioral Aspects   Systematic behavioral practice is the hallmark of social skills training and uses procedures based on operant learning theories. It is the aspect of training that is most frequently described in the social skills training literature (Bedell & Weathers, 1979). In the present model of social skills training, practice occurs only after the skill concepts that define, organize, and guide behavior have been taught.

In the current example regarding the empathic statement, the trainee would initially be given a role to enact in the context of a practice vignette. In the role-play vignette suggested above, in which Bob expresses his fears about talking to his boss, the patient would ideally practice making a statement such as "Bob, it sounds like you are really scared of what will happen when you speak to your boss tomorrow." Repeated practice is provided to the patient by the use of multiple practice vignettes and the opportunity to observe other patients who are practicing the skill being learned. Eventually, independent practice in real-life situations follows. This type of practice is described later in this chapter.

Skill-Training Component 3: Feedback

Learning cannot occur without feedback. Feedback, however, can be provided by oneself as well as others. Self-feedback takes cognitive form, and feedback from others (and to others) is generally behavioral in the form of verbal statements and non-verbal actions. We have found it useful to teach a specific feedback model. This model is used for giving cognitive feedback to oneself and verbal feedback to others.

Cognitive Self-Feedback   Cognitive feedback is self-administered. It is based on an appraisal of the match between one's performance and the skill concepts that define, organize, and guide the behavior performed. When one is teaching patients how best to give feedback, it is especially important to emphasize the usefulness of making self-statements that comment on specific aspects of thinking and behavior. That is, feedback should cite the degree to which performance *matched* the skill concepts governing that behavior. Feedback statements such as "good" or "I liked what I did" or "nice job," while providing some motivational enhancement, are not effective in providing feedback on specific skills. Statements that cite specific behaviors, such as "My empathic statement was good because it stated the other person's feeling and not my own," are more effective forms of feedback.

We also emphasize the use of feedback that comments on ways the behavior did and did not match the skill concept. When one is learning a new skill, there is often a tendency to comment only on the negative or deficient aspects of performance. The feedback model recommended encourages the individual first to comment on a positive aspect of performance (i.e., a way it matched or approximated the skill concept), and then to provide a specific recommendation for change that would improve performance (i.e., a way to better match the skill concept). For example, with regard to an empathic statement, an individual might make an erroneous response that did not match the skill concept and say, "Bob, you have so many problems, I feel sorry for you." Appropriate self-feedback would be "I liked the way I took a minute to think about the statement before I spoke, and my voice was supportive. However, since I stated how I felt, I made a sympathetic statement. My statement would have been empathic if I expressed my understanding of how Bob was feeling, not how I was feeling about Bob."

Verbal Feedback Given to Others   In addition to providing self-feedback, being able to provide feedback to others is an important aspect of social behavior. The methods used for self-feedback are adapted for use with others. Behavioral feedback to others should be specific, and explain how the observed behavior did and did not match the "skill concept" governing the skill being performed. An example of verbal feedback in response to someone's empathic statement might be: "I think your empathic statement was accurate and Bill was feeling fearful. Also, you used the "guiding phrase" "It seems like . . ." which sounded good. I think your empathic statement would have been even better if you had looked at Bill instead of at the floor."

In some cases, feedback may involve not only verbal but also motor behavior. For example, facial expressions (smiling and frowning) and body movements (approaching and leaning forward or walking away) are nonverbal forms of feedback. Since nonverbal forms of feedback are not specific, they are of value as supplements to verbal feedback.

Skill-Training Component 4: Independent Practice

Independent practice is the final step in learning a new behavior. This component of training requires the individual to perform independently all the cognitive and behavioral skills learned in the instruction and supervised-practice components of training. Thus, the patient acquires experience performing the behavior in the "natural environment" without supervision, supportive guidance, or assurance of a positive response from others. The term "independent practice" is used rather than "generalization" in order to emphasize the fact that the new skills must be performed outside the sheltered therapeutic environment. In this component of training, as in all the others, there are both cognitive and behavioral elements.

Independent Practice, Cognitive Elements   The cognitive component of independent practice requires that the individual recall the skill concepts that help him or her to define, organize, and guide behavior. Cognitive aspects of independent practice are employed prior to actual performance of the skill in order to prepare and "rehearse" the response and to create appropriate positive expectations of performance. After the behavior is performed, cognitions are oriented toward evaluation of performance and provision of self-feedback. All of these cognitive activities are, of course, performed without direct supervision and support from the therapist.

Independent Practice, Behavioral Component   The primary goal of the behavioral component of independent practice is for the patient to actually perform the social skill behaviors without direct supervision or feedback from the therapist. Patients are encouraged to practice the new behaviors in a graduated series of settings that successively approximate real-life situations, not only in terms of the situational characteristics but also regarding the degree of positive reaction likely to be received by the patient. Practice settings are graduated from situations with high probability of successful performance and positive feedback, to those that are more difficult and problematic. For instance, the patient may first be assigned the task of making an empathic statement in a setting outside the therapy group to a staff member who is associated with the skill-training program. Next, the patient may try out the new behaviors on a staff member not associated with the skill-training group, but known to be warm and supportive. The successful patient may then practice with a "socially skilled" person in his or her social network. The process proceeds with the patient practicing the new skills with other individuals who are "naive" about the social skills program. Practicing new skills in a setting where there is a high probability of conflict and rejection of the new behaviors is avoided until the skills become well integrated into the patient's repertoire.

DETAILED DESCRIPTION OF SKILL-TRAINING METHODS

Using the above model, we have developed a social skill training program described in a manual consisting of 19 chapters. Each chapter teaches a separate skill or set of skills such as (a) understanding the thoughts, feelings, and behaviors of self and others, (b) making requests of others, (c) responding to requests from others, (d) developing assertiveness skills, and (e) learning problem-solving skills.

Although the entire social skills training program is too long to be included in this chapter, two training modules have been selected for detailed presentation. These two modules will illustrate the cognitive-behavioral model of skill training described in this chapter. The first module presented teaches patients about the empathic statement, and the second teaches the empathic request. As will be seen, these two modules are sequential, and information taught in the first module is used in the second. This is illustrative of the overall strategy of this social skills training program. Basic skills are taught first, and then more complex skills are taught. Also, basic skills are combined to develop complex and sophisticated social behaviors. The two modules presented in this chapter are taken out of context, so the reader cannot be aware of the skill concepts and behavioral skills that have been taught in earlier sessions. This may make the lessons seem difficult. Rest assured, however, that all prerequisite skills and concepts needed are taught in prior sessions.

Example Module #1: Learning To Make an Empathic Statement

A. *Instructional lecture providing verbal descriptions of skill concepts.*

1 Defining the Empathic Statement   In the previous sessions, we have learned how to differentiate among our thoughts, feelings, and behaviors. Also, we defined five basic feelings in terms of the thoughts (wants and expectations) that accompany them. Learning these things is useful in helping us to understand ourselves better.

Up to this point, we have focused on applying these concepts (i.e., thoughts, feelings, and behaviors) to ourselves. That is, we have tried to develop a better understanding of our own thoughts, feelings, and behaviors. Now we are going to apply the concepts of thoughts, feelings, and behaviors to others. By applying what we have already learned in a slightly different way, we will attempt to better understand, be sensitive to, and respond to the thoughts, feelings, and behaviors of other people.

Developing a sensitivity to the thoughts, feelings, and behaviors of others is a difficult task. Communicating this sensitivity is also difficult. One of the major difficulties associated with being sensitive to another's thoughts and feelings is due to the fact that these are internal, private events that we cannot observe directly. That is, we cannot see another's thoughts and feelings. Only the behavior of the person, and the characteristics of the situation in which the behavior occurs, can be directly observed. Since these are the only two things that can be directly observed, this information is fundamental to understanding the other's thoughts and feelings. In fact, we could define an *empathic statement* as follows: "A statement that is based on the other's behavior and characteristics of the situation that expresses our attempt to understand the wants and feelings of another person."

Given this definition, there are three types of empathic statements:

    a Statement that reflects the thought(s) (i.e., wishes, wants, desires, or expectations) of another person
    b Statement that reflects the feeling(s) that another person is experiencing
    c Statement that reflects both the thought(s) and feeling(s) of another person

Thus, an empathic statement is one that attempts to communicate our understanding of another's thoughts, feelings, or both.

2 How to Understand What Another Person is Thinking and Feeling If someone tells you what he or she is thinking or how he or she is feeling, it is not difficult to make a statement that communicates our understanding of the person's wants and/or feelings. In such a situation, you simply have to listen to what the other person said, then convey your understanding of what the person said.

However, sometimes people don't communicate this information directly. They don't tell you how they feel or what they are thinking. In this case, the primary clues you have are the behaviors the other person is exhibiting (both verbal and nonverbal) and the components of the situation (i.e., Who is involved? What is the person doing? When and where is this occurring?). In other words, you can only "guess" at the other's feelings and thoughts by using other information to which you have direct access.

Here are some sources of information that you can use to understand the wants and feelings of another person.

    a What the person tells you. This is the easiest way to get an idea of another person's wants and feelings. The person may say, "I *want* to finish one task before I begin another." Based on this comment, you would know that if you asked this person to stop doing something in the middle, before the task was finished, he or she would *want* to continue the first task to completion. Similarly, a person might reveal personal feelings in a statement like "I get upset when I have to stop what I am doing in the middle." This statement would suggest that this person would *feel* angry when interrupted while doing a task.

Sometimes it is necessary to ask for information about the wants and feelings of others. For example, you may ask someone, "What is it that you want?" or "How are you feeling?"
    b Behavioral cues. Certain behaviors are associated with particular thoughts and feelings. We use our prior experience with these behaviors to help us understand the thoughts (i.e., wishes, wants, desires, expectations) and feelings associated with the behaviors we observe. For example, if we observe someone standing very close to another, leaning a bit forward with his hands on his hips,

body rigid, teeth clenched, eyes glaring, we would probably guess from these behaviors that he is angry. On the other hand, if we see our friend running toward us with her hand waving and a broad smile on her face, we could safely say, based on these behaviors, that she is *feeling happy* and she *wants to see us.* Based upon the behaviors we see and hear, we frequently pick up accurate information about the wants and feelings of others.

    c   Situational cues. Characteristics of the situation can provide information regarding another's wants and feelings. For example, people at a birthday party probably (1) want to enjoy themselves, (2) want to share in eating the cake, and (3) want to wish happy birthday to the guest of honor. Similarly, this situation (being at a party) would suggest that the person was feeling happy.

    d   How would I feel, what would I want? Sometimes we can understand other persons' wants and feelings by "stepping into their shoes." We ask ourselves, "What would I want if I was in this situation?" or "What feeling would I have if I was in that situation? To the extent that we can share the experience of the other person, we will be able to accurately guess his or her want or feeling.

    e   Prior knowledge about a person. If we have known a person for a period of time, we will have knowledge about wants and feelings based on what the person wanted or how he or she felt in similar past situations. For example, if we know from past experience that a person likes to finish tasks and not begin a new one until the current one is completed, we would expect that the person would react the same way now.

    3 **When to use an Empathic Statement** The ability to communicate empathically is a useful skill. Empathic communication allows us to relate to another person in a way that often leads to a sharing of personal experiences. Such sharing can help to create a social bond between people. To make an empathic statement, one must develop a sensitivity and concern for the wants and feelings of others. When this sensitivity is communicated to another, it can "soften" an otherwise harsh message and often elicits a more cooperative response. These desirable outcomes are due to the fact that (a) the sender of the message has demonstrated a desire to expend the energy required to understand the other person and (2) the receiver of the message will tend to recognize this attempt to be understood and will appreciate the fact that his or her wants and feelings were respected. Learning to make an empathic statement will not guarantee these positive outcomes to our social interactions, but it will maximize their likelihood of occurring.

    Examples of occasions when an empathic statement would be appropriate include:

      a   When you want to show that you are actively listening and concerned about another person

      b   When making a request to which you expect a negative reaction

      c   When refusing a request made by another person

4 Composing an Empathic Statement When expressing your understanding of another's wants and/or feelings, it is often helpful to keep in mind an example of an empathic statement you can copy. We suggest you start an empathic statement with one of the following phrases, which is then followed by a statement of the other person's wants and/or feelings.

It seems like . . .
It appears that . . .
I know you . . .
It sounds like . . .

5 Examples of Empathic Statements Imagine you are in the following situation. You are at your friend's house, and he sighs deeply as he looks down and says: "I had two interviews for that dynamite job I told you about, but they gave it to someone else."

a Empathic response to wishes, wants, and desires—"It sounds like you really wanted that job."
b Empathic response to feelings—"I know you are disappointed."

B. *Exercise used to provide supervised practice and feedback: Making an Empathic Statement*

General instructions. If there are two therapists, they should model the exercise first. If there is only one therapist, a participant can be selected to read the practice vignettes, and the therapist will model an empathic response. Following several demonstrations of this nature, the exercise is conducted as follows:

1 One statement from the list below is given to each group member. The group member reads it and writes down on a piece of paper the feeling and/or want implied by the vignette.
2 Group members are paired into dyads.
3 One member of dyad (i.e., the sender) reads and role-plays his or her statement to the other (i.e., the recipient), who replies with an empathic response.
4 Sender informs recipient whether or not the empathic response matched the feeling and/or want he or she wrote down on the paper. Participants discuss how they reached their conclusions (i.e., what information guided their response).
5 Members of dyad switch roles and follow same procedure.
6 When the exercise is completed, reassemble large group and ask for pair(s) of volunteers to demonstrate task.
7 Feedback is provided using the model taught previously (i.e., indicate specific behaviors that match and do not match the skill concept).

Statements Given to Patients To Elicit Empathic Response (Abbreviated List)

1 "I got a good grade on my test."
2 "I lost my wallet."

3 "I found a bus token on the street."

4 "I wanted to do something nice for my mother so I asked her if there was anything that I could do for her. She said, 'Nothing, I can take care of things myself, thank you.' "

5 Woman talking about her job: "One thing I always liked about this job was the regular schedule. I like to be able to plan things in advance. Now this is the third time this month that they have asked me to change my hours!"

6 "I don't want to talk about it today. It is between me and my family and it's just too personal."

Homework (independent practice of empathic statement). Group members are instructed to make at least one empathic statement to another group member on some occasion when they meet outside the group, and to record the situation, what was said, and a self-evaluation of performance. They are also asked to be prepared to present this information during the next social skills training group.

This is the end of this training module. The next training module teaches patients how to make a "simple request." This is a type of request that is used when you expect a positive or neutral response to your request. That is, there is no conflict between what you want the other to do and what the other wants to do. In this type of request, patients are taught how to state clearly what they want from the other person. It is suggested that the simple request consist of two phrases. The first phrase indicates what is wanted, and the second states the consequences if the request is granted. The "guiding phrases" for the simple request are the following: "If you . . ." followed by a statement of what is wanted from the other person.

". . . then I . . ." followed by a statement of the consequences anticipated if the request is granted.

Example Module #2: Learning To Make an Empathic Request

A. *Instructional lecture providing verbal descriptions of skill concepts*

We have learned in prior lessons to make an "empathic statement" and a "simple request." We use a "simple request" when, after appraising a situation, we determine that the reaction of the other will probably be positive or neutral. A "simple request" uses the "If you . . ., then I . . ." format. For example, I would use a simple request if I was working with you to clean up the apartment and wanted you to do a specific task. I might say, "If you start on the dishes, then I can finish dusting this room and we will get finished sooner." In this case, I would expect your reaction to be positive or neutral since we are both working on the same task and want the same thing, that is, a clean apartment. Therefore, a simple request would be appropriate.

Sometimes, however, we want to make a request that would require substantial effort on the part of the other, or would require the person to do something he or she would not have chosen to do. In these cases, we would expect at least a mildly negative reaction because the request is counter to, or conflicts with, what the other person wants. For instance, in the clean-up example, maybe the roommate would prefer to continue dusting rather than start a new task like washing the dishes. Though our overall want is the same (to have a clean apartment), my wish for my roommate to do the dishes is in conflict with his or her desire to continue dusting. Therefore, my roommate might have a slightly negative reaction to my request. Or perhaps my roommate despises washing the dishes. Then he or she would have a moderately or extremely negative reaction to the request.

In situations like these, you must "escalate" your request beyond the "simple request." The request will be better received, and the other person will be more likely to grant the request if you make an empathic statement that shows you are aware of what the other person wants in this situation. Expressing your awareness of another's wants and feelings is a good way to show that you understand and care about the person.

The type of request appropriate to this situation is the *empathic request,* in which an empathic statement precedes the "If you . . . , then I . . ." component. As we discussed earlier, an empathic statement attempts to communicate our understanding of what the other person (a) feels, (b) wants, or (c) both feels and wants. When it is used in a request, we are trying to understand the other's wants and/or feelings in relation to the request. In other words, our empathic statement expresses our understanding of the other's wants and feelings upon hearing our request.

We refer to the empathic request as an escalation because an additional component, an empathic statement, is added to the basic "If you . . . , then I . . ." statement. Thus, an empathic request is actually a combination of two skills that we have already learned: the empathic statement and the simple request. An empathic statement "softens" the simple request and helps the other person know that you are sensitive to his or her wants and feelings at the same time that you are making a request to get your own wants fulfilled. When you take the time and expend the effort to understand others' wants and feelings and communicate this information, your request will be better received and you will likely reduce the negative effect that you expect. This occurs because your empathy fulfills one of the most important and universal human needs people have: that is, to be treated in a way that shows that their wants and feelings are respected and valued by others.

For instance, in the clean-up example, suppose I know from your previous behavior that you prefer to finish one chore before starting another. My want, for you to stop dusting and start the dishes while I finish dusting, is in conflict with your want, and you might have a negative reaction to my request. Therefore, an empathic request is appropriate. It might be formulated as follows: "*I know you* would prefer to finish dusting before starting anything else, but *if you* can start on the dishes while I finish up in here, *then we* can get done a lot sooner."

As mentioned, empathy is effective in demonstrating understanding only when it is expressed "convincingly," that is, when the nonverbals show that you mean what you say. In order to do this successfully, you really have to "step into the other's shoes" temporarily and actually attempt to experience that person's wants and feelings. When you do this in preparation for making a request, you become more aware of the strength or importance of the other person's want. As a result, you may decide to modify your own want so that both you and the other person can get your wants met. We will talk more about this in future lessons.

Let's practice the format for an empathic the format for an empathic request using a made-up situation entitled "Walking to the Store" (read vignette to group).

> Practice Vignette: Walking to the Store. I am walking to the grocery store with Betty. We are both looking forward to some leisurely time together, but we're also in a hurry to get home before it starts to rain. Halfway to the grocery, I remember that I also want to mail my rent check at the post office, which is a couple of blocks out of the way. I rarely get to see Betty anymore, and today is the only opportunity I'll have all week. If she starts her shopping while I go to the post office, we'll hardly have any time to speak with each other. I turn to Betty and make an empathic request, saying . . .

The following process is used to formulate an empathic request (the concept of two separate "thinking" and "behavior" components was taught in the prior lesson on the simple request).

1 *Thinking component*
  a *My wants.* What do I want from the other person? I want her to accompany me to the post office.
  b *Consequences.* What are the consequences if the request is granted? I will be able to mail my letters.
  c *Other's wants.* What are the wants of the other person in relation to my wants?
    She wants to get home before it starts raining.
  d *Other's reaction.* How do I think the other person will react to this request?
    neutral_____ positive_____ negative __X__
    (If negative, go to e.)
    (If neutral or positive, go to f.)
  e *Modify want or offer compromise.* If I anticipate a *negative* reaction, do I want to modify my want(s) or think of a compromise that would enable both of us to get our needs met?
    No __X__ (if no, go to f.)
    Yes _____ (If yes, go back to a, repeat thinking process.)
  f *Decision #1: Simple or escalated request?:* Based on other's anticipated reaction (d), what type of request should I make? If d is:

1)   neutral or positive _____ make simple request (Go to b of Behavioral Component below.)

2)   negative __X__ make empathic statement (Go to a of Behavioral Component below.)

2   *Behavioral component: Stating the empathic request*

   a   Make an empathic statement that shows I am considering the other's wants regarding my request (see c, Thinking Component above).

   "I know you want to get home before it starts raining, but . . .

   b.   Make a positive statement of what I want from the other person (see a, Thinking Component).

   If you would come with me to the post office first, . . .

   c.   State the consequences if the request is granted (see b, Thinking Component).

   . . . then I can mail these letters."

3   *Exercise to facilitate supervised practice and feedback.* Hand out the vignette entitled "Four O'Clock Meeting" (see below), and give the following directions: "Now that you have a model for making the empathic request, I want you to practice with a made-up situation. When the exercise begins, read the practice situation, then follow the thinking and behavior steps outlined on the worksheet (Figure 5-1). Be sure to perform all six thinking steps before making your statement of the request."

When the participants have completed the worksheet, divide the group into dyads and continue with the following instructions: "Now that you have completed the request in writing, I want you to role-play the situation with your partner. Decide which person in the dyad will present a request to the other; then act out the scene. When you're done, switch roles; the person who made the request should now receive it, and the recipient should now make the request."

Sample Vignette: Four O'clock Meeting

It is four o'clock and Sharon's meeting with her therapist is just about to end. Sharon's therapist likes to leave precisely at four because she starts early and sees a lot of people during the day. They have been discussing a new job Sharon will be starting tomorrow, and Sharon is feeling very anxious about this. She thinks she wants a little more help deciding on some things she can do today and tonight to deal with her fear. As her therapist is writing out an appointment slip for their next meeting, Sharon turns to her and makes an empathic request, saying . . .

4   *Feedback to patients on supervised practice exercise*

After the dyads have interacted as described, re-form the large group and ask volunteers to act out their requests. Be sure they tell the group the thinking

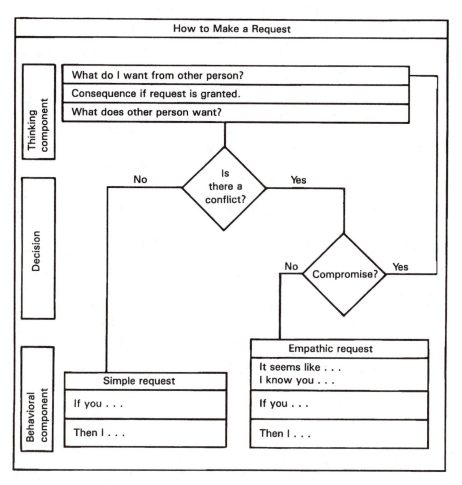

Figure 5.1   Worksheet to guide the development of an empathic statement.

process they went through as well as the request they made. Feedback should include specific information about how the response matched and failed to match the skill concepts associated with the empathic request.

   5   *Homework to facilitate independent practice*
A worksheet to guide the development of an empathic statement is given to each group member. Members are asked to make an empathic request during the week and record their thoughts and behaviors on the worksheet. Ask them to be prepared to discuss it in the next group meeting. Included in the assignment is the request that they be prepared to discuss their self-evaluation of performance according to the skill concepts.

EVALUATION OF RELATIONSHIP BETWEEN KNOWLEDGE OF SKILL CONCEPT AND BEHAVIORAL PERFORMANCE

In this chapter I have placed a heavy emphasis on the teaching of cognitive concepts to promote subsequent behavioral change. In order to provide preliminary empirical validation of the model presented, the following evaluation was conducted. The goal of this evaluation was to determine whether there was a relationship between an individual's ability to learn a skill concept and ability to perform that skill. Subjects were involved in a communication and problem-solving skill training program that employed the methods described in this chapter. Only the data regarding performance with the empathic statement will be presented here since this skill was used as an example throughout the chapter.

Subjects were 12 patients with severe and persistent psychiatric disorders and histories of extensive hospitalization. They were enrolled in a continuing day treatment program and had diagnoses of schizophrenia, major affective disorder, attention deficit disorder, and paranoid personality. They were provided five 90-minute training sessions covering the concepts and skills needed to make an empathic statement. According to the model described in this chapter, they had received three components of training (a) instruction, (b) supervised practice and (c) feedback. They had not yet engaged in independent practice. Subjects were evaluated to determine if they (a) possessed the knowledge of the defining characteristics of the empathic statement and (b) were they able to generate an empathic statement in response to four interactional vignettes. The question used to assess knowledge of the skill concept was the following:

An empathic statement is a statement that
a) tells someone how *you* feel
b) gives sympathy
c) expresses your understanding of what another person is thinking or feeling
d) asks a question

The subjects were also presented four interactional vignettes and asked to make an empathic statement in response to each. The four interactional vignettes were the following:

1   Someone says to you:
    "I finally got the "A" that I have been working on in math."
       You say:
    "It seems that you . . ."

2   Someone says to you:
    "I just looked for my wallet in all the usual places and it is not there."
       You say:
    "It sounds like you . . ."

3 Someone says to you:
   "I was looking for some money so I could take the train and I found this token on the floor."
   You say:
   "It seems that you . . ."
4 Someone says to you:
   "I got my rent paid on time this month."
   You say:
   "It sounds like you . . ."

Regarding knowledge of the skill concept (empathic statement), subjects' performance was classified into one of two categories: (a) could define concept and (b) could not define concept. Ability to generate an empathic statement in response to the vignettes was also classified into one of two categories: (a) provided at least one empathic statement, (b) did not provide an empathic statement. These data were evaluated using a 2×2 chi-square analysis. The results of the analysis yielded a significant chi-square (chi $= 5.04$ ($df = 1$), $p < .05$), indicating that accurate knowledge of the skill concept was significantly related to the ability to perform the behavioral aspect of the social skill.

Although preliminary in nature, these results indicate that "skill concepts" are significantly associated with the ability to perform skilled behavioral tasks. Of course further research is needed to determine more information about the relationship between skill concepts and behavior.

SUMMARY

Social skills training is a well-documented procedure for use in rehabilitation. Recent emphasis on the cognitive aspects of skill training has been highlighted in this chapter. The training program described consists of four components: instruction, supervised practice, feedback, and independent practice. A general explanation and a specific practical example of this model of skill training were provided. Also, a preliminary evaluation was presented that supports the idea that a positive relationship exists between the knowledge of skill concepts and behavioral performance of social skills. It is suggested that this relationship be reflected in the training procedures used in rehabilitation programs.

REFERENCES

Bandura, A. (1969). *Principles of behavior modification.* New York: Holt, Rinehart, & Winston.

Beck, A. (1976). *Cognitive therapy and emotional disorders.* New York: International Universities Press.

Bedell, J. R., & Ward, J. (1989). An intensive community-based treatment alternative to state hospitalization. *Hospital and Community Psychiatry, 40,* 533–535.

Bedell, J.R., & Weathers, L.R. (1979). A psychoeducational model of skill training: Therapist and game facilitated appreciations. In D. Upper and S. M. Ross (Eds.) *Behavioral group therapy: An annual review.* Champaign, IL: Research Press.

Bellack, A. S., Morrison, R. L., & Mueser, K. T. (1989). Social problem solving in schizophrenia. *Schizophrenia Bulletin, 15,* 101–116.

Bellack, A. S., Turner, S. M., Hersen, M., & Luber, R. F. (1984). An examination of the efficacy of social skills training for chronic schizophrenia patients. *Hospital and Community Psychiatry, 35* 1023–1028.

Benton, M. K., & Schroeder, H. E. (1990). Social skills training with schizophrenics: A meta-analytic evaluation. *Journal of Consulting and Clinical Psychology, 55,* 741–747.

Brady, J. P. (1984). Social skills training for psychiatric patients. II, Clinical outcome studies. *American Journal of Psychiatry, 141,* 491–498.

Ellis, A., & Grieger, R. (1978). *The handbook of rational-emotive therapy.* New York: Springer.

Hersen, M., & Bellack, A. S. (1976). Social skills training for chronic psychiatric patients: Rationale, research findings, and future directions. *Comprehensive Psychiatry, 17,* 559–580.

Hogarty, G. E., Anderson, C. M., Reiss, K. J., Kornblith, S. J., Greenwald, D. P., Javna, C. D. & Madonia, M. J. (1986). Family psychoeducation, social skills training, and maintenance chemotherapy in aftercare treatment of schizophrenics: One-year effect of a controlled study on relapse and expressed emotion. *Archives of General Psychiatry, 43,* 633–642.

Ladd, G. W., & Mize, J. (1983). A cognitive-social learning model of social-skill training. *Psychological Review, 90,* 127–157.

Leff, J., & Vaughn, C. E. (1980). The interaction of life events and relatives' expressed emotion in schizophrenia and depressed neurosis. *British Journal of Psychiatry, 136,* 146–153.

Liberman, R. P., & Bedell, J. R. (1989). Behavior therapy. In H. I. Kaplan, & B. J. Sadock (Eds.), *Comprehensive textbook of psychiatry* (5th ed.) Baltimore: Williams & Wilkins.

Liberman, R. P., DeRise, W. R., & Mueser, K. T. (1989). *Social skills training for psychiatric patients.* New York: Pergamon.

Liberman R. P., Mueser, K. T., Wallace, C. J., Jacobs, T. E., & Massel, H. K. (1986). Training skills in the psychiatrically disabled: Learning coping and competence. *Schizophrenia Bulletin, 12,* 631–647.

Libet, J. M., & Lewinsohn, P. M. (1973). Concept of social skill with special reference to the behavior of depressed persons. *Journal of Consulting and Clinical Psychology, 40,* 304–312.

Meichenbaum, D. H. (1977). *Cognitive-behavior modification: An integrative approach.* New York: Plenum.

Meichenbaum, D. H., & Goodman, J. (1977). Training impulsive children to talk to themselves: A means of developing self-control. In A. Ellis & R. Grieger (Eds.), *Handbook of rational emotive therapy.* New York: Springer.

Morrison, R.L. & Bellack, A.S. (1984). Social Skills Training. In A.S. Bellack (Ed.), *Schizophrenia: Treatment, management, and rehabilitation.* Orlando, FL: Grune & Stratton.

Robertson, I., Richardson, A. M., & Youngson, S. C. (1984). Social skills training with mentally handicapped people: A review. *British Journal of Clinical Psychology, 23,* 241–264.

Wallace, C. J., & Liberman, R. P. (1985). Social skill training for patients with schizophrenia: A controlled clinical trial. *Psychiatry Research, 15,* 239–247.

Wallace, C. J., Nelson, C. J., Liberman, R. P., Aitchison, R. A., Lukoff, D., Elder, J. P., & Ferris, C. (1980). A review and critique of social skills training with schizophrenic patients. *Schizophrenia Bulletin, 6,* 42–63.

Zigler, E., & Phillips, L. (1961). Social competence and outcome in psychiatric disorder. *Journal of Abnormal and Social Psychology, 63,* 264–271.

Chapter 6

Recreational and Activity Therapies in Multilevel Psychoeducationally Oriented Social Skills Training

John C. Ward, Jr., Barry J. Naster, Janice E. Pace, and Paula K. Whitaker

The past two decades have brought increasing empirical and clinical evidence of the importance of "behavioral therapies" (Craighead, Kazdin, & Mahoney, 1981) in the rehabilitation of people with severe and persistent mental disorders (Anthony, 1979; Bedell, Archer, & Marlowe, 1980; Bedell & Michael, 1985; Bellack & Hersen, 1978; Bellack, Turner, Hersen, & Luber, 1984; Goldsmith & McFall, 1975; Margules & Anthony, 1976; Wallace & Liberman, 1985). The most effective psychiatric rehabilitation programs use "multimodal" strategies that combine social skills training and other behavioral interventions with judiciously prescribed psychotropic medications. A combination of these treatments results in lower relapse rates and higher levels of social adjustment than does the use of psychoactive drugs alone (Hierholzer & Liberman, 1986). Although there is uncertainty about the typology of symptoms addressed by each modality, it generally is thought that psychiatric medications alleviate "positive signs" of the disorders, for example, hallucinations and delusions, and that psychosocial and behavioral interventions modify "negative signs," for example, social skills deficits (Andreasen & Olsen, 1982). More recently, behaviorally oriented "self-medication" skills-training groups (Crockett et al., 1989; Liberman, 1986; Verbosky, 1983) have also been shown to have indirect effects on "positive signs" by improving knowledge, skills, *and* compliance in groups of people treated with psychopharmacology (Dow, Verdi, & Sacco, 1991; Eckman, Liberman, Phipps, & Blair, 1990; Hogarty et al., 1986).

Although skills enhancement approaches have been implemented in a variety of applied settings, the techniques and procedures that comprise this type of training are not standardized in practice or in research, nor have they remained static across time. Methods of teaching skills vary greatly and are somewhat dependent on the type of skill being taught. Strategies range from practicing simple behaviors (e.g., increased eye contact or smiling as aids for communication skills) to memorizing complex cognitive strategies for analyzing problems and developing potential solutions. An important refinement to traditional behavioral methods of skills training evolved when instructional and learning strategies from the discipline of education were combined with techniques derived from the cognitive and behavioral therapies of psychology and psychiatry. An early model that exemplifies these "psychoeducational" procedures is described by Bedell and Weathers (1978). An updated refinement of this model is presented in Chapter 5. That chapter describes four components of skill training: (a) instruction, (b) supervised practice, (c) feedback, and (d) independent practice. Fundamental to the development of socially skilled behaviors, and first presented in the instruction phase, is the systematic learning of "skill concepts," which are cognitive constructs that serve to define, organize, and guide (DOG) an individual's behavior.

A variety of methodologies may be applied during the instructional phases of social skills training. Techniques borrowed from the fields of recreational therapy and education and the business community (Bedell & Weathers, 1978; Foxx, McMorrow, & Schloss, 1983; Gordon, 1979; Nash, 1975; Weathers, Bedell, Marlowe, and Gordon, 1978) are extremely useful in social skills training, especially for teaching "skill concepts." "Therapeutic games," which follow the principle that a little bit of sugar makes the medicine go down, nest the material to be learned within activities that appear more recreational than treatment oriented. Some recreational and activities-oriented psychoeducational board games are reportedly so simple that participants are able to set up and initiate play even without immediate staff supervision (Weathers, Bedell, Marlowe, & Gordon, 1978).

Although clinical researchers acknowledge the need to consider participants' levels of functioning in order to develop useful social skills training programs (Bellack et al., 1984), most psychoeducational program evaluations have been conducted only with less acutely ill individuals in outpatient, day treatment, partial hospitalization, or long-term residential settings (Agacinski & Stern, 1984; Bellack et al., 1984; Coviensky & Buckley, 1986; Hierholzer & Liberman, 1986). This may be due to a supposition that social skills training is too difficult for lower functioning or acutely mentally ill persons until they have been stabilized on medication and are able to function in less restrictive levels of care. However, the use of therapeutic games and other recreational strategies may make it possible to begin social skills training and development of skill concepts in groups of people who are more decompensated or lower functioning than those in traditional skills-training programs. Research on the rehabilitation of people challenged by severe developmental disabilities provides some support for that assumption. Skills-training programs using therapeutic games and activities are reportedly very effective in treating people exhibiting a variety of symptoms related to mild and profound mental retardation (Foxx, McMorrow, & Mennemeier, 1984; Singh & Winton, 1983). The cognitive deficits exhibited by those individuals are not unlike the impairment of thinking characteristic of people with severe and persistent mental disorders (e.g., schizophrenia) at the time of their admission to inpatient care. Although delaying their participation in basic recreational or activities-styled social skills training may be well-intentioned, this practice may cause us to miss opportunities to teach basic cognitive and behavioral tools that will assist in more rapid recovery and stabilization. Rudimentary skills, concepts, and supervised practice gained at these early stages of treatment form a base upon which more advanced learning and independent practice will depend as individuals progress to less restrictive levels in the continuum of mental health care.

Empirical support for using recreational and activities therapies to teach social skills to people during acute stages of mental health treatment comes from the evaluation of a short-term (30–35 day), inpatient, psychiatric rehabilitation program that utilized "multilevel" psychoeducational groups as a therapeutic core (Bedell & Ward, 1989; Ward & Naster, 1991). Structured, lesson-planned groups were used to teach skills associated with thinking, communicating, problem solving, and self-medicating. There were three levels of each group. The first two levels, comprising the majority of the therapeutic group activities on the unit, provided social skills training that used techniques borrowed from recreational therapy and activity therapy. Participation in these groups began the first day the person was admitted to the inpatient unit.

Each group in the multilevel program was "open-ended." That is, participants "graduated" to the next level only after demonstrating cognitive and behavioral learning of the behaviors and skill concepts taught in the lower level. This permitted participants to complete each of the three levels of groups at their own pace. The instructor's assessment of discrete cognitive and behavioral performance determined when a participant was ready to graduate to the next, more complex level of training. Performance on this evaluative task also served as a daily measure of each individual's rate of compensation and general response to treatment. Participants were found to have shorter lengths of stay and less recidivism following discharge from that program of treatment than were a comparable group admitted to a state mental health hospital.

Programs that do not allow participants to progress at their own pace have been shown to be effective with higher functioning, community-based participants

(Upper, Livingston, Conners, & Olans, 1982). However, these programs may frustrate participants who are able to progress more rapidly or those not able to learn as quickly (Agacinski & Stern, 1984; Bellack et al., 1984). Professionals in the field of occupational therapy have long been aware of this principle and have pointed out the need to structure treatment so that it minimizes stress, especially when the disability itself exaggerates the individual's sensitivity to the demands of the environment (Agacinski & Stern, 1984; Coviensky & Buckley, 1986). Occupational therapy's focus on health rather than illness is also an important concept in the application of skills-training programs. Psychoeducational skills-training programs that emphasize ability training and skills acquisition rather than disability correction encourage participants to learn new skills instead of dwelling on real or imagined deficits over which they may have little control.

Consideration of the various principles and philosophies described thus far led to the development of a comprehensive psychiatric rehabilitation program with a social skills training core that includes three instructional levels (introductory, intermediate, and advanced or "skills" level) for teaching skills in each of four content areas (self-awareness, communication, problem solving, and self-medication). Selected skill areas and procedures for teaching those skills will be described in more detail later in this chapter. Table 6-1 shows how the levels of each group were scheduled in a highly structured, intensive, short-term residential treatment program. The following is a brief description of each of the three levels of skill training.

Introductory Level   These groups use a combination of *educational* and *recreational activity* methods in structured therapeutic games to teach and assess learning of *basic definitions* related to the content of a specific skill area. This level focuses on developing rudimentary skill concepts emphasizing skill definitions. After "passing" basic performance criteria for a content area (e.g., communication), the participants graduate to the next, more advanced group within that content area.

Intermediate Level   These groups apply the basic skill concept definitions learned in the introductory level using *activity therapy* methodology. Hypothetical vignettes require participants to apply the basic definitions in role-plays, paper and pencil drawing, and other preplanned group activities. Participants in these group activities are not expected to master skills, nor are they expected to apply what they are learning to personal or emotionally threatening situations that could increase distress and delay recovery.

Advanced Level   The procedures used to teach and assess performance of participants at the "advanced level" are similar to those used in traditional social skills training groups. Each group begins with didactic review of material learned

Table 6-1 Daily schedule of short-term residential psychiatric rehabilitation program.

	Monday	Tuesday	Wednesday	Thursday	Friday	Saturday	Sunday
6:30	Wake up	Wake up	Wake up	Wake up	Wake up	Wake up for medication	Wake up for medication
7:00	Medication*	Medication*	Medication*	Medication*	Medication*	Medication*	Medication*
7:30	Breakfast	Breakfast	Breakfast	Breakfast	Breakfast	Breakfast	Breakfast
8:00	Free time	Free time	Free time	Free time	Free time	Free time	Free time
8:45	Exercise	Exercise	Exercise	Exercise	Exercise	Exercise	Exercise
9:10	Relaxation training	Relaxation training	Relaxation training	Relaxation training	Relaxation training	Relaxation training	Relaxation training
9:30	Self awareness Introductory group Intermediate group Skills group	Introductory group Intermediate group Skills group	Self awareness Introductory group Intermediate group Skills group	Client/staff community meeting	Self awareness Introductory group Intermediate group Skills group	Home management group	Free time
11:00	Outside Free time Individual counseling	Visitors 11–noon Outside Free time Individual counseling	Outside Free time Individual counseling	Visitors 11–noon Outside Free time Individual counseling	Outside Free time Individual counseling	Outside Free time Individual counseling	Individual counseling
Noon	Medication*	Medication*	Medication*	Medication*	Medication*	Medication*	Medication*
12:15	Lunch	Lunch	Lunch	Lunch	Lunch	Lunch	Lunch
1:00	Free time	Free time	Free time	Free time	Free time	Free time	Free time
1:30	Communication Introductory group Intermediate group Skills group	Self medication Introductory group Intermediate group Skills group	Communication Introductory group Intermediate group Skills group	Self medication Introductory group Intermediate group Skills group	Communication Introductory group Intermediate group Skills group	Visitors 1–4	Visitors 1–4
3:00	Relaxation training	Relaxation training	Relaxation training	Relaxation training	Relaxation training	Individual counseling	Individual counseling
3:10	Free time Individual counseling	Free time Individual counseling	Free time Individual counseling	Free time Individual counseling	Free time Individual counseling	Outside	Outside
4:45	Medication*	Medication*	Medication*	Medication*	Medication*	Medication*	Medication*
5:15	Dinner	Dinner	Dinner	Dinner	Dinner	Dinner	Dinner
6:00	Visitors 6–7	Outside	Visitors 6–7	Outside	Visitors 6–7	Free time	Free time
7:20	Relaxation training	Relaxation training	Relaxation training	Relaxation training	Relaxation training	Relaxation training	Relaxation training
7:30	Problem solving Introductory group Intermediate group	Self awareness Introductory group Intermediate group	Problem solving Introductory group Intermediate group	Self awareness Introductory group Intermediate group	Problem solving Introductory group Intermediate group	Movie/dance	Client/staff community 7:30–9
8:00	Relaxation training	Relaxation training	Relaxation training	Relaxation training	Relaxation training	Relaxation training	Relaxation training
8:10	Medication*	Medication*	Medication*	Medication*	Medication*	Medication*	Medication*
9:30	Individual counseling	Individual counseling	Individual counseling	Individual counseling	Individual counseling	Individual counseling	Individual counseling
11:00	Bedtime	Bedtime	Bedtime	Bedtime	Bedtime	Bedtime	Bedtime

*Except for clients who have passed the Self Medication skills group and take their medication during free time; 8:00—8:15 AM, 1:00—1:15 PM, and 10:00—10:15 PM.

in lower level groups. Participants are guided through the use of structured "homework assignment sheets" with instructions to describe real situations that occurred to them within the previous 24 hours. This facilitates the independent practice component of training and helps participants apply cognitive and behavioral strategies of the new skill to more personally relevant situations encountered in daily living.

By the time most participants reach advanced level groups, they will have completed 1 to 2 weeks of treatment. At this time, they are considered better able to address personal and emotional problems related to their need for treatment. In addition, a framework has been provided within which they can each begin to understand and communicate their own feelings as they develop strategies for resolving more serious problems.

The remainder of this chapter will present detailed lesson plans of introductory (recreational) and intermediate (activities therapy) groups for teaching self-awareness, communication, and problem-solving skills. Readers may choose to adopt or adapt these procedures for use in their own clinical settings. Although lesson plans for the advanced groups have been omitted, most readers are already familiar with the traditional training format that these groups follow. They are described in Chapter 5 and are also available elsewhere (Naster et al., 1991). Information about the three levels of self-medication training groups is also available (Crockett et al., 1989; Verbosky, 1983).

LESSON PLANS FOR ACTIVITY THERAPIES

I   LESSON PLANS FOR INTRODUCTORY LEVEL RECREATION GROUPS
    A   The "Self-Awareness" therapeutic game is called "Beanbag Toss."
        1   The group facilitator reviews performance objectives and criteria for passing the introductory self-awareness group and gives a description of the therapeutic game Beanbag Toss to participants. Duration: 5 minutes.
        2   "Skill concepts" are introduced. Duration: 10 minutes.
            a   Very simple definitions of thoughts, feelings, and behaviors are presented in a classroom lecture format using posters displaying definitions and examples.
               (1)   *Thoughts:* Messages from the brain, e.g., ideas, wishes, wants, judgments, hopes
               (2)   *Feelings:* Two types of "feelings," physical and emotional
                   (a)   Physical feelings (e.g., hot, cold, hunger) are the body's reactions to the internal or external environment.
                   (b)   Emotional feelings (e.g., fear, love, anger, sad, or happy) are psychological interpretations of (and may also cause) some physical feelings.
               (3)   *Behaviors:* Things that we do that can be seen or hear- e.g., walking, talking, laughing, crying

    b   Examples of thoughts, feelings, and behaviors that are "nonpersonal" are offered.

    c   The importance of knowing the difference between thoughts, feelings, and behaviors is examined.

    d   The "Thoughts, Feelings, and Behaviors: Definitions and Examples" poster is displayed.

    e   An "identification" practice session on how to recognize thoughts, feelings, and behaviors is conducted. The group facilitator reads several statements to the participants. Each statement has one specific word underlined. That word is an example of either a thought, feeling, or behavior. Each participant must indicate whether the underlined word is a thought, feeling, or behavior by circling or underlining a T, F, or B (see below).

        (1) Sam *dreamed* he would go fishing.

            <u>T</u> — F — B

        (2) Sam is *happy* about going fishing.

            T — <u>F</u> — B

        (3) Sam is *fishing*.

            T — F — <u>B</u>

3 The Beanbag Toss therapeutic game is presented.

    a   Instructions on how to play the game are given, and the game is demonstrated by the facilitator. Duration: 5 minutes.

        (1) Bean bags are tossed at scoring board. The score board is 2 feet wide and 3 feet high. It is made of quarter-inch plywood and is painted blue. It has five holes, each having a diameter of 6 inches. A hole is located near each corner of the board, and there is one in the center. Each hole has a number painted below it specifying the number of points that can be earned by tossing the beanbag through the hole. Holes are worth 3, 5, 7, 10, or 15 points.

            (a) No points are awarded if the participant misses the scoreboard with the beanbag.

            (b) Participants receive 1 point for hitting the scoreboard with the beanbag.

            (c) Participants receive the number of points marked by a hole if the beanbag goes through a hole or "catches" and hangs on a hole.

        (2) Participants must stand 10 feet from board when "tossing."

        (3) Each participant is allowed one practice toss of a bag.

        (4) Each participant takes turns tossing a total of six bags.

        (5) After each toss, the participant draws a "card" from a "deck" of playing cards (each card has a statement similar to those in 2.e. above).

        (6) The individual identifies the underlined word as a thought, feeling, or behavior.

        (7) The group facilitator reviews correctness of the answer with participant and group. When the participant correctly identifies the thought, feeling, or behavior, the score from the bean bag toss is increased.

    (a)   A toss that resulted in either 0 or 1 point is given an additional 3 points for correct identification.

    (b)   A toss that earned points listed for a hole is doubled, e.g., a score of 7 for a toss is increased to 14 points.

  b The game is played for 40 minutes. At the end of the 40 minutes, the individual scores are calculated and:

    (1)   The game winner is selected.

    (2)   The game winner is awarded a prize, e.g., an edible snack or other tangible reward.

    (3)   The game winner also receives applause from the rest of the group.

4 The group facilitator gives feedback on group process and participation.

5 After the group is dismissed, the facilitator completes a form that lists each participant, how long he or she attended the group (i.e., completed or left early) and whether or not he passed other group criteria (e.g., responded when "prompted" by facilitator during the "lecture" portion of group and participated in the "game").

  a Data are collected, calculated, and recorded.

  b Facilitator contacts and gives feedback to all individuals about whether they will continue at same level or move to next level.

B The introductory level "Communication" group therapeutic game is called "Communication Casino."

1 The objectives and criteria for the overall group and a description of the Communication Casino game are presented to participants. Duration: 5 minutes.

2 Group terms are introduced. Duration: 10 minutes.

  a Very simple definitions of passive, aggressive, and assertive communications styles are presented in a didactic format.

    (1) *Passive:* Wanting to express thoughts and feelings, but not expressing them, or expressing them in an indirect manner

    (2) *Aggressive:* Expressing thoughts and feelings in a forceful, demanding, and/or threatening or intentionally intimidating manner

    (3) *Assertive:* Expressing thoughts and feelings in an open, direct, constructive manner, without demanding, attacking, begging, or offering excuses.

  b Nonpersonal examples of passive, aggressive, and assertive communications are given.

  c The importance of "time," "place," and "person" are examined in relationship to each style of communication.

  d The "Passive, Aggressive, and Assertive: Definitions and Examples" poster is displayed.

  e The facilitator presents several statements from a deck of "Communication Cards." Each statement is either a passive, aggressive, or assertive style of communication. Each participant must indicate which style of communication the statement represents. Examples are:

(1) Give me a cigarette, right now!
PA — <u>AG</u> — AS
(2) May I have a cigarette?
PA — AG — <u>AS</u>
(3) That smoke sure smells good.
<u>PA</u> — AG — AS

3 The Communication Casino therapeutic game is described.

a Instructions are given. The facilitator describes and demonstrates how the game is played. Duration: 5 minutes.

(1) Each participant is given 30 points worth of poker chips from the casino bank:
    (a) 10 white chips worth 1 point each
    (b) 2 blue chips worth 5 points each
    (c) 1 red chip worth 10 points
(2) Player roles a "die."
(3) Player "bets" on own success at identifying the modes of communication on the communication cards.
(4) Player picks card and identifies three statements as either passive, aggressive, or assertive.
(5) Other participants place "bets" only if they believe player was correct in identifying the styles of communication from the communication card.
(6) All bets are limited to 10 points maximum.
(7) Answers are reviewed by the group facilitator for correctness.
(8) Bank pays all winning bets of participants.
(9) Bank collects bets lost by participants.
(10) Scoring
    (a) For each card answered correctly, the player who rolled the die receives a score derived from multiplying the number of points bet by the number that came up when the die was rolled.
    (b) Other participants (bettors) receive chips from the bank based on the number of points they bet only if the player correctly identified all three communication styles shown on the Communication Card.
    (c) Incorrectly identified cards result in loss of all bets.
(11) Process of rolling die and reading communication cards is repeated six times per player.
(12) Winner is determined by player with the most points at the end of the game.

b The game is played for 40 minutes.

(1) The game winner is selected.
(2) The game winner receives a tangible reward, e.g., a snack.
(3) The game winner receives applause from the group.

    4 After group is dismissed, group attendance and participation criteria are determined for each participant. Duration: 15 minutes.

        a Data are collected, calculated, and recorded.

        b Facilitator contacts and gives feedback to each participant.

C The introductory level "Problem-Solving" therapeutic game is called "Memory Round-up."

    1 The facilitator presents objectives and criteria for the introductory level problem-solving group and describes the Memory Round-up game. Duration: 5 minutes.

    2 "Skill concepts" are introduced. Duration 10 minutes.

        a Requirements that solutions to problems must be "socially acceptable" and "legal" are presented in didactic format.

        b Nonpersonal examples of socially acceptable and legal solutions that may help achieve goals and solve specific problems are given.

        c The importance of finding several alternatives for solving a problem is examined, i.e., the process of "alternative generation."

        d Methods for developing these "alternative solutions" are discussed; e.g., "brainstorming."

        e A "Problem-Solving Poster" is displayed that includes definitions of "socially acceptable," "legal," and "alternative generation."

        f "Identification session": Each participant is read a goal and three possible solutions from a deck of problem-solving cards. The participant is asked to identify solutions that are socially acceptable and legal. An example of a goal and related solutions that are printed on the problem-solving cards is:

        Goal: Find ways to get sleep.

        (1) Do breathing relaxation exercise.

            <u>Yes</u> No

        (2) Take a half bottle of sleeping pills.

            Yes <u>No</u>

        (3) Read a dull book.

            <u>Yes</u> No

    3 The problem-solving introductory level therapeutic game of Memory Round-up is played.

        a Facilitator gives instructions and demonstrates how the Memory Round-up game is played.

            (1) The Memory Round-up game is played with two decks of cards.

                (a) A standard deck of 52 playing cards

                (b) A "problem-solving" deck of 50 goals solution cards (see f. above).

            (2) The game begins by the facilitator's shuffling the standard deck of cards and spreading them face down on a table.

            (3) Players take turns selecting a card from the problem-solving deck.

(4) The player identifies whether each solution is socially acceptable and legal.

(5) Facilitator gives feedback on correctness of identifications.

(6) If a player does not correctly label all three solutions on the problem-solving card, play rotates to the next player.

(7) If player correctly labels all three solutions on a card, that player turns over two of the cards from the group of playing cards that were placed face down on the table.

(8) If the playing cards match, player takes those matching cards and repeats process until no match occurs.

(9) Depending on the size of the group (and time allowed), each player will usually have about six turns.

(10) The game may continue until all pairs of playing cards are collected.

(11) The winner is the participant with the most cards.

b Game is played. Duration: 40 minutes.

(1) The game winner is selected.

(2) The game winner receives a tangible reward (e.g., an edible snack).

(3) The game winner receives applause from the group.

4 Feedback on group participation and group process. Duration: 5 minutes.

5 Overall group criteria are determined for each person after group is dismissed. Duration: 15 minutes.

a Data are collected, calculated, and recorded.

b Facilitator gives feedback to each participant.

II Lesson Plans for Intermediate Level Activity Groups

A The therapeutic activity for the intermediate level "Self-Awareness" group is the "Who's to Blame Story."

1 The objectives and criteria for the overall group and the specific criteria of "Who's to Blame Story" are reviewed. Duration: 5 minutes.

2 "Skill concepts" covered in the introductory level self-awareness group are reviewed and new "skill concepts" are introduced. Duration: 30 minutes.

a Definitions of thoughts, feelings, and behaviors are briefly reviewed (using poster).

b Definitions of "responsibility" and "blame" are presented in a didactic format by the facilitator.

(1) *Responsibility:* Focusing on our wants, and how we view and accept whether we get or lose what we want, as the cause of our feelings.

(2) *Blame:* Focus on others or characteristics of self as cause for feelings (e.g., "You make me angry" or "I'm so stupid, I can't do anything right.")

c Nonpersonal examples of responsibility and blame are given.

d The "Thoughts—Feelings—Behaviors poster" and the "Responsibility/Blame Poster" are displayed.

e A "responsibility/Blame" practice identification session is held for distinguishing between "responsibility" and "blame" statements in describing "feelings." Each participant is given a list of statements. Each statement is to be identified as describing either "responsibility" or "blame".

   (1) Jack feels angry because Mary told him to be quiet and mind his own business.
   <u>Blame</u>   Responsibility

   (2) Jack feels fear because he believes Mary will not be his friend as he wishes.
   Blame   <u>Responsibility</u>

3 "Who's to Blame Story" is presented.

   a Instructions are given by the facilitator. Duration: 5 minutes.

   (1) Facilitator reads the "Who's to Blame Story" containing several subplots.

   Who's to Blame Story

   On Friday morning at 9:40 A.M., in the group room during the Activity group, Jack said to Mary, "You know Mary, you should come to group on time, at 9:30 instead of getting here at 9:40, so you could pass attendance criteria and wouldn't have to come to these same old groups all the time."

   Mary looked at Jack and couldn't believe her ears. She thought Jack was her friend and was shocked to hear him tell her what to do in front of the whole group. Mary said to Jack, "Why don't you be quiet and mind your own business!"

   Sue, sitting next to Jack, thought that Mary was talking to her because she had been talking with Jeanette about the colors they were using in their drawing.

   (2) Facilitator discusses possible feelings associated with each character.

   (3) Facilitator distributes "Responsibility/Blame Questionnaire" that is related to the case example, "Who's to Blame Story." Examples from the questionnaire are:

   (a) Jack feels anger because Mary told him to be quiet and mind his own business.
   <u>Blame</u> Responsibility

   (b) Sue feels anger, because she does not want Mary telling her what to do, and she is not able to stop Mary from saying anything.
   Blame   <u>Responsibility</u>

   (4) Facilitator instructs the students to identify each thought described as either a "responsibility" or a "blame" statement.

   (b) Questionnaire is completed. Duration: 10 minutes.

      (c)   Answers are reviewed with feedback on correctness. Duration: 10 minutes.

4 Feedback on group participation and group process. Duration: 10 minutes.

5 Overall group criteria are determined for each person after group is dismissed. Duration: 15 minutes.

    a Data are collected, calculated, and recorded.

    b Facilitator gives feedback to each individual.

B The therapeutic activity for the intermediate level "Communication" group is the "Baffling Behaviors Communication Story."

  1 The objectives and criteria for the overall group and the specific criteria for the "Baffling Behaviors Communication Story" are reviewed. Duration: 5 minutes.

  2 "Skill concepts" covered in the introductory level communication group are reviewed and new "skill concepts" are introduced. Duration: 15 minutes.

    a Definitions of "passive," "aggressive," and "assertive" communication styles are briefly reviewed.

    b Definitions and characteristics of "nonverbal communications" for each of the three communication styles are presented in a didactic format by the facilitator (see below).

Partial Listing of Nonverbal Communication Characteristics

	PASSIVE STYLE	AGGRESSIVE STYLE	ASSERTIVE STYLE
EYES	Downcast/Avoid	Stare (Glare)	Intermitent
EXPRESSION	Flat to sad	Tense jaw	Relaxed
BODY POSTURE	Slumped	Rigid	Open/Relaxed
PERSONAL SPACE	Distant	Invasive	Arm's length
VOICE	Soft	Loud, or forceful	Normal

    c The "skill concepts" for "nonverbal communications" are applied to nonpersonal examples for each of the three communication styles.

    d The "Verbal and Nonverbal Communications" posters are displayed

    e A practice identification session is held for recognizing nonverbal characteristics of passive, aggressive, and assertive communication styles. Identification requires recognition of passive, aggressive, and assertive nonverbal communication behaviors. For example:

      (1) Jack gets very close to Mary and talks in a loud tone of voice.
          Passive <u>Aggressive</u> Assertive

      (2) Jack is looking at the floor, his shoulders are slumped over, and he's talking to the staff in a soft voice.
          <u>Passive</u> Aggressive Assertive

(3) Jack appears to be relaxed, he is talking in a normal tone of voice, and he is looking at the person while he is talking to him.

Passive   Aggressive   <u>Assertive</u>

3   Copies of the "Baffling Behaviors Communication Story," a "Verbal Questionnaire," and a "Nonverbal Questionnaire" are distributed to the participants by the facilitator. (These questionnaires will be described later.) Duration: 40 minutes.

a   Instructions are given by the facilitator for "Baffling Behaviors Communication Story."

(1) The facilitator reads the "Baffling Behaviors Communication Story" aloud while participants follow along on their copies.

Baffling Behaviors Communication Story

Cindy has been a coworker of Donna's for a year. Cindy and Donna spend a lot of time together and are best friends at work. Cindy and Donna also worked with Jane the last year and all became good friends. Everybody who worked with Jane thought she was great. Jane left her job a week ago, moved to a new city 100 miles away to take a new job, and bought a new house. Jane's house caught on fire shortly after she moved in and Jane lost all she owned. Jane had no friends or family in that town who could help her. Donna took up a collection at work to give Jane financial help. Donna called Jane and told her that a collection of $125.00 from her friends at the office would soon arrive to aid her. Jane thanked Donna and told her how much she was counting on the $125.00. Donna told Cindy that she had called Jane to tell her about the money. Cindy said she would be willing to drive to that town to take Jane the money the following week. Donna said "great" and gave Cindy the money. Two weeks later, Jane called Donna and said that she had not received the money. The next day at work, Donna quietly (because other coworkers were in the room) approached Cindy to ask her why she hadn't taken Jane the money yet, as she had promised. Cindy shouted at Donna, in front of everyone, "Are you calling me a thief and a liar?"

(2) The facilitator describes a communication goal, for example:

(a) How can Donna communicate to Cindy, in front of her coworkers, her desire to have Cindy tell her what happened to the money?

         (b)   How can Donna communicate to Cindy her desire to have Cindy talk to her in a quiet and nonaccusatory manner?

   b   Instructions for the "Verbal Questionnaire" are given by the facilitator.

      (1)   Facilitator distributes the "Verbal Questionnaire" that is related to the case example, "Baffling Behaviors Communication Story."

      (2)   Facilitator instructs each participant to write one passive, one aggresive, and one assertive communication statement for each goal. The participant is asked to select the statement(s) that would most likely achieve the goal.

      (3)   Each participant completes the "Verbal Communication Questionnaire" following the above instructions.

      (4)   The facilitator gives feedback to the participants.

   c   The facilitator gives instructions for completing a "Nonverbal Questionnaire" (see section II.B.2.e. for examples of the types of statements and format of the questionnaire).

      (1)   The facilitator distributes the "Nonverbal Questionnaire," and explains that it is not related to the communication story.

      (2)   The facilitator instructs the participants to read each statement in the "Nonverbal Questionnaire" and identify each style of communication by the behaviors depicted in the examples.

      (3)   Participants complete the "Nonverbal Questionnaire."

      (4)   The facilitator reviews answers and gives feedback on correct responses.

 4   Facilitator gives feedback on overall group participation and group process. Duration: 5 minutes.

 5   Each participant's criteria is calculated by facilitator after group is dismissed. Duration: 15 minutes.

   a   Attendance, participation, and "activity" scores are calculated and recorded for each participant on group data sheets.

   b   Facilitator gives feedback to each participant.

C   The therapeutic activity for the intermediate level problem-solving group is called"Daily Problem Situations."

 1   The objectives and criteria for the overall group and the specific criteria of "Daily Problem Situations" therapeutic activity are reviewed. Duration: 5 minutes.

 2   "Skill concepts" from introductory level problem-solving groups are reviewed and new "skill concepts" are introduced. Duration: 25 minutes.

   a   Facilitator reviews definitions and examples of "socially acceptable" and "legal" solutions.

b   Facilitator introduces concept of "alternative generation" and "consequences" in didactic format.

    (1)   "Alternative generation" is a process in which various methods are used (e.g., brainstorming) to identify several things a person might do to achieve a goal. They must be legal and socially acceptable.

    (2)   A "consequence" is a brief description of what might happen if you choose a particular "alternative" (e.g., what you might "feel" or what others might "feel," would I really achieve my goal? at what cost?).

c   The facilitator uses nonpersonal examples to demonstrate the skill concepts of "solutions" and "consequences."

d   A "Solution/Consequence" poster is displayed which states definitions from C.2.a. and b. above. The poster is used for "prompting" during the therapeutic activity.

e   A practice session for "alternative generation" and "consequences" is conducted. This requires "brainstorming" at least three alternative solutions to any problem, and describing at least three alternative solutions to any problem, and describing at least two different consequences for each alternative.

Goal: Identify ways to lose weight
Alternative Solutions

a   I could limit calories to 1,200 per day.
b   I could not eat any desserts.
c   I could skip two of my three meals per day.

Consequences: At least two for each "Alternative"

a   I would be able to eat a lot of low calorie food.
    I would not have to limit types of food, just calories.
b   I could still have a healthy diet.
    I might start dreaming about desserts.
c   I would save lots of money.
    I would probably get sick.

3   Copies of the **Daily Problem Situations** therapeutic activity for intermediate level problem solving are:

a   Instructions are given by the facilitator, Duration: 10 minutes.

    (1)   Facilitator reads one of six Daily Problem Situations while participants follow along on their copies. These are selected because they do not represent situations that are personally disturbing to participants, but each situation allows practice in applying skill concepts, for example:

Barbara has been a housewife and mother for the past 5 years. Barbara has never worked before, as she got married right out of high school. Barbara wants to find a job but has never looked for a job. What are some ways Barbara might find a job?

(2) Facilitator discusses how to state goals. A goal statement is developed for each of the six situations and they are written on the board.

(3) Facilitator distributes blank "Daily Problem Forms" on which participants will list "alternatives" and "consequences" they develop for each of the six Daily Problem Situations, for example:

Goal Statement: *How can Barbara find a job.*

ALTERNATIVE SOLUTIONS: CONSEQUENCES:

1.	a)	b)
2.	a)	b)
3.	a)	b)
4.	a)	b)

(4) Facilitator instructs the participants to generate *six* solutions for each goal, and two consequences for each solution.

(5) The facilitator instructs the participants to select the solution (the "alternative" and resulting "consequences") that is socially acceptable, legal, and is "related" to the goal.

b   The therapeutic activity is completed by participants. Duration: 10 minutes.

c   Responses are reviewed by facilitator and feedback is given. Duration: 10 minutes.

4   Feedback on group participation and group process. Duration: 5 minutes.

5   Group criteria are calculated by facilitator for each participant after group is dismissed. Duration: 15 minutes.

a   Attendance, participation, and "activity" scores are calculated and recorded on group data sheets.

b   Facilitator gives individual feedback to each participant.

The skill areas included in these groups were selected with the specific objective of teaching participants to become more effective "self-monitors" (Kanfer, 1970). In addition to becoming more informed consumers of mental health services, participants learn how to (a) describe essential characteristics that define any situation; (b) recognize and accept emotional feelings experienced before, during, and after that situation; (c) identify, evaluate, and accept responsibility for beliefs or expectations held before, during, and after the situation; (d) establish goals, and (e) formulate, activate, and evaluate strategies designed to achieve those goals. Each group is structured to run about 75 minutes, including a 5- to 10-minute "break" (stretching, restroom, etc.) following the didactic presentation, but before the therapeutic "game" or "activity." These breaks are very important for distracted, decompensated, or lower functioning participants. The format of the groups also allows staff to monitor each participants' mental status so that they *can* progress at their own pace. For example, most participants will "pass" criteria in the introductory level self-awareness group in about one to four sessions. Very decompensated or lower functioning participants take longer. It is helpful for programs using these procedures to have "alternate" forms available for each activity to be rotated on some regular basis to maintain interest of the participants *and* the facilitators. While staff in many programs may choose to create their own alternative forms, additional games and activities (including advanced or "skills" level groups) have been developed and are available (Naster, et al., 1991).

The use of lesson-planned psychoeducational materials makes it possible to increase the role and importance of paraprofessional staff in the psychiatric rehabilitation process. Utilizing paraprofessional staff and peers as instructors also frees other professional staff to address more complex clinical issues. This may contribute to lower overall program costs.

When reasons for including lesson-planned psychoeducational materials in the psychiatric rehabilitation process are considered, it is useful to examine treatment issues related to "continuity of care." Mental health planners, administrators, and clinicians often define continuity of care by the presence or absence of certain types or levels of treatment in the health care continuum (i.e., residential, day treatment, outpatient, etc.). Unfortunately, adoption of new treatment methodology or technology within each program in a community's continuity of care system is slow and unsystematic (Bedell, Archer, Ward, & Stokes, 1985). Different programs within an array of mental health services were generally developed at different points in time, they may be based on different philosophies, and they often use very different terminology (language) and treatment methods. This has to be a confusing and stressful experience to people recovering from severely disabling symptoms of persistent mental illness as they (a) "adjust" and improve while in one level of care; (b) are discharged to a less restrictive service within that same continuum; and (c) then have to cope with a different set of philosophies, terminology, and treatment methods. Adoption of compatible psychoeducational methodologies and procedures as part of the treatment offered by *all* levels of mental health programs within a community may be the only way in which consumers of those services will perceive clear and meaningful "continuity" in their care. We are more likely to engage people in their own rehabilitation process when we provide treatments that are less confining, more interesting, and more relevant to the needs of the participants.

REFERENCES

Agacinski, K., & Stern, D. (1984). A two track program enhances therapeutic gains for chronically ill in a day hospital population. *Occupational Therapy in Mental Health, 4*(2), 15–21.

Andreasen, N., & Olsen, S. (1982). Negative versus positive schizophrenia: Definition and validation. *Archives of General Psychiatry, 39,* 789–794.

Anthony, W. (1979). *The principles of psychiatric rehabilitation.* Baltimore, MD: University Park Press.

Bedell, J., Archer, R.P., & Marlowe, H.A. (1980). A description and evaluation of a problem solving skills training program. In D. Upper & S.M. Ross (Eds.), *Behavioral group therapy: An annual review.* Champaign, IL: Research Press.

Bedell, J., Archer, R., Ward, J., & Stokes, N. (1985). An empirical evaluation of a model of knowledge utilization. *Evaluation Review, 9*(2), 109–126.

Bedell, J., & Michael, D. (1985). Teaching problem solving skills to the chronically mentally handicapped. In D. Upper, & S. Ross (Eds.), *Handbook of behavioral group therapy.* New York: Plenum Publishing.

Bedell J., & Ward, J. (1989). An intensive community-based treatment alternative to state hospitalization. *Hospital and Community Psychiatry, 40*(5), 533–535.

Bedell, J., & Weathers, L. (1978). A psycho-educational model for skill training: Therapist-facilitated and game-facilitated applications. In D. Upper & S. Ross (Eds.), *Behavioral group therapy: An annual review (Vol. 1).* Champaign, IL: Research Press.

Bellack, A., & Hersen, M. (1978). Chronic psychiatric patients: Social skills training. In M. Hersen & A. Bellack (Eds.), *Behavior therapy in the psychiatric setting.* Baltimore: Williams & Wilkins.

Bellack, A., Turner, S., Hersen, M., & Luber, R. (1984). An examination of the efficacy of social skills training for chronic schizophrenic patients. *Hospital and Community Psychiatry, 35,* 1023–1028.

Coviensky, M., & Buckley, V. (1986). Day activities programming: Serving the severely impaired chronic patient. *Occupational Therapy in Mental Health, 6*(2), 21–30.

Craighead, W., Kazdin, A., & Mahoney, M. (1981). *Behavior modification: Principles, issues, and applications* (2nd ed.). Boston: Houghton, Miflin.

Crockett, B., Gibertini, M., Hinrichs, S., Pensel, R., Potts, P., & Ward, J. (1989). *Self medication training for adult mental health patients: A psychoeducational approach.* Tampa: Florida Mental Health Institute Publication Series #120, University of South Florida.

Dow, M., Verdi, M., & Sacco, W. (1991). Training psychiatric patients to discuss medication issues. Effects on patient communication and knowledge of medications. *Behavior Modification, 15*(1), 3–21.

Eckman, T., Liberman, R., Phipps, C., & Blair, K. (1990). Teaching medication management skills to schizophrenic patients. *Journal of Clinical Psychopharmacology, 10*(1), 33–38.

Foxx, R., McMorrow, M., & Mennemeier, M. (1984). Teaching social/vocational skills to retarded adults with a modified table game: An analysis of generalization. *Journal of Applied Behavioral Analysis, 17,* 343–352.

Foxx, R., McMorrow, M. J., & Schloss, C. (1983). Stacking the deck: Teaching social skills to retarded adults with a modified table game. *Journal of Applied Behavioral Analysis, 16,* 157–170.

Goldsmith, J., & McFall, R. (1975). Development and evaluation of an interpersonal skills-training program for psychiatric inpatients. *Journal of Abnormal Psychology, 84,* 51–58.

Gordon, R. (1979). Psychotherapeutic games help patients adapt to community. *Frontiers of Psychiatry: Roche Report,* June 1, 1979.

Gordon, R., Weathers, L., Patterson, R., Bedell, J., Bates, H., & Hatcher, M. (1979). Ability and willingness of mental health workers to adopt and implement modular approaches to social skills training. In A. Slater & L. Bowan (Eds.) *Modular treatment and training* Monograph Series No. 2, Human Resources Institute, University of South Florida.

Hierholzer, R., & Liberman, R. (1986). Successful living: A social skills and problem-solving group for the chronic mentally ill. *Hospital and Community Psychiatry, 37,* 913–918.

Hogarty, G., Anderson, G., Reiss, D., Kornblith, S., Greenwald, D., Javna, C., & Madonia, M. (1986). Family psychoeducation, social skills training, and maintenance chemotherapy in the aftercare treatment of schizophrenia. *Archives of General Psychiatry, 43,* 633–642.

Kanfer, F. (1970). Self monitoring: Methodological limitations and clinical implications. *Journal of Consulting and Clinical Psychology, 35,* 148–152.

Liberman, R. (1986). *Social and independent living skills medication management module, trainers manual.* Los Angeles: Rehabilitation Research and Training Center in Mental Illness.

Margules, A., & Anthony, W. (1976). Skills training programs for psychiatric patients. *Journal of Applied Rehabilitation Counseling, 7,* 40–49.

Nash, W. (1975). The effects of warm-up activities on small group divergent problem-solving with young children. *Journal of Psychology, 89,* 237–241.

Naster, B. J., Pace, J. E., Ward, J. C., Pensel, R. K., Bedell, J. R., & Gibertini, M. (Eds.). (1991). *Cognitive behavioral training in self-awareness, communication and problem solving: Introductory, intermediate, and advanced psychoeducational groups* (Pub. Series No. 135). Tampa: University of South Florida, Florida Mental Health Institute.

Singh, N., & Winton, A. (1983). Social skills training with institutionalized severely and profoundly mentally retarded persons. *Applied Research in Mental Retardation, 4,* 383–398.

Upper, D., Livingston, L., Conners, G., & Olans, J. (1982). Evaluating a social and coping skills training group for psychiatric day-hospital patients. *International Journal of Partial Hospitalization, 1*(3), 203–211.

Verbosky, S. (1983). *The efficacy of a self medication program on a psychiatric inpatient population.* Unpublished master's thesis, University of Florida, Gainesville.

Wallace, C., & Liberman, R. (1985). Social skills training for patients with schizophrenia: A controlled clinical trial. *Psychiatry Research, 15,* 239–247.

Ward, J., & Naster, B. (1991). Reliability of an observational system used to monitor behavior in a mental health residential treatment unit. *Journal of Mental Health Administration, 18*(1), 64–68.

Weathers, L. R., Bedell, J. R., Marlowe, H. A., & Gordon, R. E. (1978). Psychotherapeutic games. *Journal of the Florida Medical Association, 65,* 891–896.

Weathers, L., Marlowe, H., Bedell, J. Gordon, R. & Reed, V. (1978). The utilization of psychotherapeutic games by mental health workers. *Occasional Paper Series,* Report #4, Slater, A., & Bowman, L. (Eds.). Tampa: Human Resources Institute, University of South Florida.

Chapter 7

Vocational Rehabilitation of the Psychiatrically Disabled

Bertram J. Black and Joseph S. Lechowicz

HISTORICAL PERSPECTIVE

It has been many years since we had to begin nearly every discussion of vocational rehabilitation with assurances that persons who were mentally ill could still be productive at work. There was then a tacit assumption, unfortunately still adhered to in many quarters, that someone who becomes "mentally ill" has left the world of real work and is unlikely, except under unusual circumstances, to return to open competitive employment. In the early 1950s, the vocational rehabilitation field, having struggled through demonstrating that persons who suffered heart attacks and survived did not require extended bed rest (the treatment of choice at the time) and could return to the strains of daily employment very quickly, turned its attention to the rehabilitation of persons discharged from mental hospitals. There was not, of course, the advantage that there had been with heart disease of having a president of the United States (Dwight Eisenhower) demonstrate rapid rehabilitation after his illness. Even today there would still be grave question about such a demonstration with mental illness.

It is not necessary to extol the virtues of work in terms of its economic or social value to the individual in our society—in fact, in any society. Work has the same values to the mentally ill person as it has to any one of us (Black, 1988). However, what is less well-known is that in psychiatric terms work represents one of the last-damaged areas of the ego. Not only do we now know that persons who have suffered from serious mental illnesses can become productive at a wide variety of work tasks, but we know that many of them can work productively in spite of the presence of symptoms.

A dozen years ago one of us spoke at a meeting of the then Center for Occupational Mental Health to an audience of industrial vice presidents and personnel directors. The subject was "The Potential Productivity of the Chronic Schizophrenic." He pointed out that epidemiological studies had determined that in our population some 12 out of every 1,000 persons in the age range 25 to 44 evidenced symptoms of schizophrenia; but only one out of every 1,000 in this age range were known to the mental health hospital and treatment system. There must, then, be a large number of persons who have psychiatric symptoms who are not in the treatment stream but who are living and working in our society. The response by the audience was confirmatory. Quite a number told of persons in their employ who were queer and difficult but highly productive individuals, who somehow controlled their behavior so that it was not a deterrent to their working.

The National Schizophrenia Fellowship in England reported what a mentally ill woman did to continue working without a break through four illness episodes. She explained that she had to start learning the five basic rules of how not to appear insane. These she called her "sanity rules."

1 Never mention any hallucinations one is having to anyone, not even to friends and relatives.
2 Never transmit messages telepathically.
3 Never discuss telepathy or psychic power with anyone.
4 Avoid fights and physical violence of any kind.
5 Secretly learn all one possibly can about defense against telepathy and psychic force.

She stated that the most important thing was to learn how to distinguish between thoughts from her own mind and dangerous thoughts put into her mind to test her sanity.

We have learned a great deal in this past decade or two about how to help those unfortunate enough to suffer mental illness cope with their symptoms, and we are beginning to understand more clearly the nature and course of the illnesses themselves. Studies over time are beginning to confirm what those of us who work with the mentally ill have surmised all along, that illness runs a course with ups and downs, never straight, but with a point of stability in 8 to 10 years

(Strauss, Hafez, Liberman, & Harding, 1985). It is not the "bottomless pit" that many clinicians even today assume serious affective and schizophrenic disorders to be. A large number of persons who become ill (about a third) become acutely ill, most often in the prime learning or working years of their lives, get well, and may never have another bout. Chemotherapies and psychotherapies do the trick. Perhaps another third of those who become ill have more extended periods of remission and relapse, but with treatment and rehabilitative efforts they too stabilize and become or continue to be productive members of society. The last third are the most difficult, for theirs are the chronic conditions, and they require longer treatment effort and greater rehabilitation resources. However, it is our firm conviction that with proper and adequate social and vocational resources and guidance the vast majority of these folks, too, can find niches in the workaday world.

It is for this last third of the mentally ill population that our formal systems of rehabilitation services have evolved. Generally speaking, vocational rehabilitation is provided through combinations of two social systems: that of the federal-state vocational rehabilitation program and that of a network of rehabilitation agencies and programs, many allied with the mental health service system, but many independent of it. There is a rich literature, so let it suffice for now to outline briefly the elements in the process we call vocational rehabilitation and the major resources utilized.

ESSENTIAL ELEMENTS OF VOCATIONAL REHABILITATION

Before we begin, however, let us explain to the reader about a concept popular in the United States but not really known almost anywhere else in the world—that of *vocational* rehabilitation. Rehabilitation of people with disabilities, by whatever definition desired, has as its essence return or development to the highest level of functioning in the everyday world that is possible for a person who is disabled at birth, by accident, or by illness. Here and in most of the world, the term "rehabilitation" embraces all techniques and methods necessary to achieve such an end, not social alone, nor residential, nor vocational. For reasons that would take too much time to go into here, we in the United States have developed a specialty called "vocational rehabilitation," with its emphasis upon return to the workaday world, and have tried hard to keep it distinct from all other aspects of rehabilitation just referred to.

This causes us problems in dealing with mental illness, for we can hardly separate the vocational needs of our patients and clients from their other social and psychological requirements. We have tried to find a way around this dilemma, for it poses problems for us in organizing and financing the array of services necessary in rehabilitation of the chronic mental patient. We therefore have coined a term that attempts to integrate the various components of the services: "psychosocial rehabilitation." In a similar attempt some years ago, we borrowed the term "productive participation" from the social anthropologists ("Productive Participation for the Mentally Ill," 1973).

There are three basic principles inherent in rehabilitation services, however they may be defined, and for whatever the illness or disability:

1   The emphasis is on the strengths an individual may possess or can develop rather than upon the handicaps presented.
2   Rehabilitation should begin as early after recognition of the illness or disability as is possible.
3   Rehabilitation belongs to no single discipline, but requires teamwork of a number of specialists, and should include the patient or client in any decision making.

Upon referral to any of the rehabilitation programs, the client participates in an *evaluation.* This will include the medical diagnosis, the social history of the illness, and also various psychological and vocational assessments. Many rehabilitation agencies also make use of placement in a simulated work environment to conduct a "situational assessment" of work habits and other behavior in the work setting. To the extent the individual appears capable, a variety of work setting models are utilized to prepare the client for the most independent work behavior he or she can achieve. The oldest such settings have been the "sheltered workshop" and the "work activity center," where the demands of productivity can be quite low (though governed by federal and state wage and hour laws specific for handicapped persons). These shops, of course, are simulations of regular work establishments. Although they are often intended to serve as transitional experiences to the "real" world of work, they very often become what the economists call "substitute permanent employment." Today, for the mentally ill, that is what most of the sheltered workshops have become. The work activity center is a combination of sheltered work and recreational/creative arts programs to suit the needs of the most functionally deteriorated chronically mentally ill, who cannot maintain concentrated continuous attention to work tasks. Such centers are used by state mental hospitals and some community mental health centers as a first stage in patients' long road to reestablishing functional capabilities.

As the locus of treatment has moved out of the big mental hospitals to community services, such places of "substitute permanent employment" have lost their attraction. Both clients and the professionals involved in treatment and rehabilitation have begun to set their sights on return to the competitive employment field. Following the lead of British psychiatry, one of our large "psychosocial clubs," Fountain House Foundation, in New York, established a "transitional employment program" cooperatively with Alexander's department store and then with other places offering opportunities for entry-level simple jobs under supervision of both the business and the mental health center. Such a transitional employment program (TEP) usually affords a client half-time work, paid for by the business, with the mental health program guaranteeing that the work will get done in a satisfactory manner by staff or another client if the first client fails. It is an important commentary on "work ability" of these chronically ill clients that there have been few reports of the need for staff fill-in among hundreds of these transitional programs by mental health centers and psychosocial clubs across the country.

Although most of the transitional employment programs are just that—after a few weeks the client goes on to other work, preferably a competitive job in regular employment—a few have arranged that a successful client remain in the business employment on a full-time basis as a regular job. The mental health staff supervisor drops out, except perhaps to remain available to the employer in consultation, if necessary. The very small proportion of clients who do remain severely limited in functioning end up in a sheltered workshop or in the day hospital work activity center, or drift out of the mental health service system.

SUPPORTED WORK

In recent years, the field of service to the mentally retarded and developmentally disabled has devised a form of permanent employment/sheltered work in industry that has come to be known as "supported work." The concept is similar to the transitional employment model, except that the work is seen as permanent, though it may be either part-time or with limited expectations of production. The setting is in normal industry or business; the supervision is by an agency "job coach," who learns the tasks and teaches them to the clients and remains available to clients and employer to ensure productivity and skills learning. Most usually, payment for production is to the service agency, which in turn pays the clients at current job rates. The costs of job coach and group transportation for those unable to use public facilities are the responsibilities of the agency. The expectation is that some of the individuals who are mentally retarded/developmentally disabled will make the grade to regular, non-agency-supervised, employment at the workplace. However, continued support by a job coach is not seen as a failure.

Supported work has become the current pet project of our federal government. The state vocational rehabilitation services are urged by the federal Rehabilitation Services Administration (RSA) to develop such programs, and Congress has allocated substantial funding to this venture. As those who are familiar with the business and industrial world can recognize, this is not an easy assignment. The business world must be willing to accept persons with disabilities in this special arrangement in its work force. The service agency must supply job coaches, a commodity in short supply in an economy that has many better paying opportunities for the young men and women who are the likely candidates; the clientele capable of filling supported-work slots must be found and prepared for them.

This latter requirement raises special issues in the vocational rehabilitation of persons who are mentally ill. First of all, the very concept of supported work suggests that it is a permanent end of the road. Therefore, it is most likely that only patients for whom traditional competitive job opportunities have failed or for whom additional treatment interventions seem most unlikely will be referred. Secondly, those patients who accept referral are allowing themselves to be identified as mentally ill, and as we discovered years ago (Meyer & Borgatta, 1959), many persons who are apparently well enough to be discharged from hospital care have no desire to be so labeled. And certainly, persons who were working before they were first diagnosed as having affective or schizophrenic illness and who are fairly quickly stabilized under treatment will expect to return to their regular occupation rather than being placed in a special rehabilitation unit. In addition, of course, there are disincentives to trying rehabilitative work programs that might jeopardize continuation of income benefits.

There are in this picture shades of the quota system by which some European countries attempt to insure employment of persons with disabilities who might otherwise remain out of the work force. These quotas, as well as the targeted job tax credit system in our country, have met with limited usefulness for the same reasons.

PREDICTING VOCATIONAL OUTCOME

When persons become mentally ill, the question does arise as to what criteria can predict whether they will be among those who recover quickly or slowly or among those who have remissions and recurrences with gradual diminution of functional powers. With modern medications and individual and group psychotherapies, we can now be fairly hopeful for those who succumb to the affective disorders, the manic-depressive syndromes. For those whose diagnoses are among the schizophrenic and schizophreniform disorders, the prognosis is less positive. A fairly recent review of outcome studies states:

> The range of disability found among persons with schizophrenia depends upon the criteria used to diagnose the disease. By most of the widely used diagnostic systems, schizophrenia is a disease with heterogeneous outcomes ranging from complete recovery to chronic and unremitting psychosis with extensive disability. . . . Attempts to find . . . predictors of chronicity and disability have been only moderately successful. (Mohs & Lesser, 1987 p. 70)

What then can be done to determine whether rehabilitation intervention is likely to lead to a successful outcome? A crucial element in assessing the chances of a successful outcome to any rehabilitation effort is the vocational evaluation. Information as to past and current cognitive strengths and weaknesses, premorbid and present behavior, the support system available through family and friends, and the patient's relation to reality is of great value. Where there has been little past work history to build on, measurements of interest and task abilities are helpful. Understanding of the effects of medication on the patient's performance is of great importance, particularly appraisal of work performance under optimal medication. This does not necessarily mean that all symptoms need be eliminated for a person to return to work. Many persons can perform adequately on a job, as did the woman who reported to the Schizophrenia Fellowship in spite of continued hallucinations and delusions. We used to tell clients of a rehabilitation workshop not to be concerned that the machines talked to them; just don't talk back! Situational assessment, using a rehabilitative work setting, is best in our opinion for such a determination. This, however, takes time, and time becomes money, and it is difficult to provide enough of such skilled evaluation.

It is here that the state agency vocational rehabilitation system becomes of great value. The state agency counselor can arrange for such a situational assessment, and should be in a position to interpret the results. While not definitive in every case, skilled vocational evaluation is the best we have to offer. Although such evaluation, and the counseling that goes with it, may seem similar to or identical with usual psychological or vocational counseling, it is really quite different. Vocational rehabilitation counseling must take into account the disability, the medical condition, and the person's assets and deficits. The counselor must be prepared to assist the client through teamwork involving the physician, health and rehabilitative personnel, and the family, as well as the patient.

REHABILITATION RESOURCES AND PROGRAMS

It is difficult to separate rehabilitation counseling for the mentally ill from the state-federal system of vocational rehabilitation, highly defined by its history in federal legislation that mandated in 1943 that service to persons with psychiatric disabilities be on a par with services to individuals with physical handicaps. Even in the 1950s, various state vocational rehabilitation programs negotiated cooperative agreements with mental health systems, rehabilitation units, and halfway houses in the state hospitals. Such units provided various prevocational services, including home economic activities of daily living, and work facilities and workshops that offered evaluation and training. As newcomers on the block, rehabilitation personnel often found themselves competing for higher functioning clients with other hospital treatment services, and were often assigned the most seriously disabled. As the community mental health centers, and later the community support programs, were increasing in number, the state vocational rehabilitation services negotiated full-, or at least part-time, inclusion of services.

As the community mental health and state hospital systems have evolved over the past number of decades, rehabilitation counseling services to persons with psychiatric disabilities have been a patchwork, depending on the relationship of state and local rehabilitation agencies and the mental health system and their ability to work together. In a sense, it may be viewed as a pull and tug between two competing philosophies, one insisting on a complete understanding and documentation of a person's symptoms and their alleviation before discharge from a hospital or other medical care, and the other seeking to maximize the person's abilities in such a way that he or she could enter or reenter paid work when "ready."

In the meantime, however, a substantial knowledge base from the many state and local cooperative programming activities has been developed, assisted by the federally funded Research and Training Centers focused on mental health.

Those traditional services of vocational assessment, counseling, adjustment, prevocational and job training, and placement have been offered in many instances not only by rehabilitation counselors but also by other mental health professionals working in the mental health system who, like their rehabilitation counterparts, discarded traditional theories in their search for practical and reality-based methods to prepare, place, and support clients in employment.

Perhaps occupational therapists recall when their colleagues were supervising prevocational activities, and prevocational assessments as well, and sheltered workshops. Such service activities were, and are no doubt still, an outgrowth of a holistic view of patients and how services might amplify patients' strengths and minimize their deficits. These attempts gave rise to training in ADL (activities of daily living), in skills-training efforts, and in group approaches in job seeking.

In addition to the activities of rehabilitation counselors and occupational therapists, departments of social work in the state hospitals and mental health centers continued in their own tradition, supervising community-based work programs as well as individual and group approaches to job placement. These activities also overlapped with those of state agency rehabilitation counselors.

In this age of interagency cooperative agreements, rehabilitation counseling has become recognized as a professional discipline of its own. With its emphasis upon the "vocationalization" of clients/patients, it nevertheless has a philosophy of holistically addressing the healing and recovering person. Rehabilitation counseling often becomes the coordinating discipline that brings together the array of services now recognized as needed to help the ex-patient in self-determination and, ultimately, in improved employment and independence.

A discussion of vocational rehabilitation for persons with psychiatric disabilities would be incomplete without mentioning two special facilities that have evolved to serve the most seriously disturbed among them. One has already been mentioned, the psychosocial clubs, offering shelter, socialization, recreation, and, with increasing frequency, sheltered, transitional, and supported employment (see Black, 1988; Rutman, 1987). The other set of facilities is what have come to be known as the Fairweather Lodges (Fairweather, 1980), named after a psychologist who devised a scheme for groups of patients to form small living and working units. Each group of eight to a dozen persons leaves the mental hospital as a living and working-together unit, centering their lives in a cooperative manner around small businesses, usually in house cleaning and yard work. Psychosocial clubs are now spreading across the country, especially in urban areas; Fairweather Lodges have become established in smaller towns and rural areas in the South and Midwest.

Summary

The best proof of what has been written here is in a comprehensive study in Britain of 1,200 ex-patients who worked in a variety of businesses and industries over a period of some time (Wansbrough & Cooper, 1980). Employers and rehabilitation specialists and hospitals and psychiatrists participated in these follow-ups. Their findings were these:

• The largest category of work performed was in semiskilled manual, non-machine work. Clerical occupations were quite numerous.
• Those with prior work history normally returned to their old jobs.
• Though machine operation was confined to a minority of the disabled persons, a third of those with psychoses in one sample did operate machines.
• Ex-patients referred directly from the hospital lasted a shorter time in employment than ex-patients referred or introduced from any other source. Even a spell of unemployment seemed to offer better preparation. The conclusion was inescapable that the transition from the patient to the worker role for those out of the hospital had been too fast.
• There appeared to be no correlation between onset of relapses and working conditions, even such conditions as noise and windowless rooms. Strict disciplinary codes in some settings were unrelated to sickness or absence.
• Jobs involving face-to-face contact with the public were successfully filled by persons with diagnoses of psychosis as well as by those diagnosed as depressed or neurotic.
• Shift work appeared to present a trying life-style for the psychologically frail, but there was no problem with overtime being worked when required.

One of the most interesting conclusions reached by the British researchers was that the most an employer risks in taking on a person who has been mentally ill is one who may be potentially a poor timekeeper and who has some awkward traits; not a dangerous maniac as protrayed dramatically on screen and television. They further concluded, and in this we definitely agree, that the employer is entitled to the best advice possible when faced with problems of an employee who shows evidences of psychiatric distress.

REFERENCES

Black, B. J. (1988). *Work and mental illness: Transitions to employment.* Baltimore: Johns Hopkins University Press.

Fairweather, G. W. (Ed.). (1980). *The Fairweather Lodge: A twenty five year retrospective* (New Directions for Mental Health Services, No. 7). San Francisco: Jossey-Bass.

Meyer, H. J., & Borgatta, E. F. (1959). *An experiment in mental patient rehabilitation.* New York: Russell Sage Foundation.

Mohs, R. C., & Lesser, J. C. (1987). Schizophrenia and disability. In A. T. Myerson & R. Fine (Eds.), *Psychiatric disability: Clinical, legal and administrative* (pp. 69–82) Washington, DC: American Psychiatric Press.

Productive participation for the mentally ill. (1973). International conference, Helsinki, Finland. Amsterdam: Excerpta Medica.

Rutman, I. D. (1987). The psychosocial rehabilitation movement in the United States. In A. T. Myerson & R. Fine (Eds.), *Psychiatric disability: Clinical, legal, and administrative.* (pp. 197–220). Washington, DC: American Psychiatric Press.

Strauss, J. S., Hafez, H., Liberman, P., & Harding, C. M. (1985). The course of psychiatric disorder III: Longitudinal principles. *American Journal of Psychiatry, 142,* 289–296.

Wansbrough, N., & Cooper, P. (1980). *Open employment after mental illness.* London: Tavistock Publications.

Wing, J. (Ed.). (1975). *Schizophrenia from within.* London: National Schizophrenia Fellowship.

Chapter 8

Supported Employment in Vocational Rehabilitation

Robert Gervey and Jeffrey R. Bedell

The preceding chapter described the increased availability during the last 20 years of psychiatric vocational rehabilitation programs for patients living in the community. Also during this period, attention has increasingly been focused on employment as a measure of the effectiveness of psychiatric treatment and as an element of psychiatric diagnosis (Strauss & Carpenter, 1972, 1974; Anthony & Jansen, 1984; Anthony & Buell, 1975). However, it would be mistaken to assume, given these developments, that vocational rehabilitation has become well integrated into traditional psychiatric treatment. On the contrary, vocational rehabilitation of the psychiatrically disabled continues to be viewed as an ancillary activity that is primarily performed by staff outside of standard psychological treatment (Harding, Strauss, Hafez, & Lieberman, 1987; Black & Kase, 1986; Anthony & Marguelos, 1974). Consequently, there has been relatively little development of vocational rehabilitation treatment approaches designed specifically for persons with psychological disabilities. Instead, psychiatric vocational rehabilitation programming has primarily been "borrowed," with only minor adaptations, from procedures employed with the developmentally and physically disabled. Supported employment, initially conceived for use with the developmentally disabled, represents one of the most recent rehabilitation approaches being applied to psychiatric patients.

This chapter is intended to review the current state of the art in supported employment and describe a supported-employment program currently in operation at the Albert Einstein College of Medicine, in New York. It is hoped this information will assist practitioners and researchers in the development and evaluation of supported-employment programs for the psychiatric population. The chapter is divided into five sections, describing supported employment's (a) background and development, (b) various models, (c) basic elements, and (d) current status, and also describing (e) the supported-employment program at Einstein.

BACKGROUND AND DEVELOPMENT OF THE SUPPORTED-EMPLOYMENT MODEL OF VOCATIONAL REHABILITATION

Dissatisfaction with Sheltered Workshops

Sheltered workshops are work-oriented rehabilitation facilities operating in controlled, segregated environments for the purpose of providing employment-related training to persons with disabilities (Whitehead, 1987). The primary goal of the sheltered workshop is to *train* clients in vocational skills and then *place* them in competitive employment. Sheltered workshops are among the oldest and most common forms of vocational rehabilitation in existence today. Originally developed for the blind in 1837 (Nelson, 1971), sheltered workshops currently serve a broad range of disability groups, including the physically ill, the developmentally disabled, and the mentally ill. Generally, work tasks are routine and menial, requiring a low level of skills. Most commonly patients are involved in materials assembly, food preparation, building maintenance, clerical tasks, or retail sales in not-for-profit businesses. Productivity is generally underemphasized in these training sites. Instead, the focus is on such generic work behaviors and attitudes as attendance, punctuality, endurance, motivation, and the appropriateness of dress and conduct. Subminimum wages are paid, and the average sheltered workshop employee earns approximately one quarter to one third of the minimum wage. In 1979, annual wages averaged approximately $414 (Department of Labor report cited in Wehman & Kregel, 1985; Whitehead, 1987).

Despite the "train-place" philosophy of sheltered workshops, clients enrolled in these programs are rarely placed in competitive employment. Several federal audits have established that persons participating in sheltered workshops have only a 1 in 10 chance of moving into the competitive labor market (Whitehead, 1987). Instead of moving out of the sheltered workshop environment, clients remain dependent on the sheltered workshop for social and recreational needs and dependent on governmental subsidies for financial assistance. Once viewed as the cornerstone of community-based rehabilitation services, the sheltered workshop is currently viewed as the equivalent of the state hospital's "back ward": Clients are maintained in a segregated environment with little opportunity or hope of moving into competitive employment.

Consumer Dissatisfaction and Rise of Consumer Advocacy

In the past, the "failure" of a client to move out of the sheltered workshop was attributed, primarily, to the client's lack of job readiness, ability, or motivation. Now, the client's lack of movement out of the sheltered workshop is understood to be a consequence also of the lack of resources dedicated to supporting client movement into competitive employment (Revell, Wehman, & Arnold, 1984). This shift in thinking about who and what are responsible for keeping clients in segregated treatment environments has come about largely as a result of a national consumer advocacy movement that has increasingly advocated for persons with disabilities to have greater access to mainstream employment and to mainstream community activities. Initiated, primarily, by families of the physically and developmentally disabled, this national consumer movement has gained support from legislative and national rehabilitation committees. The consequence of these activities is that rehabilitation agencies are increasingly being mandated to include consumers on their advisory boards and to develop programs that support clients' movement to mainstream, integrated settings (Whitehead, 1987). Supported employment, with its emphasis on placing persons with disabilities in competitive, mainstream jobs, is the type of program that consumer advocates want for themselves and family members.

Supported-Employment Legislation

As a result of consumer activism, and also in an attempt to reduce the costs of federal programs, Congress has increasingly enacted legislation to assist people with moderate and severe disabilities to become employed and be independent of federal subsidies. In this section, significant supported-employment legislation will be highlighted.

The 1984 amendments to the Education of the Handicapped Act amendments of 1973 (EH P.L. 98-199) is often credited as the initial piece of supported-employment legislation. Public Law 98-199 cited the lack of transitional services for special education students and called for programs to help the transition of special education youth out of the school and into competitive employment. In 1985, as a result of this law, the Office of Special Education and Rehabilitation Services (OSERS) provided funds to 10 states to develop supported-employment programs. In 1986, this funding was extended to 27 states.

The Developmental Disabilities Act of 1984 (P.L. 98-527) helped define supported employment as an integrated, mainstream activity and provided a mandate to the field of rehabilitation to improve employment-related activities for all severely disabled persons, not just special education students transitioning out of school.

The 1986 amendments to the Rehabilitation Act of 1973 (P.L.-506) specifically included people with severe psychiatric disabilities as being eligible for supported-employment services. While persons with psychiatric disabilities had not previously been excluded by P.L. 98-527, P.L.-506 was considered essential because historically persons with psychiatric disabilities have generally been excluded from vocational rehabilitation (VR) services.

The Americans with Disabilities Act of 1990 (ADA) supports the goals and objectives of supported-employment legislation. The ADA clearly affirms the right of the disabled person to work in nonsegregated environments and mandates that public and private employers provide reasonable accessibility to disabled workers.

Funding for supported-employment programs now exceeds 260 million dollars per year. In fiscal year 1993, the Rehabilitation Service Administration (RSA) alone has budgeted approximately 41 million dollars for supported-employment programs (Staff, "National Rehabilitation Association Newsletter," 1991). Within the RSA budget, supported-employment funding now parallels expenditures for staff development and training, independent living centers, and research. Additional funding for supported-employment programs is available through the U.S. Departments of Justice and Labor, and the Social Security Administration. State and city departments of mental health, mental retardation, alcoholism, drug abuse, education, and employment are also funding supported-employment programs.

Community-Based Rehabilitation Treatment

Although legislative and consumer demand for community-based treatments provided a positive impetus, effective clinical procedures that would successfully implement supported-employment programs still needed to be identified and developed. The original architects of supported employment (e.g., Paul Wehman of Virginia Commonwealth University) came from special education and had a background in the field of physical and developmental disabilities. Consequently, these program designers focused on models of community-based care conceived for special education students and the developmentally disabled. Since treatment for these populations historically has been based on behavioral principles, it is not surprising that supported-employment programs have also been based upon behavioral management techniques and often include psychoeducational and skills-training curricula (Wehman & Kregel, 1985; Hill, Wehman, Kregel, Banks, & Metzler, 1987; Brickey & Campbell, 1981; Rusch, Morgan, Martin, Riva, & Agran, 1985).

Parent involvement in supported-employment programs is designed to help the family adjust to and provide support for the client's movement to competitive employment. Skills training is designed to help the client learn skills that are necessary to get a job (e.g., interviewing and completion of a job application) and to keep a job (e.g., communicating effectively with coworkers and/or supervisors, and solving problems of everyday living). The techniques employed to train clients in the skills needed to get and keep a job include modeling, coaching, skill rehearsal, and practice at the job site.

Much of the traditional treatment for the psychiatric patient has been based on a medical model that places emphasis on psychopharmacology, dynamic psychoanalytic formulations, verbal interventions, and insight as opposed to skills training and behavioral coaching. One of the challenges of providing supported employment to the psychiatrically disabled is the need for mental health providers to shift from a dynamic, psychoanalytically oriented, medical model to a more skills-oriented, cognitive-behavioral, rehabilitation model. Fortunately, several researchers within the field of psychiatry have developed and evaluated community-based treatment protocols using a skills-oriented, rehabilitation approach for persons with psychiatric disabilities. Empirical data currently exist demonstrating that persons with severe disabilities can learn to work and function in the community within the context of well-described, psychoeducational, social skills training programs (Hogarty et al., 1986; Stein & Test, 1985; Bedell & Ward, 1989; Falloon, Boyd, & McGill, 1982; Liberman, Mueser, & Wallace, 1986). As the reader will see, these types of psychiatric interventions form the core of the Einstein supported-employment program that will be described later.

MODELS OF SUPPORTED EMPLOYMENT

The historical factors cited above have led to the development of four widely accepted models of supported employment: individual placement, enclave, mobile work crew, and affirmative businesses. It is reported (Kregel, Wehman, & Banks, 1989) that in the 27 states that have been funded by OSERS to provide supported-employment services, 90% of clients receive services in one of these four models.

Individual Placement Model

The individual placement model (sometimes referred to as the "supported-work" or "competitive employment model") is the most commonly used. Kregel and colleagues (1989) found that of 1,550 supported-employment clients they studied, 78.4% received services organized according to the individual placement model.

Hill and colleagues (1987) defined the individual placement model as providing individualized job placement for people who are usually not considered "job ready" and who initially require intensive on-site training to help them attain a level of performance satisfactory to the employer. A 1:1 training ratio of staff members to workers is provided for an extended period of time at the job site while the worker develops job competence. The job coach reduces the frequency and intensity of services at the job site as the client's functioning improves. Eventually, long-term follow-along is provided to ensure job retention.

This model, developed at the Virginia Commonwealth University Rehabilitation Research and Training Center (RRTC), has been well articulated in the literature, and replication has been made possible through the publication of several training and procedural manuals (e.g., *An instructional guide for training on a job site: A supported employment resource,* Barkas, Brooke, Inge, Moon, & Goodall, 1987).

A slightly modified version of the individual placement model is known as the "clustered placement model." This model places individuals in community-based job sites that are in close proximity to one another, such as in different stores within a single mall, or different departments within a single department store.

Kregel and colleagues (1989) report that clients employed in the individual placement model earned significantly higher hourly wages than clients placed using other models. This model seems to be the most effective of the four models in terms of meeting the supported employment goals for (a) increased earning, (b) integration with nonhandicapped employees, and (c) independence. The individual placement model is favored by advocates of the disabled because it provides the greatest flexibility with regard to job placement (J. H. Noble, personal communication, 1991).

Enclave Model

The second most common form of supported employment, the enclave model, is used with 9.4% of supported-employment clients (Kregel et al., 1989). The enclave model provides competitive employment for a group of up to eight persons with disabilities within a single work setting. In this approach, the job coach becomes the permanent supervisor of the work team. An example of the enclave model is illustrated by Monarch Industries Inc., a rehabilitation agency. They reported establishing a dishwashing work crew in a hospital setting in which the entire work crew consisted of patients employed by the rehabilitation agency (Como, 1984). In this example, Monarch Industries Inc. contracted with the hospital to administer and staff the dishwashing operation.

The enclave model has been confused at times with other employment models, such as "work stations in industry" or "sheltered employment without walls." These latter models fall short of the goals envisioned by supported employment in that they are designed as self-contained work enclaves, the employees having little interaction with the nonhandicapped employees of the host business (Rhodes & Valenta, 1985).

These enclaves have often been used as a means of moving those considered to be the most severely disabled from the sheltered workshop into a competitive work environment. In some cases, workers remain employees of the rehabilitation agency and are paid subminimum wages. In other cases, workers are assigned work that is not at all related to the work being performed by the host industry.

Perhaps as a result of the misclassification of some enclave programs, Kregel and colleagues (1989) report that, compared to clients in the individual placement model, those enrolled in enclaves worked more hours but were paid less per hour and had less integration with nonhandicapped coworkers. Although the group enclave model seems to be well suited for the more severely handicapped (Rusch & Hughes, 1989), use of this model must comply with the basic components of supported employment.

Mobile Work Crew Model

Kregel and colleagues (1989) report that 8.6% of supported-employment clients are employed in mobile work crews. The mobile work crew model provides employment in a small, single-purpose business operated by a rehabilitation program. Each work crew is staffed by one supervisor and up to eight workers. Typically, mobile work crews perform building maintenance contract work obtained through competitive bids. The job coach functions as the direct and permanent work supervisor.

The authors' experience with the mobile work crew model suggests that insufficient outside contract work often results in the work crew's being employed by the rehabilitation agency to perform sheltered work.

Kregel and colleagues (1989) report that work crew members often earn and work less and have less opportunity for social contact with nondisabled workers than do persons placed within the individual placement model. This model was also found to be the least cost-effective of the four supported-employment models.

Affirmative Business Model

Only 3.7% of supported-employment clients have jobs in an affirmative business, which makes it the least-used model (Kregel et al., 1989). Affirmative businesses are for-profit enterprises that hire up to 50% of their work force from the disabled population. This model of supported employment is uncommon in the United States. The affirmative business model is more frequently used in countries where there are government incentives and hiring quotas established for the disabled population. For example, in Japan and Australia, affirmative businesses are more common, and are established as subsidiaries of large businesses in order to comply with government quota policies (Cho, 1984).

Natural Supports in the Workplace: Another Alternative

Nisbett and Hagner (1988) have identified a number of difficulties associated with each of the four supported-employment models described above and have proposed a fifth, alternative model. Their major criticism has to do with the use of a rehabilitation staff person (job coach) to help clients adjust to the competitive work site. Specifically, they suggest that the client may become too dependent on the job coach, making withdrawal of this support difficult. Second, clients may perform differently in the presence of the job coach, which may lead to inaccurate assessments of how well the client is performing on the job. Third, the presence of a job coach may increase rather than decrease the stigmatization of the client worker in the workplace. Finally, the use of a job coach may increase the cost of supported employment to the point that it is not cost-effective.

To overcome these problems, Nisbett and Hagner (1988) suggest the development of natural supports within the job site. Specifically, it is suggested that nonhandicapped coworkers be identified and trained to take responsibility for facilitating the client-worker's adaptation to the workplace. Some authors have suggested paying these nonhandicapped, coworker mentors a stipend for their training responsibilities (Buckley, 1991).

Summary

Since there are no research data available comparing the different models of supported employment, it is not possible for the authors to suggest one particular model. In the absence of evaluation data, the present authors recommend use of models that best integrate handicapped workers with nonhandicapped workers. In addition, it is recommended that the model chosen be carefully constructed to conform to the basic elements of supported employment described below.

BASIC ELEMENTS OF THE SUPPORTED-EMPLOYMENT MODEL OF VOCATIONAL REHABILITATION

As indicated above, supported employment appears in many forms. The basic elements and characteristics of supported employment, however, have been defined by legislation. For example, legislation demands that supported-employment programs place a high value on (a) immediate placement and (b) acceptance of all applicants interested in vocational placement. In addition, supported-employment programs are required to place clients in competitive employment sites in the community that provide (a) payment of at least minimum wage, (b) a minimum of 20 hours of work per week, (c) integration with nonhandicapped persons, (d) on-the-job skills training provided by a job coach, and (5) long-term job-coaching services at least biweekly (Developmental Disabilities Act of 1984).

The 1986 amendments of the Rehabilitation Act defined the target population to be served by supported-employment programs as those persons with severe handicaps for whom competitive employment has not traditionally occurred, or for whom competitive employment has been interrupted or intermittent as a result of a severe disability and who because of their handicap need on-going support services to perform such work (Rusch & Hughes, 1989). Further, the target population is to include handicapped clients enrolled in adult day activity centers, those in sheltered workshops, and youth in transition from school to work.

CURRENT STATUS AND EVALUATION OF SUPPORTED-EMPLOYMENT PROGRAMS

A review of the literature on supported employment was conducted in order to determine the degree to which supported-employment programs met the implicit and explicit service goals cited in the previous section.

Immediate Placement

Supported employment, often referred to as the "place-train model," is expected to place persons immediately into job sites in the community. Despite the value given to the goal of immediate placement, no published article has reported the use of this practice. Instead, published reports indicate the use of some form of preplacement screening and evaluation program that takes several weeks and sometimes months to complete. While it seems that programs have employed preplacement evaluation periods lasting weeks and months, it is often not clear how long clients must wait prior to their placement on a competitive work site. Two supported-employment programs serving persons with psychiatric disabilities have reported a discrete "preplacement" service prior to competitive placement. Fabian and Wiedefeld (1989) describe a 7-week orientation program prior to placement and Cook and colleagues (1990) describe a program that uses several transitional employment placements lasting an average of 8 months prior to competitive employment. As will be described in the next section, the present authors have utilized a 4-week evaluation and orientation program prior to placing clients in supported employment.

The absence of programs reporting an immediate placement procedure raises obvious questions about the feasibility and practicality of this goal. Since there is at present an absence of adequate data regarding the feasibility of immediate placement, programs demonstrating immediate placement or minimum amounts of "readiness training" are needed to provide information on this issue.

However, not everyone endorses the goal of immediate placement. For example, Anthony and Blanch (1987) advocate a preplacement period for psychiatric patients. They argue that a preplacement period permits clients to become more educated about the job placement process, and thereby more active in choosing the types of jobs at which they might want to work.

Zero Rejection

A second goal of supported employment is to serve all clients who express an interest in employment. In consistency with this goal, persons are not to be denied supported employment for reasons such as a poor prior work history.

Despite the "zero-rejection" philosophy, most programs evaluate and screen patients. There seem to be two universal forms of screening. The first requires successful attendance at and performance in a program prior to placement, and the second requires clients to meet performance standards considered to be related to job execution. A recent review indicates that programs often set additional standards such as parental support, agency support, client interest in job placement, job availability near client, travel availability, and SSI eligibility (Wehman, Hill, Wood, & Parent, 1987; Noble, 1991). Unfortunately, screening practices have not always been well described in the literature.

The present authors have found that the use of even minimal screening methods leads to a substantial reduction in the number of persons served. In the Einstein College of Medicine supported-employment program, simple enrollment requirements (i.e., signed parental informed-consent forms, a recent medical examination, birth certificate, social security card, proof of address, and working papers), resulted in only 60% of those referred being enrolled. The additional 4-week evaluation period used in this program resulted in an additional 40% reduction in the number of clients deemed eligible for job placement. The present authors' two-tier screening process (i.e., basic admission standards and success in an evaluation program) resulted in only 36% of those referred for services being placed in competitive employment.

Minimum Wage

Table 8-1 reveals that supported-employment programs are succeeding in placing most of their clients in minimum wage jobs. Programs such as those carried out by Wehman and his associates in Virginia clearly set minimum wage as a prerequisite of supported-employment services. There remain, however, a substantial number of supported-employment clients earning less than minimum wage. In one of the largest studies to date, Kregel and colleagues (1989) report that 81.4% of the clients served in supported employment earned at least minimum wage. Nearly 50% of the sample in the McDonnell, Nofs, Hardman, and Chambless (1989) study, and 30% in the Wacker, Fromm-Steege, Berg, and Flynn (1989) study, earned less than minimum wage. Rhodes and Valenta (1985) report that none of their clients received minimum wage in what they reported to be a supported-employment enclave.

The data suggest that minimum wage salaries are available for individuals placed in supported employment. It seems appropriate to recommend that programs placing persons in jobs paying less than minimum wage not be considered supported-employment programs since they do not meet an important standard for that type of designation.

Table 8-1 Review of Performance of Supported-Employment Programs Regarding Legislative Service Goals

Published Study	Sample Size	Minimum Wage Earners(%)	Work 20 hr/ wk(%)	Measure Integration	Type of Disorder	Mean Age
Kregel et al. (1989)	1,411	81.4	71.8	N.R.	DD	30
Wacker et al. (1989)	51	70	N.R.	N.R.	DD	22
McDonnel et al. (1989)	120	52	88	Scale	DD	33
Rhodes & Valenta (1985)	8	0	100	Anecdotal	DD	30
Brickey & Campbell (1981)	17	100	100	Anecdotal	DD	28
Wehman et al. (1985)	167	100	100	Scale	DD	30
Noble (1991)	1,305	100	N.R.	Scale	Mixed	29

Abbreviations: DD = developmentally disabled.

Hours Worked

Table 8-1 reveals that supported-employment programs are placing most of their clients in jobs that average 20 hours or more per week. However, a significant number of supported-employment clients work less than 20 hours per week (Kregel et al., 1989; McDonnell et al., 1989). In fact, it is reported that some clients worked as little as 3 or 4 hours per week.

Recently, legislation has been proposed to eliminate the requirement that supported-employment clients work at least 20 hours per week. The 20-hour-per-week standard would become a minimum "goal" to be attained prior to the case being considered a successful VR closure. The authors strongly disagree with the proposed legislation and suggest that the 20-hour minimum be maintained so as not to dilute the distinction between the supported-employment model and other forms of vocational rehabilitation.

Integration with Nonhandicapped

Although a number of articles strongly suggest that supported employment is having a positive effect on the integration of persons with handicaps in the community, information on social integration is often absent from reports of supported-employment programs. Table 8-1 reveals that only half of the published articles report data on integration. Two of these studies report only anecdotal information. Only Wehman and colleagues (1985) and McDonnell and colleagues (1989) use quantitative methods to describe the degree to which their samples were interacting with nonhandicapped coworkers and supervisors. Clearly, there is a need for additional information concerning the social integration of supported-employment clients.

The present authors find that although their clients are in close proximity to nonhandicapped workers, and may be rated on some scales as being integrated, the clients often remain isolated and uninvolved in the informal social life at work. We have found, for example, that clients (a) are infrequent participants in informal company parties, (b) are unlikely to share break time with others, (c) do not join betting pools, (d) are not part of social cliques, and (e) do not participate in social events occurring after work hours. As indicated by previous research on mainstreaming, placing persons with disabilities in integrated settings does not necessarily lead to integration. It seems that a great deal more attention needs to be placed on enhancing the integration of handicapped persons working in integrated settings.

On-the-Job Coaching

The supported-employment literature reveals a serious lack of discussion concerning the use, function, or credentials of job-coaching staff employed by these programs. Given that job coaching is the most important distinguishing feature of supported employment, the lack of discussion of this process is most disconcerting. It has led one of the leaders in the field to refer to supported-employment programs as, being a "place and pray" model (F. R. Rusch, personal communication, 1992). The "place and pray" analogy is based on the fact that the nature of the job-coaching services provided in most supported-employment programs is not known. Since job coaching takes place in a "black box," it is difficult to evaluate these practices and replicate successful programs. Clear standards for job coaching have been well articulated by Wehman and his associates at the Virginia Commonwealth University RRTC. Therefore, it seems reasonable for supported-employment programs to describe how their job-coaching practices compare to this standard model. The authors suggest that programs report on the credentials of their job coach staff, the job-coach-to-client ratio, and the percentage of time that clients receive job-coaching services at the competitive work site.

Serving the Most Severely Handicapped

Table 8-1 reveals that nearly all of the supported-employment programs reported in the literature serve persons with developmental disabilities (DD). Nearly 9 out of 10 persons who were provided supported-employment services were mentally retarded according to Kregel and colleagues (1989).

Several authors have examined the diagnoses of supported-employment clients and found that the majority had been diagnosed as either moderately or mildly retarded. Only 10% were found to be profoundly retarded. This finding has led these authors to suggest that few individuals with severe handicaps are being employed with support (Rusch & Hughes, 1989; Kregel et al., 1989).

The present authors suggest that functional assessments and work history inventories be used instead of diagnostic classification to evaluate "severity of disability." This procedure is recommended because studies have repeatedly demonstrated this approach to be superior to diagnostic classification in predicting employment outcome.

Wehman and associates (1985) developed an innovative method of assessing the severity of the disabilities of their clients. They required that clients be interviewed by VR services and rated in terms of their prognosis for employment. This procedure, which resulted in a measure of severity of handicap, demonstrated that a majority of their clients were considered so disabled as to be ineligible for VR services. Thus, their clients clearly met the "most severely handicapped" criteria.

The authors have employed an extensive work history questionnaire to help determine how severe the population's disability has been in relation to work functions. The work history questionnaire asks each client to report (a) number of jobs held, (b) longest job held (in months), (c) total length of past jobs, (d) highest hourly wage earned, (e) most hours worked per week, (f) average hours worked per week, (g) number of months worked in last year, (h) time since last job, (i) number of times fired, (j) number of times quit, and (k) reasons for leaving jobs. Using data of this type, Bedell, Prange, and Otten (1985) found that a history of losing jobs for not being on time for work and having trouble getting transportation as a reason for quitting were significantly predictive of employment. These variables, in fact, significantly increased the degree of prediction compared to that obtained when only the number of days of previous employment was used.

In addition, the authors use the Preliminary Diagnostic Questionnaire (PDQ; Moriarity, Wall, & McLaughlin, 1987), which is a functional assessment of employability for persons with severe disabilities. The PDQ has been shown to predict employment among persons with disabilities and provides a score that can be used to compare clients across different supported-employment programs.

Serving Persons in Transition

As may be seen in Table 8-1, supported-employment programs seem to have been provided mostly to adults (mean age = 30 years), not persons transitioning from school to work. Most supported-employment clients in the literature are enrolled in day activity centers or sheltered workshops.

The supported-employment program operated by the present authors is for 15- to 25-year-olds. We have identified a number of difficulties associated with programming for school-aged youth. First, differences in funding categories make it difficult to develop a program for youth and young adults. In mental health funding, adult and child services are typically divided at the age of 18, whereas the children enrolled in special education are considered eligible for services

until the age of 21. The Department of Employment funds school-to-work programs that serve clients up to the age of 21. However, the state vocational agencies
do not like to enroll persons who are still in school. The divergence that exists
among funding agencies needs to be remedied if supported-employment programs
are to be developed for persons in transition from school to work.

Furthermore, in order for more youth to be served by supported employment,
adult vocational agencies need to be encouraged to program their adult services
so that in-school youth can be served. Similarly, schools need to become more
flexible in their programming so that students can be enrolled in school-to-work
supported-employment programs that operate during the school day.

Job Retention

Although supported-employment legislation does not explicitly address job retention, in order to be cost-effective, supported-employment programs must provide
clients with long-term, stable employment or at least effective reemployment
services. Paul Wehman and his associates at the RRTC at the Virginia Commonwealth University are among the few groups that have consistently provided data
on job retention. Their 8-year follow-up of clients placed in supported employment
revealed that 70% of those placed remained employed at least 6 months. The
average length of employment was 21 months for 214 clients served (Hill et al.,
1987). More studies need to report the job tenure of supported-employment
clients and the length of time that is required to re-place clients in jobs.

The above findings suggest that as a model of vocational rehabilitation
supported employment has great promise in the area of placing severely handicapped persons in integrated work settings in the community where they earn
minimum wage. Clearly, however, not all programs portrayed to be providing
supported-employment services are in fact providing services that meet the minimum standards required. At this early stage in the research and development of
supported employment, it is important to maintain clear and consistent standards
regarding wages earned and hours worked, as decreed by legislative authoriza-
tions.

Additionally, greater emphasis should be placed on enhancing integration
of handicapped persons in the work setting and describing job-coaching activities.
The authors strongly support the practice of including data of clients who meet
the minimum standards of supported employment (i.e., earn minimum wage,
work for at least 20 hours per week, receive job-coaching services, and be in a
work force that includes no more than eight handicapped persons).

Thus, while there are abundant claims in the literature of the success of
supported employment, these claims are premature. There are no published studies
using random assignment to compare supported employment to other types of
vocational rehabilitation programs. Instead, studies have used single-group
designs (Wehman et al., 1985) or cross-sectional designs comparing supported-

employment outcomes to those of supposedly similar clients served in traditional programs (Conley, Rusch, McCaughrin, & Tines, 1989). While research studies using these uncontrolled designs suggest that supported employment is better than traditional sheltered or day activity programs (Noble & Conley, 1987; Conley et al., 1989; Wehman et al., 1985; Hill et al., 1987), they are inconclusive because inadequate experimental designs were employed.

DESCRIPTION OF EINSTEIN SUPPORTED-EMPLOYMENT PROGRAM

The Einstein supported-employment program is designed to serve seriously emotionally disturbed youth aged 16 to 25. It is part of a controlled research project that includes three different vocational treatment programs: (a) individual placement using job coaching, (b) individual placement using natural supports in the workplace, and (c) traditional sheltered workshop training. Only the individual placement model using job-coaching services will be described in this chapter, since it is more widely used than the natural supports model.

The supported-employment program consists of the following discrete rehabilitative components. Each will be described in the following section. The components are (a) enrollment, (b) vocational and social skills training and assessment, (c) job development, (d) job coaching, (e) long-term problem-solving group, (f) multiple family therapy, and (g) individual therapy.

Enrollment

Enrollment procedures were designed to be as simple as possible. Information is required that documents the fact that prospective participants are minimally eligible to receive treatment services, are certified to work, and agree to participate in the research. Referred clients and their legal guardians are required to (a) sign a research informed consent, (b) provide evidence of a recent physical examination, (c) have current working papers (if under 18), (d) have a social security card, (e) show proof of residence, (f) provide a birth certificate, (g) verify selective service registration (if male and over 18), and (h) have a vocational goal stated in their Individual Education Plan (IEP) or mental health treatment plan prior to referral. We also require that referred clients have not been suspended from the referral program during the month prior to enrollment.

Vocational and Social Skills Training and Assessment

Persons providing the above information are enrolled in a program to evaluate vocational and social skills. Clients attend the program 5 days per week, 5 hours per day, for 4 weeks. Clients are paid about $85 for the approximately 100 hours that they are in the training and evaluation program.

Vocational Training and Assessment   Clients receive 60 hours of placement in one of five vocational training sites, including food service, clerical, building maintenance, thrift shop, or assembly program. In these settings, a job coach provides training similar to that provided to clients placed in competitive jobs. Training was designed to teach skills identified by a task analysis performed on each of the five work settings. Clients are given daily feedback on (a) ability to perform each task correctly without support, (b) percentage of on-task time, and (c) amount of productivity compared to that of a "job-ready" person.

Social Skills Training and Assessment   Clients are presented 22 social skills training lessons focused on assertive communication and problem-solving skills training. The training covers topics including how to have more self-awareness of feelings and expectations, how to express feelings and expectations to others, how to make requests of others, how to respond to requests from others, and how to behave assertively toward others considering one's own wants and needs as well as those of the others. This skill training follows the procedures described in Chapter 5.

Clients' ability to perform these various skilled behaviors is assessed using structured behavioral exercises conducted in the training groups. The training sessions are videotaped, and review of these tapes also aids in the evaluation of the social skill behaviors.

Individual Training and Assessment   Clients meet for 1 hour each week with a staff member to evaluate work adjustment, social skill generalization, time management, and other issues, such as the often-expressed desire to "hang out" rather than work.

Standardized Assessment   In addition to the above assessment situations, clients are administered 5 hours of standardized tests, including the Talent Assessment Program (TAP), (Nighswanger, 1971), a videotaped behavioral assessment (see Chapter 4), the Preliminary Diagnostic Questionnaire (Moriarity et al., 1987), the WRAT-R, the Structured Clinical Interview for DSM-III-R (SCID-P; Spitzer, Williams, Gibbon, & First, 1989), the Diagnostic Interview Schedule for Children (DISC-2.1C; Schaeffer, Fisher, Piacentini, Schwab-Stone & Wicks, 1989), the Vocational and Mental Health Questionnaire (Bedell et al., 1985), and a battery of psychological self-report measures that evaluate emotions (e.g., depression) and cognitions (e.g., irrational beliefs).

The results of these tests are not used specifically to determine the client's ability to proceed to work placement. They are included as part of the research evaluation of this project. Once the research is completed, it is possible that scores on these tests may be shown to be predictive of vocational success. In that case, they can be used as part of the screening process.

Family Conferences   During the month, two family conferences are held to review the client's performance and current status in the program.

Summary of Training and Assessment Phase of Program

A great deal of information is obtained on each client during the month of vocational and social skills training and assessment. In the spirit of the "zero-rejection" philosophy of supported employment, clients are not expected to master the skills presented to them in order to be placed in employment with a job coach. Performance in five basic skills is used to determine suitability for job placement: (a) attendance at scheduled meetings, (b) punctuality at scheduled meetings, (c) preparedness (e.g., bringing tools to work, notebook to class), (d) making at least one on-target comment during each training session, and (e) completion of off-site homework assignment (e.g., practicing social skills tasks). Clients are frequently and systematically provided feedback and instruction on these five categories of performance.

The criteria for "passing" the training and assessment phase are simple and straightforward. Clients are required to attend and be punctual at scheduled activities a minimum of 75% of the time. In addition, they are required to be prepared for scheduled activities, provide on-target comments in groups, and complete off-site homework assignments at least 80% of the time. In the work setting, they are required to remain on-task 80% of the time, perform 80% of the work task without error, and perform at 80% of productivity.

Job Development

After clients complete the preliminary training and assessment phase, job development and placement services begin immediately. Matching a client to a job is facilitated by the use of data obtained during the training and assessment phase, including an assessment using the *Job/Worker Compatibility Analysis* (JCA), (VCU-RRTC, 1987). The analysis indicates the client's work interests and any restrictions that should be placed on the work schedule. The Talent Assessment Program (TAP), which assesses 10 basic worker traits, was also administered. Finally, the Situational Assessment, which measures the client's performance in a real work setting, is administered.

Job development proceeds quickly because a large amount of information is available on each client and also because a positive relationship has been established between the job developer and client during the training and assessment period. Clients meet with the job developer twice each week. They prepare for job interviews using videotapes of practice interviews. The job developer accompanies clients to all employment interviews and provides coaching throughout the interview process. Interview coaching includes prompts to help clients complete applications, respond to questions, and make requests of employers for additional information or clarification concerning the job.

The job developer is required to make two placements per month, 24 placements per year. In order for a developer to accomplish this task, it has been found that each day 30 prospective employers must be contacted by telephone and one client-employer interview must occur. On the average, 30 calls are needed to obtain one interview, and 12 interviews are needed for a client to secure a job placement.

To facilitate clients' learning the job search process, they are instructed to use a job development notebook in which they record all job leads and notes regarding follow-up activities on each job. In addition, the job developer conducts a daily job club meeting where job candidates are assisted in developing résumés, completing employment applications, learning interviewing skills, identifying job leads, and pursuing interviews.

Job Coaching

Once a client is employed, job-coaching services begin. Job-coaching interventions used in this program are based on the model developed by Paul Wehman and his associates at the Virginia Commonwealth University RRTC and are also influenced by the recent work of Rusch and Minch (1988) concerning coworker involvement and collateral training.

When possible, the job coach completes a task analysis of the job duties prior to the client's first day at work. In addition, the client's ability to travel to the work site is assessed. If necessary, training regarding employment tasks and travel is provided prior to the first day at work. Also prior to the first day of work, clients are escorted from their home to the work site in order to acquaint them with the work environment.

An orientation checklist is used as a means of introducing the client to the important areas of the work environment. Use of this checklist alerts the job coach to areas of strength and weakness. For example, if the client is unfamiliar with the use of time cards, the job coach will note the need for training in this area.

A reinforcement questionnaire is administered within the first few days of employment to assess the client's wants and interests. Information from this questionnaire is used to sustain motivation on the job in the event that the natural rewards of working and being paid are not sufficient.

All work duties assigned to the client are task analyzed. The written task analyses provide a detailed sequencing of all job duties. The task analyses become the basis for job coach training and assessment. Throughout the client's training, these task analyses are used to assess the client's (a) knowledge of the job duties, (b) percentage of on-task time, and (c) productivity. The job coach provides daily feedback to the client on performance.

The job coach gradually fades from the job site as the client demonstrates increased competence. Generally, during the first month of employment, the job coach is present 75% of the time while a client works. The presence of the job coach decreases to 40% to 50% during the second month, 25% to 40% during the third month, and 20% during the fourth month. During subsequent months, the job coach is present approximately 10% of the time. In order to provide ongoing support, the job coach continues to visit the client at the job site at least once every 2 weeks for as long as the client is employed.

Long-Term Problem-Solving Group

Clients meet with staff weekly in a problem-solving group. This group facilitates ongoing practice and generalization of adaptive and socially skilled behaviors in work, home, school, neighborhood, and/or treatment environments. The group starts by learning additional, more advanced communication and problem-solving skills not presented during the 4-week evaluation period. These lessons teach clients how to cope with anxiety through anxiety management techniques such as relaxation training and cognitive restructuring. Skills are also developed in the application of a problem-solving process including problem recognition, problem definition, generation of alternative problem solutions, evaluation of alternatives, and decision making. After the advanced training is completed, these groups focus on application of a structured problem-solving model to issues related to employment and seek to facilitate peer as well as professional support for clients on the job (see Bedell & Michael, 1985; Bedell, Archer, & Marlowe, 1980; or Chapter 10, for detailed presentation of a problem-solving group).

Multiple-Family Therapy

Clients and families participate in a multiple-family group, as described in Chapter 10. The rationale for providing multiple-family therapy to these clients and families is to (a) help clients extend their newly acquired social skills behaviors to the family environment, (b) provide a forum for the families to become active participants in the clients' rehabilitation, and (c) provide the families a natural support and advocacy network for themselves and their children.

Individual Therapy

Once placed on the job, clients attend weekly individual therapy sessions. These sessions are directed to continue training in and generalization of effective communication and problem-solving skills to current problems experienced by the client. One important value of this modality is that it allows for greater individualization of the social skills training to the needs of the client.

PRELIMINARY RESULTS OF A CONTROLLED EVALUATION OF SUPPORTED EMPLOYMENT

Purpose of Study

This study examined the placement rate and employment tenure of 34 severely disabled youth randomly assigned to one of three treatment programs: (a) supported employment using job coaches, (b) supported employment using natural supports in the workplace, and (c) sheltered-employment training.

Subjects

All subjects were diagnosed using the Diagnostic Interview Schedule for Children (DISC-2.1C, Child's Version) and Structured Clinical Interview for the DSM-III-R (SCID-R). Psychiatric disabilities included schizophrenia, major affective disorder, attention deficit disorder, paranoid personality disorder, and oppositional defiant disorder. All of the subjects were drawn from a low-income, densely populated urban center. Two thirds of the subjects were male. The average age of the sample was 19, and ranged from 16 to 25 years of age. Fifty percent of the sample was Afro-American, 33% was of Hispanic background, and 17% was Caucasian. Eighty percent of the subjects had been enrolled in special education classes or self-contained special education schools. Forty percent scored below the seventh grade reading level on the WRAT-R reading test. Only 20% had any previous work experience.

Participation in the study was voluntary. All subjects and family members provided institutionally approved informed consent.

Independent Variables

Subjects who completed the vocational and social skills training and assessment phase of the program were randomly assigned to one of the following three vocational training programs: (a) *supported employment with job coaching* consisted of job placement and job-coaching services, with weekly individual, family, and peer group therapy; (b) *supported employment using natural supports* in the workplace consisted of job placement services with weekly individual, family, and peer group therapy; and (c) *sheltered employment* consisted of training in a sheltered workshop setting with weekly individual, family, and peer group therapy.

The supported-employment treatments placed clients in competitive work sites that paid at least minimum wage and provided at least 20 hours of work per week. Clients were placed using the individual placement model. All counseling sessions were based on clinical procedures described within a set of cognitive-behavioral social skills treatment manuals. Treatment sessions were videotaped and reviewed in clinical supervision meetings to assure compliance with these protocols.

Dependent Variables

Job placement and job tenure (defined as the number of consecutive days of employment) data were obtained for each subject via records maintained by the job developers of the supported- and sheltered-employment programs and from monthly interviews with each subject. Dates employment began and terminated were determined from this information. In addition, each month subjects were telephoned and asked about their current employment status, hourly wages, work schedule, and any changes that had occurred in their employment status during the previous month. Reasons for job terminations were determined and recorded.

Results

Job Placement   During the first year of this research, a total of 34 subjects were randomly assigned to the three treatment groups: 14 with job coaches, eight with natural supports in the workplace, and 12 in sheltered-employment training. Subjects were classified as "placed in employment" or "not placed in employment," and a 2 × 3 chi-square analysis was conducted to compare the three treatment groups. This analysis yielded significant results [chi(2, N = 34) = 9.82, p < .01], indicating that a difference existed among the three groups. A series of subsequent analyses were conducted to compare the various groups to each other. Results indicated there were significantly more job placements in the job-coached group than the sheltered workshop group [chi(1, N = 26) = 5.75, p < .01], significantly more job placements in the natural supports group than the sheltered workshop group (Fisher's Exact Test, p < .01), but no difference in placement rate between the groups receiving job coaching and natural supports. A review of the data showed that 73% (16 of 22) of those assigned to supported employment were placed in competitive employment during the year of the study, compared to only 17% (2 of 12) of those assigned to sheltered-employment training.

Job Tenure (Number of Days of Employment)   The numbers of days of employment during the year of this study were analyzed using one-way analysis of variance (ANOVA) statistics to compare supported employment with job coaching, supported employment with natural supports, and sheltered workshop training. The mean number of days of competitive employment for subjects receiving supported employment with job coaching was 117 days (17 weeks). Subjects receiving supported employment with natural supports in the workplace worked 80.25 days (11 weeks), and subjects receiving sheltered-employment training worked 14.92 days (2 weeks). The results of the ANOVA of this data were significant [$F(2, 34)$ = 3.65, p < .03]. The Duncan Range statistic was used to evaluate the means associated with the three treatment groups. This analysis revealed that subjects receiving supported employment with job coaching were employed more days than subjects who received the sheltered-employment training. There was no significant difference in the number of days of employment between supported employment with job coaching and supported employment with natural support or between natural support and sheltered employment.

DISCUSSION

The results of this study of supported employment using random assignment to treatment groups clearly indicated the superiority of the supported-employment with job-coaching model over the sheltered workshop regarding the number of clients placed in competitive employment (71% vs. 17%) and their job tenure, measured in days of employment (128.8 vs. 43.1). Supported employment with natural supports was also superior to the sheltered workshop in placement rate (75% vs. 17%), but not in job tenure (days of employment: 80 vs. 14 days). Comparisons between supported employment with job coaches and that with natural supports indicated they were not significantly different on either placement rate or job tenure.

However, the small cell size associated with these preliminary data may have resulted in insufficient statistical power to detect some differences between experimental groups. Determination of the relative effectiveness of job coaches and natural supports must wait until a more powerful test of these treatments is available. This reservation notwithstanding, the supported-employment model appears to be superior to sheltered workshop training and produce outcomes consistent with contemporary vocational goals set in recent legislation. Further refinements of the supported-employment model, and more stringent experimental evaluations, are currently under way at Einstein. We are optimistic that the results of these more complete studies will support those found in this preliminary evaluation of supported employment.

REFERENCES

Anthony, W. A., & Blanch, A. (1987). Supported employment for persons who are psychiatrically disabled: A historical and conceptual perspective. *Psychosocial Rehabilitation Journal, 11*(2), 5–23.
Anthony, W. A., & Jansen, M. A. (1984). Predicting vocational capacity of the chronically mentally ill: Research and policy implications. *American Psychologist, 34*(5), 537–544.
Anthony, W. A., & Buell, G. L. (1975). The relationship between patient demographic characteristics and psychiatric rehabilitation outcome. *Community Mental Health Journal, 11*(2), 208–214.
Anthony, W. A., & Marguelos, A. (1974). Toward improving the efficacy of psychiatric rehabilitation: A skills training approach. *Rehabilitation Psychology, 21*, 101–105.

Barkas, M., Brooke, V., Inge, K., Moon, S., & Goodall, P. (1987). *An instructional guide for training on a job site: A supported employment resource* (Monograph). Richmond: Virginia Commonwealth University, Rehabilitation Research and Training Center.

Bedell, J. R., Archer, R. P., & Marlowe, H. A., Jr. (1980). A description and evaluation of a problem-solving skills training program. In D. Upper & S. M. Ross (Eds.), *Behavioral group therapy: An annual review.* Champaign, IL: Research Press.

Bedell, J. R., & Michael, D. D. (1985). Teaching problem-solving skills to chronic psychiatric patients. In D. Upper & S. M. Ross (Eds.), *Handbook of behavioral group therapy.* New York: Plenum Press.

Bedell, J. R., & Ward, J. C. (1989). An intensive community-based treatment alternative to state hospitalization. *Hospital and Community Psychiatry, 40,* 533–535.

Bedell, J. R., Prange, M., & Otten, C. (1985). *Predicting post-hospital employment of chronic psychiatric patients.* Paper presented at the annual meeting of the Southeastern Psychological Association, Atlanta, Georgia.

Black, B. J., & Kase, H. M. (1986). Work as therapy and rehabilitation for the mentally ill: Changes in programs over two decades. *Professional Monograph Series of the Altro Institute for Rehabilitation Studies, 1,* 3–37.

Brickey, M., & Campbell, K. (1981). Fast food employment for moderately and mildly mentally retarded adults: The McDonald's Project. *Mental Retardation, 19*(3), 113–116.

Buckley, J. (1991). *Issues in developing company support.* Presentation to the Coalition of Mainstream Employment Programs, New York.

Cho, D. W. (1984). An alternative employment model for handicapped persons. *Journal of Rehabilitation Administration, 10,* 55–63.

Como, P. (1984). *A course guide for work stations in industry—video course.* Syracuse, NY: Program Development Associates.

Conley, R. W., Rusch, F. R., McCaughrin, W. B., & Tines, J. (1989). Benefits and costs of supported employment: An analysis of the Illinois Supported Employment Project. *Journal of Applied Behavioral Analysis, 22*(4), 441–447.

Cook, J. A., Solomon, M. L., Jonikas, J. A., & Frazier, M. (1990). *Supported competitive employment program for youth with severe mental illness.* Final Report to the U.S. Dept. of Education. Grant #G008630404. Chicago: Thresholds, Inc.

Fabian, E., & Wiedefeld, M. F. (1989). Supported employment for severely psychiatrically disabled persons: A descriptive study. *Psychosocial Rehabilitation Journal, 13*(2), 53–60.

Falloon, R. I., & Boyd, H. L., & McGill, C. W. (1982). Family management in the prevention of the exacerbation of schizophrenia. *New England Journal of Medicine, 306,* 1437–1440.

Harding, C. M., Strauss, J. S., Hafez, H., & Lieberman, P. B., (1987). *The Journal of Nervous and Mental Disease, 175*(6), 317–326.

Hill, M. L., Wehman, P. H., Kregel, J., Banks, P. D., & Metzler, H. M. D. (1987). Employment outcomes for people with moderate and severe disabilities: An eight year longitudinal analysis of supported competitive employment. *JASH, 12*(3), 182–189.

Hogarty, G. E., Anderson, C. M., Reiss, D. J., Kornblith, S. J., Greenwald, D. P., Javna, C. D., & Madonia, M. J. (1986). Family psychoeducation, social skills training and maintenance chemotherapy in the aftercare treatment of schizophrenia. *Archives of General Psychiatry, 43,* 633–642.

Kregel, J., & Wehman, P. (1989). Supported employment: Promises deferred for persons with severe disabilities. *JASH, 14*(4), 293–303.

Kregel, J., Wehman, P., & Banks, R. D. (1989). The effects of consumer characteristics and types of employment models on individual outcomes in supported employment. *Journal of Applied Behavior Analysis, 22*(4), 407–415.

Liberman, R. P., Mueser, K. T., & Wallace, C. J. (1986). Social skills training for schizophrenic individuals at risk of relapse. *American Journal of Psychiatry, 143*, 523–526.

McDonnell, J., Nofs, D., Hardman, M., & Chambless, C. (1989). An analysis of the procedural components of supported employment programs associated with employment outcomes. *Journal of Applied Behavior Analysis, 22*(4), 417–428.

Moriarity, J. B., Wall, R. T., & McLaughlin, D. E., (1987). The Preliminary Diagnostic Questionaire (PDQ): Functional assessment of employability. *Rehabilitation Psychology, 32*(1), 5–15.

Nelson, N. (1971). Workshops for the handicapped in the United States. Springfield, IL: Charles C Thomas.

Nighswanger, W. (1971). *Talent Assessment Program (TAP)* (rev.) Jacksonville, FL: Ben Gorden Company, Talent Assessment, Inc.

Nisbett, J., & Hagner, D. (1988). Natural supports in the workplace: A re-examination of supported employment. *JASH, 13*(4), 260–267.

Noble, J. H. (1991). *The benefits and costs of supported employment for persons with mental illness and with traumatic brain injury in New York State* (Monograph Contract No. C-0023180). New York: Research Foundation of the State University of New York.

Noble, J. H., & Conley, R. W. (1987). Accumulating evidence on the benefits and costs of supported and transitional employment for persons with severe disabilities. *JASH, 12*(3), 163–174.

Revell, W. G., Wehman, P., & Arnold, S. (1984, Oct.–Dec.). Supported work model of competitive employment for persons with mental retardation: Implications for rehabilitation services. *Journal of Rehabilitation*, 33–38.

Rhodes, L. E., & Valenta, L. (1985). Industry-based supported employment: An enclave approach. *JASH, 10*(1), 12–20.

Rusch, F. R., & Hughes, C. (1989). Overview of supported employment. *Journal of Applied Behavioral Analysis, 22*(4), 351–363.

Rusch, F. R., & Minch, K. E. (1988). Identification of co-worker involvement in supported employment: A review and analysis. *Research in Developmental Disabilities, 9*, 247–254.

Rusch, F. R., Morgan, T. K., Martin, J. E., Riva, M., & Agran, M. (1985). Competitive employment: Teaching mentally retarded adults self-instructional strategies. *Applied Research in Mental Retardation, 6*, 389–407.

Schaeffer, D., Fisher, P., Piacentini, J., Schwab-Stone, M., & Wicks, J., (1989). *Diagnostic Interview for Children* (DISC-2.1, Child's Version). New York: Biometrics Research Department, New York State Psychiatric Institute.

Spitzer, R. L., Williams, J. B., Gibbon, M., & First, M. B. (1989). Structured Clinical Interview for DSM-III-R: Client Version (SCID-P). New York: Biometrics Research Department, New York State Psychiatric Institute.

Staff (1991, October). Washington update: Appropriations update. *Newsletter for the National Rehabilitation Association,* p. 7.

Stein, L., & Test, M. A. (Eds.) (1985). The training in community living model: A decade of experience. *New Directions in Mental Health.* San Francisco: Jossey-Bass.

Strauss, J., & Carpenter, W. (1972). The prediction of outcome in schizophrenia: Part One. *Archives of General Psychiatry, 27,* 739–746.

Strauss, J., & Carpenter, W. (1974). The prediction of outcome in schizophrenia: Part Two. *Archives of General Psychiatry, 31,* 37–42.

Wacker, D. P., Fromm-Steege, L., Berg, W. K., & Flynn, T. H. (1989). Supported employment as an intervention package: A preliminary analysis of functional variables. *Journal of Applied Behavior Analysis, 22*(4), 429–439.

Virginia Commonwealth University Rehabilitation Research and Training Center (VCU-RRTC). (1987). Test Development Unit. Richmond, VA: Author.

Wehman, P., Hill, M., Hill, J. W., Brooke, V., Pendleton, P., & Britt, C. (1985). Competitive employment for persons with mental retardation: A follow-up six years later. *Mental Retardation, 23*(6), 274–281.

Wehman, P., & Kregel, J. (1985). A supported work approach to competitive employment of individuals with moderate and severe handicaps. *Journal of the Association for Persons with Severe Handicaps,* 10, 3–11.

Wehman, P., Hill, J. W., Wood, W., & Parent, W. (1987). A report on competitive employment histories of persons labeled severely mentally retarded. *JASH, 12*(1), 11–17.

Whitehead, C. W. (1987, July–Sept.). Supported employment: Challenge and opportunity for sheltered workshops. *Journal of Rehabilitation,* 23–28.

Chapter 9

Case Management as a Rehabilitation Intervention

Andrea K. Blanch and Richard C. Surles

Case management may become an important modality for delivering mental health services in the community. Despite considerable variation in the nature, purpose, and organization of case management programs, state mental health administrators increasingly look to case management as an effective strategy in responding to a fragmented community service system. Case management has also emerged as a vehicle for assisting in the rehabilitation and recovery of persons with long-term psychiatric disabilities.

HISTORY

National emphasis on case management in mental health is relatively recent (OBRA, 1986). In the early years of the community mental health movement, the need for case management services was rarely articulated. Case management did not become a major topic of conversation for state mental health commissioners until the late 1970s, and did not appear in a majority of state mental health service plans until the 1980s (Blanch, 1986).

Case management was not specifically mentioned in the federal Community Mental Health Center (CMHC) Act of 1963, nor was it included as one of the "five essential services" specified in federal CMHC regulations published in 1964 or as one of the "twelve essential services" defined in the 1975 amendments (Wagenfeld & Jacobs, 1982).[1] Although "service coordination" was required, this tended to be implemented by referring clients to services within the CMHC itself. Moreover, the expectation was that once a referral was made, the client or the client's family would be responsible for following the treatment plan.

Historically, CMHCs appear to have served clients who were less seriously disabled than the state hospital population (Robinson, Bergman, & Scallett, 1989). In the sixties and early seventies, most case management for persons with serious disabilities was performed (if at all) primarily by state-operated aftercare programs or through projects funded by the National Institute of Mental Health (NIMH) Hospital Improvement Program (HIP). In the first 5 years of the HIP program, over 120,000 long-term hospital clients were transitioned to the community, often through case management and outreach services (Ozarin, 1982). The HIP program was eventually phased into the NIMH Community Support Program, which specified case management services as one of 10 essential elements in a comprehensive community support system (Turner & Ten Hoor, 1978).

In the initial years following passage of the Community Mental Health Center Act, individual therapy remained the dominant outpatient treatment response. Case management generally was composed of paperwork and other administrative activities required to conduct therapy. As researchers began documenting the difficulties faced by former state hospital clients living in the community, the need for a case management system to ensure access to needed services and supports and to maintain continuity of care over time became clear (e.g., Caton, 1981; Test, 1981).

During the early 1980s, case management was increasingly conceptualized as a means for linking and coordinating a wide range of services. An early advocate for client-centered case management, John Talbott, described the need for support to assist clients in "finding their way among a multitude of services" (1980 p. 48). Considerable debate ensued over the role of case managers as direct service providers/therapists versus independent service coordinators. Advocates argued that outpatient clinicians doing "case management" as part of their routine activities were not likely to engage in the out-of-office advocacy and negotiating functions critical for seriously disabled persons to succeed in the community. Clinicians argued that "service coordination" without a high level of client trust and a strong clinical relationship would ultimately be ineffective (Love, 1984).

---

[1]The "five essential services" were inpatient, outpatient, and emergency services; aftercare; and consultation and education. The 1975 amendments added partial hospitalization, diagnostic services, screening, services for children and the elderly, transitional services, and services for alcohol and drug abusers.

This debate continues today, as the term "case management" is used to refer to a wide range of activities and approaches (Bachrach, 1989; Hyde, 1990).

During the period prior to 1986, both federal and state financing for case management was limited. Few state mental health agencies could afford an independent case management system. Instead, states generally assigned case management activities (such as planning, monitoring, linking) to existing staff (Love, 1984). Similarly, aspects of case management were allowed as an activity within Medicaid, but case management was not funded as a discrete service. Prior to 1986, federal financial participation could be claimed in any of the following four areas (Department of Health and Human Services, 1988):

1 *Component of another service.* Case management services such as preparation of treatment plans could be included as an integral part of another covered Medicaid service. *Separate* reimbursement could not be made, but was included in the payment made for the service at the Federal Medical Assistance Percentage (FMAP) rate.

2 *Administration.* Case management activities such as utilization review, prior authorization, and preadmission screening could be provided as a function necessary for the proper and efficient operation of the Medicaid state plan. Such activities could be reimbursed as an administrative expense, at either the 50% matching rate or the 75% rate for medical personnel.

3 *Section 1915 (b) waivers.* Case management could be provided through a waiver of the freedom of choice requirements of section 1902. To qualify for such a waiver, the case management project needed to demonstrate cost-effectiveness, efficiency, and consistency with the objectives of the Medicaid program. The primary purpose of this waiver was to allow the establishment of "primary care case management" in order to restrict the provider from whom an individual could obtain medical care services.

4 *Section 1915 (c) waivers.* Case management could be provided as part of a "home and community-based services waiver," under a written plan of care approved by the state. Services were reimbursed at the FMAP rate.

With increasing experience, it became clear that simply linking clients to existing services was not enough to achieve desired outcomes for seriously disabled individuals. In many cases, the range of needed services was not available (Taube, Morlock, Burns, & Santos, 1990). Often clients needed active coaching and support simply in order to use available services or to adjust to minor changes in the environment. In some cases, clients became overly dependent on the case manager, and needed training in self-advocacy skills (Thompson, Griffith, & Leaf, 1990). Moreover, a very assertive case management response was clearly necessary if utilization patterns were to be changed. Early case management programs that demonstrated successful reduction of inpatient care were characterized by both a philosophical orientation and a program structure that encouraged case managers not just to "coordinate" services, but to be aggressive in influencing both client and provider behavior. As Thompson and colleagues (1990) state about Dane County, Wisconsin: "The flow of clients through this system is scrutinized to ensure that the level of service corresponds to the level of need. This scrutiny is especially emphasized at the interface with inpatient services" (p. 630).

By the mid-1980s, a number of characteristics of successful case management programs had been identified (Robinson et al., 1989). Although research had been limited to studies in a few sites, a consensus emerged that effective case management systems shared three overall features. First, access to the case management system was controlled, generally by targeting the most disabled clients. Second, programs were designed to actively influence service utilization. Case managers were explicitly instructed to advocate for access to needed services and to prevent or reduce the unnecessary use of inpatient care through 24-hour mobile crisis response. To assist in these tasks, they were often given structural authority and flexible funds to purchase or stimulate the development of needed services and supports. Third, program leadership emphasized the potential for clients to make progress and eventually to become less dependent on services. Although case management models were structured differently and emphasized different clinical techniques (e.g., skills teaching, modeling effective problem solving, client empowerment), successful programs appeared to share an active rehabilitation orientation (Robinson et al., 1989).

Case management has thus emerged as a mechanism for managing care, with the responsibility for both ensuring positive client outcomes and ensuring effective resource utilization (i.e., reducing costs). The Medicaid amendments of 1985 and 1986, which created the first national funding stream for case management services, reinforced this emerging concept of case management as "managed care." The Consolidated Omnibus Budget Reconciliation Act of 1985 (P.L. 99-272) added case management to the list of optional services that could be provided under Medicaid. The Omnibus Budget Reconciliation Act of 1986 (P.L. 99-509) allowed case management services to be limited to AIDS patients or to the chronically mentally ill, thus encouraging states to target these populations.

Public Law 99-272 defined case management as services that assist individuals eligible under the plan in gaining access to needed medical, social, educational, and other services. Any state plan amendment request to provide optional case management services was required to specify a "target group" (e.g., by age; type or degree of disability, illness, or condition; or other identifiable characteristics), indicate whether services would be available statewide or to a limited geographic area, assure that there would be no restriction of freedom of choice of providers of other Medicaid services, establish minimum qualifications for case managers, and assure nonduplication of payments and coordination with other reimbursed case management services.

Language in the 1986 OBRA legislation indicates that Congress viewed case management as both an effective program strategy and a mechanism to contain costs. The House report accompanying the OBRA legislation stated that community-based case management services could be easily implemented and were favored by recipients of services, effective in enhancing levels of functioning, and affordable. Further, the report stated that these services were expected to yield lower acute hospitalization costs as a result of shorter lengths of stay and fewer readmissions.

By 1989, 15 states had approved plans for providing case management mental health services with Medicaid funding (Vischi & Stockdill, 1989). It is important to note, however, that approval of state plans is predicated upon states documenting a reasonable expectation that the service will be cost neutral to the Medicaid program.

Further impetus for the development of case management came with the passage of the Comprehensive Mental Health Services Plan Act of 1986 (P.L. 99-660). Public Law 99-660 requires states to develop and implement comprehensive mental health plans including providing case management services to each person with a serious and persistent mental illness who received significant amounts of public funds or services. The National Institute of Mental Health was charged with assisting states in meeting the requirements of the planning legislation.

The case management technical assistance document prepared by NIMH illustrates the evolution of case management since the 1960s (NIMH, 1989). Sections of the report are devoted to identifying a specific target population (particularly those who were using existing services ineffectively at substantial cost of public dollars), defining desired client outcomes, and establishing feedback mechanisms so the case manager can monitor progress. The report also recommended designing case management programs to incorporate flexibility, variable level of intensity, unlimited duration, and primacy of the case manager–client relationship.

RESEARCH

Recent literature reviews have continued to report the effectiveness of case management in reducing inpatient hospitalization and controlling short-term costs (Taube et al., 1990). The long-term cost-benefit impact of case management remains less clear.

Studies of the effects of case management on three variables, client symptoms, social functioning, and occupational functioning, have been mixed. The original research on the Training in Community Living (TCL) model in Madison, Wisconsin (later referred to as the Program for Assertive Community Treatment), demonstrated effective outcomes in all three areas, as have several replications (Olfson, 1990). Other studies have been unable to document improvements in client functioning. Olfson (1990) suggests that negative findings may reflect inadequate program implementation, clients in different phases of illness, or a narrowing of the gap between case management and "traditional" interventions.

Negative findings may also reflect an inappropriate conceptualization of case management as a "program." Case management may be more appropriately considered a strategy for targeting and tailoring services to the needs of specific populations—that is, for managing the care of high-risk groups—rather than a program model.

NEW YORK'S INTENSIVE CASE MANAGEMENT PROGRAM

In New York, the statewide Intensive Case Management (ICM) program has been funded since 1989 through the Medicaid case management option. This program attempts to incorporate principles of rehabilitation in a program targeted to identifiable subgroups of individuals with long-term psychiatric disabilities.

New York's ICM program was designed to meet three overall goals:

1 To increase access to services for specific groups of persons currently excluded from or choosing not to use existing mental health services
2 To decrease inappropriate utilization of emergency services and inpatient care, thereby reducing unnecessary expenditures
3 To assist clients in meeting a variety of unmet needs and in making progress toward their own goals.

Admission to the program was controlled through a "rostering" process and clearly defined target populations, and expected outcomes were explicitly stated. In addition, a partially capitated financing strategy was adopted in order to maximize case manager flexibility, and a pool of "service dollars" was made available to help fill gaps and meet emergency needs.

The ICM program thus incorporates three aspects of a "managed-care" model of case management—control over access (including both rostering and active engagement efforts); planned impact on utilization patterns; and expected rehabilitation outcomes. The ICM program is not intended to substitute for other services, nor is it intended solely to "maintain" clients in community settings. Rather, ICM has been designed specifically as a rehabilitative program for individuals who cannot be effectively reached through other service modalities. Several structural characteristics of the ICM program illustrate why case management has potential as a rehabilitation intervention.

Design of the ICM program began with identification of persons in four specific target groups: (a) heavy users of emergency services; (b) individuals who are homeless as well as mentally ill; (c) those with histories of extended inpatient care; and (d) seriously emotionally disturbed children and youth. Identifying target groups is required under the Medicaid case management option. Doing so also allows policymakers to focus the program on groups with problematic service utilization patterns that might be altered through case management and rehabilitation.

The issue of controlling access to services is a critical aspect of all managed-care systems, including case management. Often this issue is framed as one of denying access to services to those judged "less disabled" or "less needy." Intensive case management accomplishes the same goal (targeting scarce resources where they have potential for positive outcomes) by rostering members of the target population and ensuring through active engagement efforts and access to needed services that the most disabled/least well served are in fact brought into treatment, support, and active rehabilitation. Early results indicate that the ICM program is a particularly useful approach for disaffiliated groups who will not readily present for services, but tend to require significant public resources such as acute inpatient care.

Specifying a target population also encourages program design based on clinical and demographic characteristics. Many of the principles of New York's ICM program were based on current understanding about effective strategies for meeting the needs of the four target groups. Program parameters such as caseload size, availability of crisis response, site of service delivery, and qualifications of case managers will vary with different target populations.

The rehabilitative nature of New York's ICM program required a commitment to evaluation. Rather than specifying detailed guidelines or regulations, OMH issued a series of 24 "principles" that programs were expected to meet, and required that a client outcome evaluation form be completed for all clients. Six-month follow-up forms are completed on a statewide sample. In addition, direct client feedback on the effectiveness of program implementation (i.e., congruence with the principles and philosophy) was obtained.

The outcome evaluation is particularly important because it clearly identifies the domains in which intensive case managers are expected to have an impact. These domains include the following:

1   Unmet needs in the areas of housing, health care, dental care, social supports, work, leisure, education, and mental health care
2   Emergency services and hospital utilization
3   Psychiatric symptoms and problem behaviors, including substance abuse and encounters with law enforcement

The evaluation also requires the intensive case manager to report the key environmental barriers and client barriers to meeting each unmet need. These questions direct attention to issues of availability and accessibility of housing, health care, and so on, as well as to client skill deficits. The evaluation thus reinforces the intensive case manager's role as a rehabilitation practitioner and as the "manager" of a client's overall package of services and supports.

PRELIMINARY FINDINGS FOR NEW YORK

Results from the New York State evaluation of the Intensive Case Management program are preliminary. Because of different rates of implementation, baseline data do not yet adequately represent the entire state. Follow-up data are available only on a sample (n = 219), and control group results are not yet available. Nonetheless, early descriptive data are informative.

In terms of target population, it appears that the New York State ICM program is in fact reaching a very needy and difficult-to-serve group. Statewide, 8% of the ICM clients are homeless at admission; in New York City this number rises to 15%. Eighty-eight percent of ICM clients are classified as "heavy users" of emergency and inpatient services; and 21% are "extended-stay inpatients." Most are single (90%), unemployed (89%), and diagnosed with a major mental illness (90%). A surprisingly high proportion (79%) have more than one disabling condition: 40% and 37% have alcohol or substance abuse problems, respectively; 12% are physically disabled, and 6% are mentally retarded in addition to their psychiatric disability.[2] Virtually all ICM clients (99%) have been previously hospitalized. Preliminary comparisons indicate that the ICM program is serving people who are younger, who are more symptomatic, and who have more serious problems than individuals served in other New York State programs for persons diagnosed with serious and long-term mental illness.

At intake, clients have an average of four areas of "unmet needs." The highest levels of unmet need are in the areas of leisure, work, and social supports, with approximately three quarters of all clients indicating unmet needs in these areas. Almost half have needs for housing or education. The lowest areas of unmet need are for mental health services (39%), dental care (38%), and medical care (25%).

After the first 6-month follow-up assessment, the number of unmet needs had decreased significantly. Greatest progress was reported in the areas of mental health treatment, housing, and medical care, with approximately three quarters of the clients having these needs met within the first 6 months. The least progress was made in those areas that had the highest level of overall need at intake—leisure, work, and social supports.

In addition, a number of "new unmet needs" emerged at follow-up. Further investigation is required to determine whether these emergent needs resulted from the loss of supports that had existed at entry (e.g., the loss of housing) or a redefinition of what is possible for an individual (e.g., the recognition that now that living conditions are stabilized, the need for work could be seriously considered).

At 6 months, intensive case managers reported encountering environmental barriers to meeting clients needs 66% of the time, and client-centered barriers 79% of the time. Overall, lack of family support, adequate income, and transportation were the most frequently cited environmental barriers (25%, 23%, and 21%, respectively). The most common client-centered barriers were that the client disagreed with the case manager about the need (44%) or lacked necessary

[2]Total exceeds 100% as a result of multiple responses.

interpersonal skills (41%). Lack of adequate cognitive or instrumental skills was cited infrequently (16% and 15%, respectively).

It appears from the initial unmet-needs analysis that intensive case managers are dealing simultaneously with issues of access and client reluctance to use services. For example, while insufficient income or insurance was a major barrier to accessing health and dental care (80% and 73% of reported cases), clients also refused these services in a high percentage of cases (57% and 68%). Similarly, while restrictive program eligibility requirements were a barrier to accessing mental health services for a quarter of all clients with unmet needs in this area, 45% of these clients refused the services that were available.

In terms of utilization of inpatient treatment, both total inpatient days and total admissions decreased significantly when the first 6 months after ICM enrollment were compared to the 6 months prior to enrollment (for individuals who had at least one admission during either the pre- or post-ICM period). Although cost of the ICM program is high, early results suggest that significant cost reductions are being realized. In addition, several county-based evaluations have reported significant decreases in the number of days in jail for ICM clients and in the number of emergency room contacts.

Changes in symptoms and behaviors were also noted. At 6 months, reported incidents of alcohol and substance abuse had significantly decreased, as had the number of reported "behavioral problems." At 1 year, "potentially harmful behaviors" had also decreased significantly from baseline.

After 6 months, there were no significant differences seen on any of the symptom scales of the Brief Psychiatric Rating Scale. After a year, however, clients were reported to be significantly less withdrawn ($p < .05$), and a trend was seen toward a reduction in anxiety/depression ($p = .056$).

CONCLUSIONS

There are many reasons why individuals with serious, long-term psychiatric disabilities have at times failed to thrive in community settings. Many have not had access to community mental health services (either by choice or exclusion), or to basic social supports such as adequate housing. For some, lack of a continuous helping relationship has led to loss of critical community supports during crises or rehospitalizations. For others, opportunities for positive growth have been limited by the lack of care givers skilled in the technology of psychiatric rehabilitation.

Case management offers a potential vehicle for rehabilitation, defined broadly as the process of helping people with disabilities to develop the skills and supports they need to accomplish their life goals. Although not originally conceived as a rehabilitation intervention, case management has evolved as a social policy response to the fact that persons with serious disabilities often have difficulty in accessing the basic supports that are necessary for successful community living. Until such access is ensured, rehabilitation efforts are difficult.

Case management is essentially program structure. In order to be effective with persons with psychiatric disabilities, case managers must have a wide variety of skills, including the attitudes and skills necessary to perform rehabilitative activities (Anthony, Cohen, Farkas, & Cohen, 1989). Nonetheless, as a modality for service delivery, case management has several distinctive features that increase its potential as a rehabilitation intervention.

Case managers are the single point of responsibility for ensuring a broad range of outcomes for their clients, are expected to take a holistic approach to their clients' needs, and have the autonomy to provide flexible, individualized interventions. Case management programs are often designed to provide outreach to persons who will not use more formal or structured programs, thereby engaging them in the initial phases of rehabilitation. The tasks of case management also require an effective integration of clinical sensitivity and attention to concrete issues, a combination that appears to be critical to the successful rehabilitation of persons with serious disabilities or multiple, complex problems.

Case management is also appealing to policymakers, who see it as a potential mechanism for more effectively managing the care and rehabilitation of high-risk, hard-to-serve populations. Case management simultaneously attempts to reduce unnecessary expenditures on inpatient care and to increase access to services and supports that are necessary for rehabilitation. To the extent that case managers succeed, both the individual and the mental health system should benefit.

REFERENCES

Anthony, W. A., Cohen M., Farkas M., & Cohen, B. F. (1988). Case management—more than a response to a dysfunctional system. *Community Mental Health Journal, 24*(3), 219–228.

Bachrach, L. (1989). Case management: Toward a shared definition. *Hospital and Community Psychiatry, 40*(9), 883–884.

Blanch, A. (1986). *Community mental health ideology and administration of state mental health services: Changes in state mental health agencies from 1960–1984.* Unpublished doctoral dissertation.

Caton, C. L. M. (1981). The new chronic patient and the system of community care. *Hospital and Community Psychiatry, 32*(7), 475–478.

Department of Health and Human Services, Health Care Financing Administration. (1988). *State Medicaid manual: Pt. 4. Services* - at ¶ 14, 604C, revised 9-90. Washington, DC: Author.

Hyde, P. (1990). Defining case management. *Hospital and Community Psychiatry, 41*(4), 453.

Love, R. E. (1984). The Community Support Program: Strategy for reform? In J. A. Talbott (Ed.), *The chronic mental patient—five years later.* Orlando, FL: Grune and Stratton.

National Institute of Mental Health. (1989). *Guidelines for planning and implementing case management systems, P.L. 99-660, Title V.* Rockville, MD: Adamha Publications.

Olfson, M. (1990). Assertive community treatment: An evaluation of the experimental evidence. *Hospital and Community Psychiatry, 41*(6), 634–641.

Omnibus Budget Reconciliation Act of 1986 (OBRA). P.L. 99-509, October 21, 1986.

Ozarin, L. D. (1982) Mental health in public health: The federal perspective. In M. O. Wagenfeld, P. V. Lemkaw, & B. Justice (Eds.), *Public mental health perspectives and prospects.* Beverly Hills: Sage Publications.

Robinson, G. K., Bergman, G. T., & Scallett, L. J. (1989). *Choices in case management.* Washington, DC: Policy Resources Incorporated.

Talbott, J. A. (1980). Toward a public policy on the chronic mentally ill patient. *American Journal of Orthopsychiatry, 50*(1), 43–53.

Taube, C. A., Morlock, L., Burns, B. J., and & Santos, A. B. (1990). New directions in research on assertive community treatment. *Hospital and Community Psychiatry, 41*(6), 642–647.

Test, M. A. (1981). Effective community treatment of the chronically mentally ill: What is necessary? *Journal of Social Issues, 37*(3), 71–86.

Thompson, K. S., Griffith, E. E. H., & Leaf, P. J. (1990). A historical review of the Madison model of community care. *Hospital and Community Psychiatry, 41*(6), 625–634.

Turner, J. C., & Ten Hoor, W. J. (1978). The NIMH Community Support Program: Pilot approach to a needed social reform. *Schizophrenia Bulletin, 4,* 319–348.

Vischi, T. R., & Stockdill, J. (1989). The financing of comprehensive community support systems: A review of major strategies. *Psychosocial Rehabilitation Journal, 12*(3), 83–92.

Wagenfeld, M. O., & Jacobs, J. H. (1982). The community mental health movement: Its origins and growth. In M. O. Wagenfeld, P. V. Lemkaw, & B. Justice (Eds.), *Public mental health perspectives and prospects.* Beverly Hills: Sage Publications.

Part Three

Group and Family Therapy in Rehabilitation

Chapter 10

Behavioral Group Therapy in Rehabilitation Settings

Dennis Upper and John V. Flowers

An important development in psychiatric rehabilitation has been the increasing use of behavioral group therapy techniques, which combine psychological and educational methods to change behavior and to teach a variety of adaptive skills. The term "behavioral group therapy" has had three primary definitions during the course of development of this field. In its first (and most common) meaning, behavioral group therapy refers to the application in a group setting of behavior change techniques that initially were developed in individual therapy, such as systematic desensitization. When defined in this way, behavioral group therapy usually is directive, interpretive, and focused on the behaviors of individual group members. Goldstein, Heller, and Sechrest (1966) have referred to this as the process of doing behavior therapy *in* groups, as opposed to doing it *through* groups.

A second meaning of behavioral group therapy has been the use of specific behavioral interventions within an existing therapy group, regardless of the therapeutic orientation being used. Usually, one behavioral intervention (such as conditioning against silence or reinforcing the use of "I" statements) is used, and all of the other interventions are not specifically behavioral. Although this therapy is done *through* groups, it is not really behavioral group therapy. Instead, it is some form of traditional group therapy that is made potentially more effective by the limited use of behavioral principles.

A third type of behavioral group therapy, which does not fully exist at present but is still emerging and developing, involves both applying behavioral techniques in a group setting in the most effective and cost-efficient manner and attempting to enhance therapeutic outcome by manipulating group-process variables in some planned ways. In this case, the patients, problems may be homogeneous or heterogeneous, but the interventions are specific and systematic, matched to the problems of the individual patients, executed by the entire group, and based on learning principles (Flowers, 1979).

The specific behavior therapy techniques used to help a patient are often quite similar in individual and group work. In fact, the majority of behavioral group therapy cases reported in the early literature involved the direct transfer of individually oriented procedures (such as systematic desensitization) to a group of patients with similar problems (such as phobias or problems with assertiveness).

However, in spite of similarities among the behavioral methods used in individual and group therapy situations, it is clear that communicating the techniques to the patients often requires differences in timing and presentation, and that the group therapist has to assume the additional task of structuring the group experience in such a way as to enhance patients' chances of reaching their treatment goals (Frankel & Glasser, 1974). Specifically, this involves establishing group goals that create an atmosphere that encourages and reinforces patients' helping each another. The therapist can establish these goals by attending carefully to the selection of patients, the specific problem areas to be dealt with in the group, and the techniques that will be used to reinforce cohesiveness, cooperation among members, attendance, and other appropriate group-related behaviors.

ADVANTAGES OF DOING BEHAVIOR THERAPY IN GROUPS

There are a number of distinct advantages to doing behavior therapy in a group setting. For one, in addition to saving the therapist's time and effort, the group therapy situation offers greater opportunities for behavioral rehearsal and modeling. Systematic role-playing can be used in the group to help patients practice new behaviors in a therapeutic atmosphere before testing these behaviors in their natural environments. Behavioral rehearsals provide the opportunity for vicarious learning by all the group members and may result in further saving of therapy time. The group situation also offers unique opportunities to facilitate generalization of new behaviors because of the variety of participants with whom the patient can practice new ways of behaving. The other group members also can provide controlled behavioral feedback, which often is more effective than a single therapist's feedback in helping the patient to develop more appropriate behaviors, and frequently a greater number of alternate solutions to problems can be generated from group discussion than from individual therapy.

Another advantage of the group approach is that group members can support and help one another in their attempts to achieve their treatment goals. One side benefit of this is that members may learn that their problems are not unique and that they are not alone in their unhappiness. In some behavioral groups, members are encouraged to remind each other outside of the therapy situation to fulfill their behavioral assignments, and this type of approach can be extended, using structured homework assignments, so that group members can observe and reinforce each other in actual problem situations. For example, one group member with appropriate assertiveness skills can be paired with another member who is weak in this area in order to help the latter perform a behavioral assignment, such as returning an item to a department store. Further research of this type may demonstrate that pairing two differently skilled group members in this manner will increase the probability that behavioral assignments will be completed by both.

Another advantage of the group therapy is that it offers the opportunity for a far more thorough behavioral analysis than does individual therapy. When dealing with patients individually, the therapist is able to observe their behavior in relation to only one person, the therapist, which gives little information about their possible responses to other people. Patients may be able to report a great deal about other interactions, but there may be certain behavior patterns of which they are hardly aware, either of the behavior itself or of the relationship between their behavior and the feelings, attitudes, and behavior of others in response to it. The group situation gives both patients and therapist (as well as the other group members) an opportunity to directly observe their behavior in a variety of interpersonal situations, thus providing information that can significantly enhance the formulation and application of treatment strategies.

Another benefit derived from the group approach is the increased opportunity for social reinforcement and motivational stimulation. For example, just as group pressure motivates patients to attempt new behaviors, group approval serves as a powerful reinforcer of those behaviors, further increasing the probability that they will be repeated and will generalize to other situations. A patient who has begun to respond to group pressure not only receives reinforcement through direct statements of approval but, more importantly, is reinforced by being accepted for having tried, which makes him or her feel more a part of the group. The feeling of belonging or cohesiveness that develops may further increase the motivational and reinforcing power of the group (Goldstein & Wolpe, 1971).

In addition to the general benefits deriving from the group approach, there are a number of ways in which the group situation may serve to enhance the effectiveness of a particular treatment technique. For example, Paul and Shannon (1966) gave several reasons why a group approach is valuable when applying systematic desensitization: (a) the construction of hierarchies through group discussion is particularly effective, since hierarchies are set up to include the most common situational elements of all the patients in the group, with items geared to the most anxious members; (b) individuals can practice new skills in the group setting after a degree of relaxation has been achieved; and (c) there is immediate reinforcement from the other members for changes in behavior and attitudes, which is not possible in individual systematic desensitization.

Rose and LeCroy (1985) noted that one of the major advantages of the group as the context of treatment for children is the opportunity to provide the members with a large number of reinforcing activities that usually are unavailable to the isolated child in treatment. Even such individualized activities as the making of airplane models appear to be more reinforcing when others are present. Except for the highly withdrawn or autistic child, who usually is not treated in groups, most young patients value interactive over isolated activities. As a result, interactive social activities or group tasks comprise one of the major opportunities for reinforcement in group treatment.

Another example of the ways in which the group situation may serve to enhance the effectiveness of a particular type of treatment was offered by Connors, Maisto, Sobell, and Sobell (1985). They noted that, in the treatment of drunk-driving offenders, group input to individualized problem-solving exercises and drink-refusal training can significantly enhance the acquisition of new drinking-related behaviors.

Although much has been written about the advantages of doing behavior therapy in groups, potential disadvantages of behavioral group therapy have been pointed out by a number of authors. For example, Lieberman (1975) argued that the therapist may have difficulty remaining in control of the group situation and that whether the group reinforces appropriate behavior or not may be more a function of group norms than of group therapist input. Another potential problem with group therapy was raised by Kelly (1982), who stated that skills training in groups may be difficult with individuals who exhibit varying rates of skills acquisition; a pace geared for slow learners may bore the quicker learners, whereas a faster pace may frustrate slow learners. Finally, Trower, Bryant, and Argyle (1978) specified two possible disadvantages of group social skills training: (a) the poor or inappropriate modeling that might be exhibited by group members; and (b) loss of flexibility in dealing with individual problems.

THEORETICAL FOUNDATIONS OF BEHAVIORAL GROUP THERAPY

Behavioral group therapy as it currently exists is the result of a coming together of data and methods from a variety of theoretical, clinical, and research sources. An important early influence among these was the inquiry of traditional group therapists into the curative factors operating in group therapy, which had the underlying rationale that the identification of these factors would lead to the development of systematic guidelines for the tactics and strategy of the therapist.

For example, Corsini and Rosenberg (1959) abstracted the curative factors from 300 pre-1955 group therapy articles and found 175 factors, which they clustered into nine major categories:

1 Acceptance (or group cohesiveness)
2 Universalization (or perceived similarity to others)
3 Reality testing
4 Altruism (or helping one another)
5 Transference
6 Spectator therapy (or imitative behavior)
7 Interaction (or interpersonal learning)
8 Intellectualization (or imparting of information)
9 Ventilation (or catharsis)

Not satisfied merely to identify curative factors in group therapy, clinicians and researchers went on to investigate a number of factors thought to be related to these curative factors. For example, the issue of whether the therapist's theoretical orientation affected the curative factors operating in the group was investigated by Fiedler (1950), Heine (1953), and Truax and Carkhuff (1967). Studies that compared patients' views of the curative factors operating in the group with therapists' views were carried out by Berzon, Pious, and Parson (1963) and Dickoff and Lakin (1963). Yalom (1970), in his comprehensive book on group therapy, outlined further studies of how different curative factors operate in different types of groups, at different stages of the group's development, inside and outside of the group, and with different types of patients. Out of these fundamental attempts to identify the curative factors in group therapy and their various parameters grew a series of studies in which group therapists attempted to *manipulate* some aspects of the group process in a systematic way, with the eventual goal of enhancing the group's therapeutic effectiveness.

There are four main therapeutic movements that appear to have converged with the increasing use of behavioral techniques to provide treatment in groups and to enhance its effectiveness: (a) the operant conditioning approach of Skinner; (b) the systematic experiential learning of Truax and Carkhuff and of Bandura; (c) the cognitive-behavioral rehearsal of Wolpe and Lazarus; and (d) didactic teaching approaches.

Operant Conditioning

In the case of operant conditioning, a variety of approaches (used singly or in combination) have proved effective in modifying rate of speech, speech content, duration of silences, group cohesion, and a number of other variables relevant to the group therapy process. One of the earliest group studies that demonstrated that rate of speaking could be modified as a function of reinforcement was reported by McNair (1957), who used a bell tone to signify "approval." Other studies have shown that, by using a tone to indicate approval and a buzzer to indicate disapproval, one could transfer the leadership role within a group (by increasing a target member's rate of speaking), modify members' sequence of speaking, and increase the amount of disagreement among members (Shapiro, 1963, 1964; Shapiro & Leiderman, 1964).

Oakes, Droge, and August (1960, 1961) used signal-light flashes, which were visible to all group members and described as indicating the degree of "insight" of their remarks, to reinforce various response classes. They demonstrated that the conclusions reached by group members could be manipulated, that the prestige of the signaler exerted significant influence on the reinforcing properties of the light, and that a specific class of behavior (e.g., giving opinions) could be increased by using this type of signal-light reinforcement.

Heckel, Wiggins, and Salzberg (1962) showed that negative reinforcement (that is, the turning off of a negative stimulus) could be used effectively to eliminate long silences in a therapy group; the procedure consisted of surreptitiously introducing a noxious noise (a drilling noise from the hallway) whenever the group fell silent for more than 10 seconds, and then turning off the noise as soon as a group member broke the silence.

Liberman (1970a), in a classic study involving two matched groups of neurotics, trained one group of therapists to use social reinforcement to facilitate the development of group cohesiveness (also referred to as intimacy, solidarity, and affection), while a second, control group of therapists used conventional group therapy methods. Results indicated that patients in the social reinforcement groups showed significantly more cohesiveness and earlier symptomatic improvement than patients in the conventional groups. In a related study (Liberman, 1970b), prompting and social reinforcement from the therapist proved effective in increasing the frequency of verbal expressions of hostility toward the therapist, which was seen as another measure of group cohesiveness. Liberman argued that data from these studies indicated the potency of the therapist in shaping and modifying group dynamic behaviors and supported the usefulness of a reinforcement or learning approach to the understanding of group therapy.

Systematic Experiential Learning and Modeling

Another theoretical trend that has been incorporated into the behavioral group process is systematic experiential learning and modeling. Carkhuff (1971) has asserted that training patients and "significant others" in their environments using systematic programs in interpersonal skills can be more effective than unstructured learning in producing lasting increases in adaptive behaviors. As far as group therapy is concerned, the systematic experiential learning approach of Truax, Carkhuff, and their colleagues has emphasized such variables and techniques as role-playing exercises; feedback; and enhancement of empathy, warmth, and genuineness in a variety of populations of therapists and patients.

For example, Truax (1962, 1962a) has proposed *vicarious therapy pretraining* (VTP) as a means of providing standard cognitive and experiential structuring of "how to be a good patient" and as a way of quickly engaging the patient in the group therapy process. VTP simply involves presenting to prospective patients a 30-minute audiotape recording of excerpts of "good patient" in-therapy behavior. It provides a vicarious experience of how patients explore their problems and feelings, as well as of how they can prove helpful to each other during group therapy. A study by Truax and Carkhuff (1965b) indicated the therapeutic value of VTP aimed at teaching new group therapy patients those behaviors that are thought to be desirable in a therapeutic encounter.

Similar modeling/reinforcement techniques have been shown to be effective in increasing or decreasing patients' verbal expressions of feeling (Schwartz & Hawkins, 1965), modifying the degree to which patients admitted to having problems (Marlatt, Jacobsen, Johnson, & Morrice, 1966), and producing significant increases in social interactive behaviors (Gutride, Goldstein, & Hunter, 1973).

Goldstein and his colleagues (1967) discussed the advantages of using "planted" patients in a therapy group to enact those behaviors that would be most therapeutic for the other group members to copy. During the course of two ongoing therapy groups, a wide variety of potentially therapeutic roles for the planted patients was developed. When necessary, the planted patients reassured, attacked, befriended, argued with, yielded to, or encouraged other patients, or elaborated in detail on their own supposed psychopathology. The planted patients aided in quieting monopolizers, permitted themselves to be "intimidated" by patients in need of assertiveness experiences, augmented feelings of group cohesiveness, assisted in clique busting and clique formation, and encouraged other patients to bring material that had been revealed to the plants before or after sessions into the group sessions proper. Data from a post-therapy-session questionnaire indicated that, while neither of the two planted patients was chosen as the most popular or best-liked group member, both were consistently seen across sessions as the most protherapeutic patients in their respective groups.

Cognitive-Behavioral Rehearsal

A third set of therapeutic techniques adapted from individual behavior therapy to comprise an important foundation for behavioral group therapy involve cognitive-behavioral rehearsal. The potential for simultaneous group cognitive rehearsal by individuals with similar problems was demonstrated by an impressive early study by Lazarus (1961), who randomly assigned matched groups of phobic patients to either a group desensitization or a group interpretation condition. In the desensitization groups, several patients with the same phobia (e.g., claustrophobia) were treated simultaneously, and the therapist took an upward step in the hierarchy only when each patient in the group could endure a particular imagined scene without anxiety. The group desensitization procedures were found to be significantly more effective than the group interpretation methods in overcoming the phobic reactions. About two thirds of the desensitization group patients overcame their phobias in a mean of 20.4 sessions, as opposed to only 2 of 17 interpretation group patients who were symptom-free after a mean of 22 sessions.

Lazarus extended this treatment procedure, with equally impressive results, to a group of four patients who had four different phobias. These patients, after participating in group relaxation training, received the items of their relevant anxiety hierarchies on slips of paper. Each group member was instructed to read the description of the scene, and with closed eyes to try to imagine that situation without feeling anxious. Those who were able to imagine the situation without undue anxiety were then handed a description of a more difficult anxiety situation. In this manner, the group members were able to proceed at their own pace.

Group systematic desensitization and cognitive-behavioral rehearsal (often including in vivo exercises) have also been found to be effective in treating fear of flying (Denholtz & Mann, 1974), sexual dysfunction (Lobitz & Baker, 1979), test anxiety (Russell & Lent, 1982), snake phobia (Odom, Nelson, & Wein, 1978), and a variety of other behavioral disorders. In general, group desensitization using imagery has proved to be about equally as effective as individually administered desensitization, but often more sessions are required for groups because the group procedure is slower than individual treatment. Emmelkamp and Kuipers (1985) have noted, however, that because imaginal systematic desensitization is less effective than other behavioral procedures (e.g., in vivo exposure), group-administered systematic desensitization is probably for the most part of historical interest.

Didactic Teaching

A fourth stream of influence for behavioral group therapy has been didactic teaching, which can include not only specific information about behavioral problems or treatment techniques but also advice, suggestions, or direct guidance about life problems that is offered by the therapist or other patients. An early example of this was the early group work of Maxwell Jones (1944), who lectured his group patients about the structure and function of the central nervous system and its relevance to their psychiatric symptoms. Marsh (1935) and Klapman (1950) also reported forms of didactic group therapy in which formal lectures, homework assignments, and grading procedures were employed.

Recovery, Inc., a self-help group organized along didactic lines, was founded in the 1930s by Abraham Low. There is no formal professional guidance at Recovery, Inc., meetings, and leaders are chosen from among the membership. However, the proceedings of the meetings are highly structured, and parts of Low's textbook *Mental Health through Will Training* (1950) are read aloud and discussed at each meeting.

Didactic instruction in therapy groups not only has been employed to impart information, to structure the group, and to explain the nature of psychological problems, but often functions as the initial binding force in the group until the other curative factors become operative (Yalom, 1970). And, in part, explanation and clarification can serve as curative agents in their own right. For example, Malamud and Machover (1965) set up what they called "workshops in self-understanding" for patients drawn from a psychiatric clinic's waiting list. The workshop consisted of 15 two-hour sessions, and its goal was to prepare patients for group psychotherapy by clarifying reasons for psychological dysfunction, as well as to teach methods for self-exploration. This format not only was successful in preparing patients for subsequent group therapy but proved to be an effective treatment modality in and of itself; after completing the workshop, many patients felt sufficiently improved that no further treatment was required.

Probably the first type of behavioral groups that relied primarily on didactic and skills-training procedures as relaxation training groups, but it wasn't long before these so-called psychoeducational groups were being used effectively to treat a wide variety of patients with a broad range of behavioral problems. For example, psychoeducational groups have been used effectively in the areas of stress management and coping skills, social skills (for both children and adults), weight reduction, smoking, Type A behavior, alcohol abuse, panic anxiety and agoraphobia, headaches, chronic pain management, irritable bowel syndrome, marital and parenting skills, depression, and eating disorders, among others. All of these groups, however, have similar components: bibliotherapy and the use of structured treatment manuals, self-monitoring and behavioral recording, assignment of homework exercises, and reinforcement of attendance and compliance.

OPERATIONALIZING AND MANIPULATING GROUP-PROCESS VARIABLES

It has been only relatively recently that group therapy researchers have attempted to develop operational definitions of certain group-process variables or to manipulate them in some systematic ways in order to determine how this would affect treatment outcome, with the eventual goal of enhancing the group's therapeutic effectiveness. This section of the chapter will be devoted to reviewing such efforts with regard to five group-process variables: cohesiveness, self-disclosure, valence of messages (positive or negative), syntax of messages, and amount of activity within the group.

Cohesiveness

Cohesiveness (or cohesion) is a widely researched but poorly understood basic property of groups. Several hundred research articles exploring cohesiveness have been written and contain a variety of definitions of the term. In general, however, there is agreement that therapy groups differ from one another in the amount of cohesiveness present. Members of groups with greater cohesiveness tend to value the group more highly and to defend it against internal or external threats; voluntary attendance, participation, and mutual help all are said to be greater in more cohesive groups. Cohesiveness appears to grow out of shared group experience, a process that results in earned trust and a feeling of safety in the group. A cohesive group is supposed to provide the basis for meaningful self-exploration, the giving and receiving of interpersonal feedback, and a sense of being understood and valued (Sansbury, 1979). In this sense, some authors have hypothesized that cohesiveness in group therapy is the analogue of the "relationship" in individual therapy.

One of the first authors to examine the process of cohesiveness from a social learning point of view was Bernice Lott, who wrote an article entitled "Group Cohesiveness: A Learning Phenomenon" in 1961. Lott defined cohesiveness in terms of the number and strength of mutual positive attitudes among the members of the group. She used reinforcement theory to explain how these mutual positive attitudes develop, as well as to derive a number of hypotheses about what the consequences of different levels of group cohesiveness will be. Among these are (a) that more cohesive groups will be characterized by higher levels of communication among members and by a higher level of activity in general; (b) that more efficient learning will take place in high-cohesion than in low-cohesion groups; and (c) that the more cohesive the group, the greater the probability that members will develop uniform opinions and other behaviors with respect to matters of importance to the group.

There followed in the group therapy literature a series of studies in which various independent variables were manipulated in order to try to increase group cohesiveness. Although there has been little or no replication, some tentative conclusions can be drawn from these studies. Liberman's studies (1970a, b, 1971) suggest that group cohesiveness can be increased by socially reinforcing patients' verbal statements that contain high cohesive content, such as "we" statements. Studies by Dies and Hess (1971) and by Snortum and Myers (1971) suggest that frequent or sustained interactions among group members can increase cohesion. A Yalom and Rand study (1966) indicates that original compatibility among members (i.e., choosing patients who are similar to begin with) helps to build group cohesiveness, and a Kahn and Rudestem study (1971) suggests that increased self-disclosure enhances the development of cohesiveness.

Most studies of this type, however—whether inferential or correlational—have tended to treat cohesiveness as if it were a single variable and to measure it by a single measure. Flowers and his colleagues have carried out a series of studies (reviewed in Flowers, 1979) based on the belief that cohesiveness is a construct that can best be understood by identifying and operationalizing a set of variables that can be studied systematically over group sessions. Flowers and his group have identified the following eight variables, which seem to differ significantly between high-cohesion and low-cohesion sessions and which can produce greater feelings of cohesiveness when manipulated:

1 Increased percentage of eye contact with the person who is speaking
2 Increased percentage of patient-to-patient interactions (vs. patient-to-therapist or therapist-to-patient)
3 Increased use of negative feedback by the entire group
4 Deceased number of group members who repeatedly give or receive negative messages
5 Increased disclosure of problems
6 Increased flexibility in patients' patterns of activity from session to session
7 Increased number of group members trusted
8 Increased self-reported satisfaction with sessions or groups

In some of these cases, it is quite clear how a given component may influence group cohesiveness and affect treatment outcome, while in other cases, the effects may not be so apparent. For example, increasing attentiveness to the speaker could increase the amount of attention the speaker receives when disclosing problems, thus reinforcing the behavior of self-disclosure. As for its effect outside of the group, attentiveness to the speaker is a skill often taught by assertion trainers in order to improve social communication.

Increasing self-disclosure (within limits) gives the group the material with which to work and operationally demonstrates the disclosing member's trust of the group. Outside of the group, appropriately increased disclosure can lead to more intimate and presumably more fulfilling relationships.

To understand the beneficial effects of an increased use of negative feedback, however, we must take into account that there is also a decreased number of group members who repeatedly give or receive negative messages in the higher-cohesion sessions. In other words, negative feedback is distributed more "democratically" across the group in higher-cohesion sessions. Moreover, negative feedback is employed as help-intended communication, which means behaviorally that negative statements are delivered with accompanying positive feedback for the purpose of teaching discrimination to both the giver and the receiver. Thus, negative feedback is increased in a higher-cohesion session because it is safer and because group members want to tell each other what they agree and disagree with, and what they think will work and will not work. An additional way in which the increase of negative feedback may be helpful is in terms of desensitizing the patient to criticism received outside of the group, in the natural environment.

In addition to its importance in the process analysis of group therapy, cohesiveness also is important because studies have shown that patients improve more on problems they discuss in higher-cohesion groups or sessions than on problems they discuss in low-cohesion groups or sessions (Flowers, Booraem, & Hartman, 1981). Simply put, increased group cohesiveness leads to increased group effectiveness in terms of patient outcome. Operationalizing cohesiveness allows the therapist to manipulate this important variable. As more operational components are found to be a part of the cohesiveness network, more methods of influencing group process will be available to the group leader.

Self-Disclosure

Another variable that has been given increasing attention of late by behavioral group therapists is self-disclosure. Self-disclosure, which is both feared and valued by group participants, plays an integral part in all group therapies. Culbert (1967) offered the following definition:

> Self-disclosure refers to an individual's explicitly communicating to one or more others some personal information that he believes these others would be unlikely to acquire unless he himself discloses it. Moreover, this information must be personally private; that is, it must be of such a nature that it is not something the individual would disclose to everyone who might inquire about it. (p. 18)

The content of the self-disclosure may include past or current events in one's life, fantasy or dream material, hopes or aspirations for the future, or current feelings toward other individuals.

A number of research studies have indicated the general importance of self-disclosure in group therapy. For example, Hurley (1967) found that patients who are high disclosers in the early sessions of a therapy group often assume high popularity in their group, and popularity has been shown to correlate positively with treatment outcome. Peres (1947) demonstrated that successfully treated patients in group therapy had made almost twice as many self-disclosing personal statements during the course of the group as did unsuccessfully treated patients, and Truax and Carkhuff (1965a) also found that patients' success in group therapy correlated with their "transparency" (or degree of self-disclosure) during the course of the group. Lieberman, Yalom, and Miles (1973) found that, in encounter groups, individuals who had negative outcomes revealed less of themselves than did the other participants.

While self-disclosure obviously is a part of all group therapy, very little work has been done on how to systematically elicit frequent and relevant disclosures. This may not seem to be an important issue to therapists working with moderately troubled, intelligent, verbal patients; however, most mental health services are delivered to patients who are more disturbed, less verbal, and less intelligent. A number of studies have indicated that self-disclosure occurs more frequently in groups with a high proportion of patient-to-patient interactions (Flowers, Booraem, Brown, & Harris, 1974), which suggests the strategy of attempting to increase this type of interaction directly through the use of techniques such as vicarious therapy pretraining, planted patients, modeling, and social reinforcement. Since self-disclosure also occurs more frequently in groups with higher levels of cohesiveness, this suggests the programmed use of some of the techniques noted above for increasing session or overall group cohesiveness.

Beyond encouraging patient-to-patient interactions and facilitating the development of group cohesiveness, another technique that can be used to increase self-disclosure rates is the use of problem cards, as suggested by Goodman (1969). Prior to the group session, each member may be asked to write down on an index card two current problems, one judged to be more difficult or immediate and one judged to be less difficult or immediate. When asked to disclose, the patient can choose to discuss either written problem, to disclose something else that has come to mind, or to disclose nothing at all. The problem cards serve multiple purposes. First, they serve as a prompt and a pregroup preparation. In comparing groups with no cards, groups with one problem on a card, and groups with two problems listed, it has been found that (a) members disclose least frequently in groups without problem cards, and each disclosure takes longer for the group to assess; (b) problems are disclosed somewhat more frequently in groups where members write one problem prior to group and problems are easier to assess, but some members still may refuse to disclose; and (c) the highest rate of self-disclosure and the lowest rates of refusal to disclose occur in groups where members bring in cards with two problems written.

Second, listing problems on the card serves as an initial method of operationalizing the problems. Using index cards rather than sheets of paper requires greater brevity and often clearer operationalization by the writer. Finally, use of a card with two problems gives the patient a choice other than "I will" or "I will not" share with the group. Studies by Flowers and his group have shown that the combined use of cohesion facilitation, increased patient-to-patient interaction, and problem cards elicits two to four times as many disclosures as in comparison groups, thus giving the therapist and the group more of the initial material they need to conduct the therapy group (Flowers, 1975).

Instructions and modeling also may be employed to facilitate self-disclosure. Whalen (1969) studied the degree of self-disclosure in leaderless groups of four students each under four different experimental conditions. One set of groups was exposed to a filmed model of interpersonal openness, a second to detailed written instructions concerning self-disclosure, a third to both instructions and the film, and a fourth to neither instructions nor the film. The 12-minute film portrayed four students talking at a highly personal level, describing their anxieties and feeding back their impressions, whether positive, negative, or neutral, to the other group members. Results indicated that exposure to both instructions and the filmed model was the only condition effective in facilitating self-disclosure and inhibiting impersonal discussion; there were virtually no differences between the groups receiving only the film or only the instructions and control groups. The implication of this and similar studies for the group therapist is that it may be necessary to accompany the modeling process with some form of instruction to the patients in order to facilitate maximally the individual and group process variable being modeled.

Valence of Messages

Another group process variable that has been studied involves the frequency and distribution patterns of positive, negative, and neutral messages exchanged by group members and the effects of these patterns on members' behavior both in and out of the group. These patterns can be assessed in two ways: external raters can be used to judge whether a message sent during the group was positive, negative, or neutral, or group members can gather these data themselves as the group is proceeding. Because external raters (whether rating live or from video-tapes or audiotapes) are not always available, the following procedure was developed by Flowers and his coworkers to allow group members to collect this information.

In each session, patients and therapists are given 20 red and 20 blue tokens (2 inch × 2 inch pieces of stiff construction paper) and are instructed to give these tokens along with verbal statements they make to other group members. A blue token is given with each statement intended as positive (e.g., a compliment) and a red token with each statement intended as negative (e.g., a criticism). All tokens received by a patient are deposited in a container in front of the patient for a later count. Each group member has a can for this purpose, and each patient's tokens are numbered, so that the following information is available after each group session: the total number of red and blue tokens each patient distributed, to whom the patient gave them, how many tokens of each type the patient received, and from whom the patient received them.

From the number of tokens given and received, an objective rating of each patient's role during each session can be determined in the following manner:

1 Patient input role is determined by the percentage of blue and red tokens received. When a patient's percentage of blue tokens received is one standard deviation above the group mean for that session, that performance is labeled *positive input* (i.e., the patient got proportionately more positive feedback than the average group member for that session). When a patient's percentage of red tokens received is one standard deviation above the group mean for that session, the performance is labeled *negative input* (i.e., the patient got more negative feedback than the average group member for that session).

2 Patient output role is determined by the proportion of blue tokens to total tokens given. With the same guidelines as above, the patient's output is labeled as positive, negative, or balanced for each session.

Data from various studies that employed this procedure (Flowers & Booraem, 1976; Flowers, Booraem, Brown, & Harris, 1974; Flowers, Booraem, & Seacat, 1974) yield a set of consistent findings:

1   Overall, group therapy is more effective in terms of patient change if there is an increase in the percentage of valenced (positive and negative) messages employed by the entire group. Individual patients demonstrating the most improvement are those with the highest levels of such valenced input.

2   On specific problems, input can be more powerful (i.e., more effective in terms of patient change) if it is from other patients rather than from the therapists.

3   A high proportion (when compared to the group session mean) of negative messages delivered to a single patient reduces that patient's ability to hear the delivered messages; however, negative messages delivered to the therapists are heard very clearly, probably because of different learning histories.

4   Individuals (including therapists) who deliver a high proportion of negative messages also are less receptive to group input than are other group members.

In summary, an increase in the proportion of positive to negative messages, especially if that increase is from other group members, is beneficial to the group in terms of patient change. However, any imbalance in valenced messages compared to the group norm, in terms of messages either sent or received, is not beneficial. Thus, the most effective groups are those that employ a high proportion of valenced messages but employ them "democratically," that is without a disproportionate number being either sent or received by any particular group member.

Behavioral Analysis of Syntax

A behavioral analysis of the syntax of messages exchanged in groups is important because differences in syntax often determine differences in therapeutic approach. Of the most common forms of speech—questions, interpretations, self-disclosures, reflections, and advice—one would expect to find a high proportion of interpretations in analytic group therapy and a high proportion of reflection in Rogerian or "active-listening" groups. One would also expect to find a high proportion of advice (often in instructional form) in behavioral groups. All types of groups probably would employ questions for information gathering; however, within the large class of questions, one would expect analytic groups to emphasize "why" questions and behavioral groups to employ "what" questions.

Results from an early study (Flowers, 1975) were somewhat different from this prediction. Analytic group therapists did use more interpretation than behavioral group therapists; however, so did patient-centered therapists. Among the three group therapy types, there were no differences in the amount of advice used, but there was a clear difference in the type of advice used. Both analytic and patient-centered therapists used more pure advice, whereas behavioral therapists used more instructions and alternatives. "Instruction" is used here to mean a clear step-by-step procedure that a patient can follow to accomplish a specified task, and "alternatives" is used to mean at least two choices of action that the patient is offered rather than being told what to do.

In the analytic groups, the most common advice was in the form of "You should . . . ," whereas the most common advice in the patient-centered groups was in the form of "If I were you, I would. . . ." In both the analytic and the patient-centered groups, the time in this phase of the group was spent in various forms of persuasion; in the behavioral groups, time was spent primarily either in generating alternatives or in clarifying instructions. The behavioral group therapists in this study were not doing behavior therapy in the group but were attempting to conduct group therapy employing behavioral principles. Thus, the data may not be representative of behavior therapists doing a single behavioral intervention (e.g., assertiveness training) in a group of homogeneous patients.

Additionally, behavioral group therapists employed more questions than did either analytic or patient-centered group therapists. However, the time a patient spent answering behavioral group therapists' questions was significantly less than that spent answering either analytic or patient-centered group therapists' questions. Patient-centered group therapists did employ more reflection than did other group therapists, but all group therapists used comparable amounts of reflection in the assessment phase of a problem.

Three points suggested by this study are important. First, interpretations, which are used very frequently in analytic and patient-centered group therapy, are judged positively by the sender but negatively by the receiver. Second, "why" questions, which are used more frequently in analytic and patient-centered groups, elicit very long and time-consuming responses from patients. Behavioral group therapists ask significantly more questions, and yet the total patient response time is significantly less than in other forms of group therapy, which leads to the conclusion that "what" questions get clearer and shorter answers. Third, it was found that therapists could be trained to use alternatives and instruction instead of advice. More importantly, patients improved more on problems where alternatives and instruction were employed than they did when advice was used.

Since this study also showed that direct advice was judged as being more reinforcing by the sender but less by the receiver, whereas alternatives and instruction were judged as being less reinforcing by the sender but more by the receiver, it is clear why advice continues to be employed. In fact, direct advice continues to be employed in almost all forms of therapy despite the common assumption (Frank, 1964; Strupp & Wallach, 1965) that it does not work well in therapy. Data from the studies reported above indicate that this common assumption is true, but that other forms of advice, such as alternatives and instruction, do work. It is hoped that precisely this type of behavioral analysis of group process will lead to the development of a behavioral group therapy model that will not be subject to the allegation that behavior therapy is "too simple" to deal with complex human problems.

It is clear that more work needs to be done both in classifying the syntax used in various groups and in assessing which syntactical forms elicit which types of group behaviors and outcomes. The important issue is that different types of therapy groups differ in their use of syntax and that different types of syntax lead to different results. If group therapists are going to be trained to understand and to do what is effective, this type of analysis must be continued.

Behavioral Analysis of Type and Amount of Activity within Group

The relationship of individual activity within the group to other aspects of group process and to individual change is another necessary area of analysis. With as simple a question as whether or not participation leads to patient improvement, mixed results have been found (Bassin, 1962; Sechrest & Berger, 1961). Using the token procedure described above, one can use the present form of analysis to easily identify four individual participation variables: total amount of token use (where "use" refers to giving and receiving tokens), type of use (input vs. output), input valence (percentage of tokens the individual was given that were positive), and output valence (percentage of tokens the individual gave that were positive).

With relation to the first variable—the total tokens given and received—experimental data indicate that more active patients improve more than do less active patients (Flowers & Booraem, 1976; Flowers, 1975). A more recent study (Flowers, Hartman, & Booraem, 1977) indicates that total token use correlates very highly with a separate count of statements made. Thus, a count of total token use indicates total activity, as well as valenced activity.

The variable of giving versus receiving tokens indicates whether the patient is in the role of "shaper" or "shapee" in any session. Results show that group members who adopt both roles over sessions change more than those who adopt predominantly one role or the other. The advantage of this token methodology with relation to both total activity and role is that easily collected data give the group leaders an objective count of what has occurred, rather than the leaders having to rely solely on their subjective impressions of such data.

The research on input and output data yields complicated results. One repeated finding (Flowers, Booraem, & Seacat, 1974; Flowers, Kenney, & Rotheram, 1974; Flowers, 1975) was that a group member who gives a high proportion of negative messages is less sensitive than other group members in the session in which those messages were given ("sensitivity" here means the match between the subject's recall of events and the objective data).

A second finding is that a negative message delivered without an accompanying positive message is not heard clearly. A high proportion of such messages sent to a patient (when compared to other patients in the session) reduces that patient's sensitivity during the entire session. The exception to this latter finding is that experienced therapists increase in sensitivity when they receive a high proportion of negative messages in any session.

This is not to say, however, that negative feedback "does not work." In fact, too high a percentage of overall positive feedback reduces positive outcome results (Flowers, Booraem, & Seacat, 1974). The data indicate that, when negative feedback either given or received is out of proportion for a patient in relation to other patients in that session, that patient does not demonstrate change on problems discussed in that session. Furthermore, if this pattern continues, the patient often drops out of the group before the group is over. Again, the token methodology provides the therapists with an accurate assessment of which patients may be "at risk" by giving an additional visual signal of which behaviors are being reinforced and punished and which messages are being delivered in solely negative ways.

SUGGESTIONS FOR RUNNING MORE EFFECTIVE GROUPS

Based upon the research covered above and the clinical experience of the authors, the following suggestions are offered as possible ways of running more effective behavioral therapy groups in rehabilitation settings:

1   Screen patients for the group. This pregroup step is important for a number of reasons. First, the pregroup screening session provides a behavior sample that can be used to screen out potentially disruptive patients or those who may have difficulty in keeping up with the other members, as well as to achieve a beneficial mix of patients for the group. Second, the screening session can be used to shape patients' expectations about what is going to occur in the group, which can be helpful in terms of both desensitizing them to the group situation and beginning to teach them about "good patient" in-group behaviors.

2   Employ two therapists. Using two therapists allows one therapist to present material or to respond verbally to patients' statements while the other observes individual and group behavior, which permits a more thorough behavioral assessment and more consistent reinforcement. The therapists also can take different, preplanned roles within the group, which helps in assessing patients' responses to various types of people, permits greater flexibility in conducting modeling and role-playing exercises, and works to promote generalization.

3   Clearly specify required group behaviors. It makes sense to specify clearly to group members, both at the initial group session and whenever possible during the course of the group, those in-group behaviors that are believed to enhance therapeutic outcome. These include attendance, verbal participation, self-disclosure, and completion of homework assignments, among others. This clear specification simplifies the tasks of reinforcing patients when these behaviors occur and reminding them when the behaviors are absent.

4   Actively promote group cohesion. This can be accomplished by having the therapists model and socially reinforce the following types of behavior: statements that have high-cohesive content (such as "we" statements), eye contact with the speaker, patient-to-patient statements, self-disclosure, and statements indicating satisfaction with sessions or with the group.

5 Actively promote self-disclosure. Beyond encouraging patient-to-patient interactions and facilitating the development of group cohesiveness, having patients, prior to the group session, write down on an index card two problems that they may want to disclose seems to be the most promising strategy for increasing self-disclosure.

6 Shape expectations of positive outcome. Having expectations that group participation will have a positive outcome serves to reinforce patients' motivation to attend the group regularly, to participate actively, and to complete homework assignments. The therapists can shape these positive expectations by describing the progress made by patients in previous groups, by presenting research data on the effectiveness of previous groups run by those therapists or described in the literature, and even by having a successful patient from a previous group come in to describe which aspects of the group training proved to be most useful for him or her; however, this last procedure should focus on specific positive behaviors that the former patient learned in the group rather than simply being a "testimonial" to the group's effectiveness.

7 Use reading material to reinforce group instruction. The actual time spent in group each week will be proportionately quite short compared to the rest of the patients' lives. Written material—handouts, behavioral recording charts, structured treatment manuals—can increase the therapeutic effect of the group by promoting active listening rather than note taking during group sessions, by clearly outlining the main points covered in each session, and by allowing patients to review the material covered in the group between treatment sessions and even after the group is over.

8 Focus on shaping behavioral change rather than solely on outcome. This is particularly important when using a time-limited psychoeducational group (e.g., 8–12 sessions) to treat long-standing maladaptive behaviors (e.g., compulsive overeating). Patients often become discouraged when progress toward a therapeutic goal is slow, and this can lead to expressed pessimism and even dropouts. By emphasizing the gradual process of behavioral shaping and by directing patients' attention to and reinforcing them for small, progressive changes, therapists can maintain group morale and motivation.

9 Encourage patients to build outside support. Whether a behavioral group is time-limited or open-ended, it eventually will end, and group patients often express anxiety about whether they will be able to continue to progress after losing the consistent focusing and support that the group offers. They should be encouraged from the very first session to identify and to build outside supports—family, friends, self-help organizations, other group members—which will continue to reinforce motivation and effort after the group ends.

10 Learn from your successes and mistakes. No matter how many times a therapist has run a particular group, even a very structured psychoeducational group, events will occur during current group sessions that indicate ways in which the group format and presentations can be improved. One way of obtaining feedback that may lead to this type of improvement is to ask each patient, during the final group session, to cite one specific concept or technique that he or she learned during the group and found to be particularly effective and helpful. Another way is to ask patients to complete a written posttreatment questionnaire on what they found most and least helpful about the group and what suggestions they may have for improving future groups.

SUMMARY AND CONCLUSIONS

In this chapter, we discussed the three primary definitions the term "behavioral group therapy" has had in its history and noted that the third type of behavioral group therapy is still emerging and developing. We reviewed the many advantages of doing behavior therapy in groups, as well as several disadvantages, and noted how early research aimed at identifying the curative factors in group therapy evolved into attempts to manipulate such factors and to study the results.

We explored four important theoretical movements—operant conditioning, experiential learning and modeling, cognitive-behavioral rehearsal, and didactic teaching—that contributed to the emergence of behavioral group techniques, and we described more recent clinical and research efforts designed to operationalize and manipulate group process variables such as cohesiveness, self-disclosure, valenced messages, syntax, and in-group activity. Finally, we offered 10 suggestions for running more effective groups.

There are many questions about behavioral group therapy that remain to be asked and answered, and it is hoped that the proliferation of such groups in the rehabilitation setting will lead to a concomitant proliferation of well-designed studies for investigating the parameters of their use.

REFERENCES

Bassin, A. (1962). Verbal participation and improvement in group therapy. *International Journal of Group Psychotherapy, 12,* 369–373.

Berzon, B., Pious, C., & Parson, R. (1963). The therapeutic event in group psychotherapy: A study of objective reports of group members. *Journal of Individual Psychology, 19,* 204–212.

Carkhuff, R. (1971). Training as a systematic experiential learning preference mode of treatment. *Journal of Counseling Psychology, 18,* 123–131.

Connors, G. J., Maisto, S. A., Sobell, L. C., & Sobell, M. B. (1985). Behavioral group therapy with drunk-driving offenders. In D. Upper & S. M. Ross (Eds.), *Handbook of behavioral group therapy* (pp. 473–487). New York: Plenum Press.

Corsini, R., & Rosenberg, B. (1959). Mechanisms of group psychotherapy: Processes and dynamics. *Journal of Abnormal and Social Psychology, 51,* 406–411.

Culbert, S. A. (1967). The interpersonal process of self-disclosure: It takes two to see one. In S. A. Culbert (Ed.), *Explorations in applied behavioral science.* New York: Renaissance Editors.

Denholtz, M. S., & Mann, E. T. (1974). An individual program for group desensitization. *Journal of Behavior Therapy and Experimental Psychiatry, 5,* 27–29.

Dickoff, H., & Lakin, M. (1963). Patients' views of group psychotherapy: Retrospections and interpretations. *International Journal of Group Psychotherapy, 13,* 61–73.

Dies, R., & Hess, A. (1971). An experimental investigation of cohesiveness in marathon and conventional group therapy. *Journal of Abnormal and Social Psychology, 77,* 258–262.

Emmelkamp, P. M. G., & Kuipers, A. C. M. (1985). Behavioral group therapy with anxiety disorders. In D. Upper & S. M. Ross (Eds.), *Handbook of behavioral group therapy* (pp. 443–471). New York: Plenum Press.

Fiedler, F. (1950). A comparison of therapeutic relationships in psychoanalytic, non-directive and Adlerian therapy. *Journal of Consulting Psychology, 14,* 436–445.

Flowers, J. V. (1975). Role playing and simulation methods in psychotherapy. In F. H. Kanfer & A. P. Goldstein (Eds.), *Helping people change.* New York: Pergamon Press.

Flowers, J. V. (1979). Behavioral analysis of group therapy and a model for behavioral group therapy. In D. Upper & S. M. Ross (Eds.), *Behavioral group therapy, 1979: An annual review.* Champaign, IL: Research Press.

Flowers, J. V., & Booraem, C. D. (1976). The use of tokens to facilitate outcome and monitor process in group psychotherapy. *International Journal of Group Psychotherapy, 26,* 191–201.

Flowers, J. V., Booraem, C. D., Brown, T. R., & Harris, D. E. (1974). An investigation of a technique for facilitating patient-to-patient interactions in group therapy. *Journal of Community Psychology, 2,* 39–42.

Flowers, J. V., Booraem, C. D., & Hartman, K. (1981). Patients' improvement on higher and lower intensity problems as a function of group cohesiveness. *Psychotherapy: Theory, Research and Practice, 18,* 246–251.

Flowers, J. V., Booraem, C. D., & Seacat, G. F. (1974). The effect of positive and negative feedback on members' sensitivity to other members in group therapy. *Psychotherapy: Theory, Research and Practice, 11,* 346–350.

Flowers, J. V., Hartman, K. A., & Booraem, C. D. (1977, April). *Group therapist training: An objective assessment of individuals' leadership ability.* Paper presented at the Western Psychological Association Convention, Seattle.

Flowers, J. V., Kennedy, B. J., & Rotheram, M. J. (1974, April). *The effects of differing proportions of positive and negative feedback on sensitivity, satisfaction and trust of group members.* Paper presented at the Western Psychological Association Convention, San Francisco.

Frank, G. H. (1964). The effect of directive and non-directive statements by therapists on the content of patient verbalizations. *Journal of General Psychology, 71,* 323–328.

Frankel, A. J., & Glasser, P. H. (1974). Behavioral approaches to group work. *Social Work, 19,* 163–175.

Goldstein, A. P., Glassner, S., Greenberg, R., Gustin, A., Land, J., Liberman, B., & Streiner, D. (1967). The use of planted patients in group psychotherapy. *American Journal of Psychotherapy, 21,* 767–773.

Goldstein, A. P., Heller, K., & Sechrest, L. (1966). *Psychotherapy and the psychology of behavior change.* New York: Wiley.

Goldstein, A. P., & Wolpe, J. (1971). Behavior therapy in groups. In H. I. Kaplan & B. J. Sadock (Eds.), *Comprehensive group psychotherapy.* Baltimore: Williams & Wilkins.

Goodman, G. (1969). An experiment with companionship therapy: College students and troubled boys—assumptions, selection and design. In B. G. Guerney (Ed.), *Psycho-*

therapeutic agents: New roles for nonprofessionals, parents and teachers. New York: Holt, Rinehart & Winston.

Gutride, M. E., Goldstein, A. P., & Hunter, G. F. (1973). The use of modeling and role playing to increase social interaction among asocial psychiatric patients. *Journal of Consulting and Clinical Psychology, 40,* 408–415.

Heckel, R. V., Wiggins, S. L., & Salzberg, H. C. (1962). Conditioning against silences in group therapy. *Journal of Clinical Psychology, 28,* 216–217.

Heine, R. W. (1953). A comparison of patients' reports on psychotherapeutic experience with psychoanalytic, non-directive and Adlerian therapists. *American Journal of Psychotherapy, 7,* 16–23.

Hurley, S. (1967). *Self-disclosure in small counseling groups.* Unpublished doctoral dissertation, University of Michigan.

Jones, M. (1944). Group treatment with particular reference to group projection methods. *American Journal of Psychiatry, 101,* 292–299.

Kahn, M. H., & Rudestem, K. E. (1971). The relationship between liking and perceived self-disclosure in small groups. *Journal of Psychology, 78,* 81–85.

Kelly, J. A. (1982). *Social-skills training: A practical guide for interventions.* New York: Springer.

Klapman, J. W. (1950). The case for didactic group psychotherapy. *Diseases of the Nervous System, 11,* 35–41.

Lazarus, A. A. (1961). Group therapy of phobic disorders by systematic desensitization. *Journal of Abnormal and Social Psychology, 63,* 505–510.

Liberman, R. P. (1970a). A behavioral approach to group dynamics: I. Reinforcement and prompting of cohesiveness in group therapy. *Behavior Therapy, 1,* 141–175.

Liberman, R. P. (1970b). A behavioral approach to group dynamics. II. Reinforcing and prompting hostility-to-the-therapist in group therapy. *Behavior Therapy, 1,* 312–327.

Liberman, R. P. (1971). Reinforcement of cohesiveness in group therapy: Behavioral and personality changes. *Archives of General Psychiatry, 25,* 168–177.

Lieberman, M. A. (1975). Group methods. In F. H. Kanfer & A. P. Goldstein (Eds.), *Helping people change.* New York: Pergamon Press.

Lieberman, M. A., Yalom, I. D., & Miles, M. B. (1973). *Encounter groups: First facts.* New York: Basic Books.

Lobitz, W. C., & Baker, E. L. (1979). Group treatment of single males with erectile dysfunction. *Archives of Sexual Behavior, 8,* 127.

Lott, B. E. (1961). Group cohesiveness: A learning phenomenon. *Journal of Social Psychology, 55,* 275–286.

Low, A. A. (1950). *Mental health through will training.* Boston: Christopher Publishing House.

Malamud, D. I., & Machover, S. (1965). *Toward self-understanding: Group techniques in self-confrontation.* Springfield, IL: Charles C. Thomas.

McNair, D. M. (1957). Reinforcement of verbal behavior. *Journal of Experimental Psychology, 53,* 40–46.

Marlatt, G. A., Jacobsen, E. A., Johnson, D. L., & Morrice, D. J. (1966, May). *Effect of exposure to a model receiving varied informational feedback upon consequent behavior in an interview.* Paper presented at the Midwestern Psychological Association Convention, Chicago.

Marsh, L. C. (1935). Group therapy and the psychiatric clinic. *Journal of Nervous and Mental Diseases, 82,* 381–390.

Oakes, W. F., Droge, A. E., & August, B. (1960). Reinforcement effects on participation in group discussion. *Psychological Reports, 7,* 503–514.

Oakes, W. F., Droge, A. E., & August, B. (1961). Reinforcement effects on conclusions reached in group discussion. *Psychological Reports, 9,* 27–34.

Odom, J. V., Nelson, R. O., & Wein, K. S. (1978). The differential effectiveness of five treatment procedures on three response systems in a snake phobia analog study. *Behavior Therapy, 9,* 936–942.

Paul, G. L., & Shannon, D. T. (1966). Treatment of anxiety through systematic desensitization in therapy groups. *Journal of Abnormal Psychology, 71,* 124–135.

Peres, H. (1947). An investigation of non-directive group therapy. *Journal of Consulting Psychology, 11,* 159–172.

Rose, S. D., & LeCroy, C. W. (1985). Improving children's social competence: A multidimensional behavioral group approach. In D. Upper & S. M. Ross (Eds.), *Handbook of behavioral group therapy* (pp.173–202). New York: Plenum Press.

Russell, R. K., & Lent, R. W. (1982). Cue-controlled relaxation and systematic desensitization versus non-specific factors in treating test anxiety. *Journal of Counseling Psychology, 29,* 100–103.

Sansbury, D. L. (1979). The role of the group in behavioral group therapy. In D. Upper & S. M. Ross (Eds.), *Behavioral group therapy, 1979: An annual review* (pp. 39–54). Champaign, IL: Research Press.

Schwartz, A. N., & Hawkins, H. L. (1965). Patient models and affect statements in group therapy. *Proceedings of the 73rd Annual American Psychological Association Convention, 1,* 265–266.

Sechrest, L. B., & Berger, B. (1961). Verbal participation and perceived benefit from group psychotherapy. *International Journal of Group Psychotherapy, 11,* 49–59.

Shapiro, D. (1963). The reinforcement of agreement in a small group. *Behavior Research and Therapy, 1,* 267–272.

Shapiro, D. (1964). Group learning of speech sequences without awareness. *Science, 144,* 74–76.

Shapiro, D., & Leiderman, P. H. (1964). Acts and activation: A psychophysiological study of social interaction. In P. H. Leiderman & D. Shapiro (Eds.), *Psychobiological approaches to social behavior.* Stanford, CA: Stanford University Press.

Snortum, J., & Myers, H. (1971). Intensity of t-group relationships as a function of interaction. *International Journal of Group Psychotherapy, 21,* 190–201.

Strupp, H. H., & Wallach, M. S. (1965). A further study of psychiatrists' responses in quasi-therapeutic situations. *Behavioral Science, 10,* 113–134.

Trower, P., Bryant, B., & Argyle, M. (1978). *Social skills and mental health.* Pittsburgh: University of Pittsburgh Press.

Truax, C. B. (January, 1962). *Patient-centered group psychotherapy.* Workshop presented at the American Group Psychotherapy Association Meeting, New York City.

Truax, C. B. (1962a). *The therapeutic process in group psychotherapy: A research investigation.* Madison: Wisconsin Psychiatric Institute.

Truax, C., & Carkhuff, R. (1965a). Patient and therapist transparency in the psychotherapeutic encounter. *Journal of Consulting Psychology, 12,* 3–9.

Truax, C. B., & Carkhuff, R. (1965b). Personality change in hospitalized mental patients during group psychotherapy as a function of alternate sessions and vicarious therapy pretraining. *Journal of Clinical Psychology, 21,* 225–228.

Truax, C. B., & Carkhuff, R. (1967). Toward effective counseling and psychotherapy: Training and practice. Chicago: Aldine.

Whalen, C. (1969). Effects of a model and instructions on group verbal behaviors. *Journal of Consulting and Clinical Psychology, 33,* 509–521.

Yalom, I. D. (1970). *The theory and practice of group psychotherapy.* New York: Basic Books.

Yalom, I. D., & Rand, K. (1966). Compatibility and cohesiveness in therapy groups. *Archives of General Psychiatry, 13,* 267–276.

Chapter 11

Rehabilitation-Oriented
Multiple-Family Therapy

Jeffrey R. Bedell, Peter Provet, and Jeffrey A. Frank

Since certain interactional patterns within the family are related to relapse (e.g., Leff & Vaughn, 1976), rehabilitation treatment directed solely toward the identified patient is not always sufficient to obtain maximal benefit. Treatment with the entire family unit is frequently desirable to maintain and promote progress of the emotionally disturbed patient. With its roots in both group therapy and family therapy, multiple-family therapy (MFT) is a treatment that creates a unique learning environment and shows considerable promise when applied to patients with severe disabilities.

Multiple-family therapy has been the subject of two comprehensive reviews (Strelnick, 1977; O'Shea & Phillips, 1985). These reviews suggest that, although MFT is not well-defined as a unique treatment and empirical studies are few, it has a strong following of practitioners and shows promise as an innovative treatment technique. Recently, the work of Anderson, Reiss, and Hogarty (1986) and McFarlane (1990) has more clearly articulated a clear model of psychoeducational MFT, and they have reported empirical research demonstrating the effectiveness of this approach. For example, McFarlane (1990) presented research suggesting that psychoeducational MFT was more effective in preventing hospital relapse than either single-family therapy or psychodynamic multiple-family approaches. The effectiveness of MFT appeared to persist for a period of at least 3 years. McFarlane's preliminary research findings are impressive and indicate that MFT is worth consideration as part of array of effective rehabilitation treatments.

The information presented in this chapter is based on 5 years of clinical and research experience using and refining MFT. Our approach is strongly influenced by the work of Anderson and colleagues (1986), McFarlane (1990), and Falloon, Boyd, and McGill (1984), but considers a variety of additional treatment perspectives. These authors have developed treatments for severely and chronically disturbed patient populations, and their approaches are therefore appropriate for application in a psychiatric rehabilitation program. However, since no single model of MFT has been shown to be superior to any other, we have combined what we consider to be the best aspects of a variety of programs. We have also integrated into this family treatment some of the latest ideas and techniques from psychiatric rehabilitation, social skills training, social learning, and cognitive-behavioral perspectives. This integration has enabled us to develop an innovative multiple-family treatment that may be applied to a wide range of patients being treated in a rehabilitation program, and consequently we call our approach rehabilitation-oriented multiple-family therapy (ROMFT).

The goal of this chapter is to provide a description of a rehabilitation-oriented multiple-family therapy program. The following topics will be discussed: (a) goals and therapeutic elements of MFT, (b) group membership, (c) duration of treatment, (d) roles of therapists and members, (e) description of therapy procedures, and (f) case reports. Divergences between our rehabilitation-oriented MFT model and the more traditional psychoeducational MFT are pointed out and discussed wherever significant.

GOALS AND THERAPEUTIC ELEMENTS OF MULTIPLE-FAMILY THERAPY

When one is selecting therapeutic interventions, it is desirable to identify treatments that will facilitate the specific goals set for the patient. As a hybrid of family therapy and group therapy, MFT will tend to accomplish the goals traditionally associated with these two formats of treatment. On the basis of their reviews of the literature, both Strelnick (1977) and O'Shea and Phelps (1985) specify the following goals as being appropriate for MFT: (a) reduction of alienation and social isolation, (b) enhancement of communication, (c) increased awareness of family interactional patterns, and (d) resolution of role conflicts. Other researchers have cited goals such as reduction of stigma, reduction of expressed emotion, and creation of a social network (e.g., McFarlane, 1990). These goals, however, may be described as "intermediate" or "process" goals leading eventually to the treatment goals identified by Strelnick and O'Shea and Phelps. For example, use of the MFT format to reduce stigma and to create a social network is a means of reducing alienation and social isolation.

MFT not only shares many therapy goals with other forms of group and family therapy, it also shares many therapeutic elements. Yalom (1970) has cited 10 therapeutic elements associated with group therapy: (a) imparting of information, (b) instillation of hope, (c) universality, (d) altruism, (e) recapitulation of family, (f) development of socializing techniques, (g) imitative behavior, (h) interpersonal learning, (i) group cohesiveness, and (j) catharsis. MFT embraces these 10 characteristics, each of which should be maximized by the group leaders, perhaps using some of the procedures described in Chapter 10.

Although many therapeutic goals and elements of MFT are shared with other group and family therapies, this does not mean that there is nothing unique about MFT. Most practitioners agree that MFT creates a learning environment that is different from that created by traditional group and family therapies. For example, establishing a social support network among the families participating in MFT is a distinct, powerful, and innovative way to draw families out of their isolation. The opportunity for families to learn from other families is unique to MFT. Practicing weekly problem solving with a group of families is a significant motivator, not only to learn about problem solving, but to receive input and alternative solutions from families who have shared experiences and dealt with similar problems in the past. Thus, MFT may be characterized as a treatment, with clear therapeutic goals and treatment elements, that is executed using a unique format that may result in increased effectiveness compared to more traditional types of group and family therapy.

Group Membership

For the most part, the literature reports the application of MFT with groups homogeneous with regard to broad diagnostic categories. Thus, studies focus on populations such as schizophrenic individuals (McFarlane, 1983, 1990), substance abusers (Kaufman & Kaufman, 1977), children with behavioral problems (Hardcastle, 1977), dialysis patients (Steinglass, Gonzalez, Dosovitz, & Reiss, 1982), and developmentally disabled adolescents (Szymanski & Kiernan, 1983). Relatively little attention is given to other client variables such as age, severity of illness, diagnostic subtype, and stage of illness.

Forming groups composed of members with one diagnosis is especially important to the psychoeducational type of MFT. In that more traditional MFT model, a psychoeducational workshop is presented that provides information to families about the etiology and course of the disability from which the client members suffer. Such a workshop would be difficult to present if a heterogeneous group of diagnoses were represented by the group members since etiology and course of different diagnostic groups vary. Thus, homogeneous groups are necessary for certain forms of MFT.

However, MFT groups based on common functional disabilities (see Chapter 2) and treatment goals do not require members to share the same diagnostic label. Such is the case in the rehabilitation-oriented MFT groups that will be described in this chapter. Issues of patient selection based on functional and rehabilitation assessment have not been adequately considered in the MFT research literature. Ideally, MFT groups would be composed of patients and families for whom it appears that some aspect of their treatment goals would best be accomplished by participation in MFT rather than some other type of treatment. Thus, there are two nondiagnostic considerations when forming an MFT group. First, it is important to determine if the therapeutic goals of the MFT group are consistent with those of the patient. The goals of MFT should be clearly specified; a set of suggested goals for MFT have been presented earlier in this chapter. Second, it should be determined if the therapeutic methods associated with MFT are likely to best facilitate the achievement of the patient's goals.

Another aspect of group membership frequently discussed is which family members should be involved in MFT. We have begun to evaluate the utility of MFT when the client's functional rather than biological family participates. We have established MFT groups comprising a heterogeneous mixture of patients and relatives including parents, spouse, siblings, aunts, uncles, and cousins; and on occasion, we have included a biologically unrelated person such as a close, supportive friend. One common feature of all participants in MFT should be a commitment to actively participate in the group and assist the patient in the accomplishment of treatment goals.

Duration of Treatment

MFT groups have been designed with both long-term and short-term duration of operation. Short-term MFT is employed when the primary treatment goal is to inform patients and family about such issues as treatment rules, definitions of mental disorders, and general coping strategies.

A long-term MFT group operating for at least a year is much better able to capitalize on the unique therapeutic qualities of this method of treatment. Not the least of these qualities is the ability to develop a cohesive and stable membership that is capable of learning and teaching new skills and developing enduring supportive networks that function outside of the regular group meetings. McFarlane (1990) has suggested that, for patients recently experiencing an acute schizophrenic episode, groups operate for 3 to 5 years. Such a long duration may not be practical in many settings. We have found that 1 year of MFT, as described in this chapter, allows most of the goals of treatment to be accomplished.

Roles of Therapist and Members

Given the size and complexity of MFT groups, it is generally suggested that two therapists be utilized. These two individuals must assume many diverse roles in the course of running a multiple-family group. Initially they are educators, teaching members about the goals of the group, and how it will operate. As educators, the therapists use the group therapy situation as an instructional setting to teach factual information, model new skills, structure and guide the practice of skills, and promote generalization to real-life settings. In the role of educator, therapists are initially very directive in providing information and teaching skills. Over time, however, the therapists begin to operate more as facilitators than as educators. They strive to "give the skills away," and once the group or a member is capable of performing a skill, the therapist should allow the member(s) to do so. For example, initially the therapist may select the family problem to be discussed by the group, but selecting a problem should eventually be transferred to the family members of the group.

Facilitating competence on the part of families is more important than and takes precedence over therapists demonstrating their own competence and maintaining the role of "expert." In fact, the role of expert should be gradually transferred to the group members as they develop the skills being targeted by the MFT group.

DESCRIPTION OF REHABILITATION-ORIENTED MULTIPLE-FAMILY THERAPY PROCEDURES

After discrete goals for the group have been set, appropriate members selected, a duration of treatment set, and group leaders prepared for the complex roles of teacher, therapist, and member, the MFT group is ready to begin. There are a number of discrete procedures that constitute MFT as we have evolved the program. Each of these procedures is designed to help produce an environment in which the goals of MFT can be most effectively accomplished. The main components are (a) joining, (b) teaching self-awareness and communication skills, (c) socializing, (d) monitoring progress toward goals (the "go-around"), (e) problem solving, and (f) development of a social support network.

Joining

This is a process in which the group leader (a) seeks to establish a therapeutic alliance with families on an individual basis, prior to beginning the MFT, (b) determines the functional problems within the family, and (c) educates the family about the goals and procedures of MFT. This is an important phase of multiple-family therapy, usually comprising about three single family meetings. It is clearly the time when patients and families decide if they will commit themselves to this therapy for an extended period of time. Families that are not motivated to participate fully in the therapy and work toward the therapeutic goals, such as participating in a social support network, will not complete the "joining" process. Families should be supported for their willingness to become involved in treatment, and each family's unique and indispensable role in the rehabilitative effort should be emphasized.

A few specific objectives are accomplished in these individual meetings with families. First of all, a detailed psychosocial assessment (as described in Chapters 1 and 2) should be performed. Specific information regarding prior hospitalizations is obtained in an attempt to identify a pattern of prodromal symptoms (Herz, 1984) critical to future relapse prevention. The family is encouraged to discuss prior experiences with mental health systems and providers since the present program may be quite different. Families are provided a set of realistic and accurate expectations regarding (a) what they will be expected to do, (b) the role of the therapists, and (c) the goals of treatment. Each aspect of treatment is carefully described, emphasizing the goals and objectives.

As part of joining, the therapist obtains a genogram from the family members. This task should be seen primarily as a means for the therapists to become acquainted with the family. What often emerges is the description of a progressive increase in avoidance of social activities over time. The family may be informed that this is a common and understandable pattern of behavior observed in families that try to adjust to strains, pressures, and burdens of living with the disruptive effects of mental illness. It should be stated that the special skills and support needed for coping with these problems in a more adaptive way will be acquired through participation in the MFT group.

Teaching Self-Awareness and Communication Skills

Once the families have "joined" with the therapists, a series of eight to 10 structured skills-training sessions are held. These sessions teach (a) a cognitive-behavioral system of understanding the relationships among thoughts, feelings, and behaviors, (b) how to be aware of one's own and others feelings and wants, (c) how to make an empathic statement, (d) how to make requests of others, (e) how to respond to requests from others, (f) understanding assertive behavior and the consequences of being passive, aggressive, and assertive, and (g) a detailed, explicit problem-solving model that guides a patient from problem recognition to selecting problem solutions and evaluating their effectiveness. These skills are taught in the manner described in Chapter 5. In addition to teaching important skills that will be used by families both in the therapy group and at home, these activities provide an environment in which the group begins to develop cohesiveness through shared learning experiences and self-disclosure. Learning the new skills leads to a positive sense of accomplishment for the group members.

Groups that share common learning experiences generally become cohesive and supportive.

Teaching a set of clearly defined skills also serves as a period of informal assessment as group leaders observe the members' ability to learn the skills, and how they interact with other family members and with other families. The routine of the group and the educational role of the therapists are established. At the same time, the ability of the families to learn skills and gain competence is demonstrated.

A cohesive philosophy of mental illness and rehabilitation is blended into the skill-training sessions. This practice is important because patients and families often believe that the way they think and feel about things and the way they interact with each other are due to stable, rigid, and unchangeable personality traits. These beliefs are discouraging, imply that little or nothing can be changed, and suggest that individuals have no power or ability to change themselves. Since these are false beliefs, it is important to attempt to rectify them.

In place of these self-defeating beliefs, the following logical argument is presented to the members. It is suggested that (a) one's typical pattern of communicating, solving problems, and interacting with others is determined by a combination of the situation and one's "personality," (b) personality consists of the sum total of one's behaviors and the associated underlying thoughts and feelings, (c) thoughts, feelings, and behaviors are to a large extent learned, (d) human beings are always capable of new learning, and therefore (e) as one learned to relate to others in the past by learning to think, feel, and act in certain ways, one can learn new more effective ways of thinking, feeling, and behaving. Learning new ways of thinking, feeling, and behaving is a central goal of the MFT group.

As clearly described in Chapter 1, the rehabilitation model emphasizes the strengths of the patient and the family while recognizing the limitations imposed by the handicapping condition. It is important that families accept the fact that dysfunctional interactive patterns within the family are not caused by the presence of a "diseased person," but are established through prior learning histories of everyone involved in an attempt to cope with problem situations. Although no one can be blamed for what happened in the past, the process of changing these dysfunctional patterns does involve the active participation of the family and the patient and is the responsibility of all those involved. That is, the family (including the client) is responsible for learning new, better ways of coping with problems as they occur in the future.

Teaching communication skills as described above is a method of MFT that is divergent from methods described by Anderson et al. (1986) and McFarlane (1990), but similar to the work of Falloon et al. (1984). We use the social skills training approach of Falloon because it is more consistent with the positive rehabilitation orientation of our approach. Rather than teaching skills at this phase of treatment, the psychoeducational model employed by Anderson and colleagues and McFarlane uses a daylong "survival skills workshop" to explain the biological basis of mental illness. Practitioners who use this type of workshop believe that a medical or disease model explanation of psychological disorder, which focuses on the physiological predisposing factors that are supposedly genetically transmitted, helps to destigmatize the family and remove blame from the patient. However, while helping to relieve "stigma" and "blame," the "disease model" often imparts the message that the mentally disabled person cannot exercise voluntary control over life events because of the overpowering influence of the "mental illness." Further, this model tends to mislead group members into automatically construing family problems as symptomatic of the "identified patient's" mental illness. This can be very counterproductive to problem solving and therapeutic movement and sometimes leads to some very dysfunctional solutions to family problems. For example, the belief that a mental illness exists can become an excuse for group members' not being motivated for therapy and participation in behavior change. Thus, a major strength of the disease model, absolving the patient and family of personal responsibility for problem behaviors, often leads these individuals to assume the passive role of victim. In fact, research (Fisher & Farina, 1979) indicates that, in comparison with those who were given a social learning explanation of their disorder, individuals given a constitutional explanation felt that they could do less personally to cope with their problems. Since one of the objectives of MFT is to empower patients through developing skills and a social support network, we see no reason to start with a potentially self-defeating explanation of disorder that may provide a dysfunctional cognitive set.

Family stigma and patient guilt can be alleviated by acceptance of the positive rehabilitation and cognitive-behavioral philosophy of mental illness presented above. This philosophy absolves the family of blame for past problems but does not impart the "victim" role with the accompanying passivity and perception of lack of personal control and responsibility. In fact, families come to believe that change can occur now that they are learning clear and practical new skills that they never learned before.

Notwithstanding the above described divergence from the work of Anderson and colleagues and McFarlane, the effectiveness of their programs is not questioned. Their research, however, evaluates a multifaceted program and does not indicate the specific role of the survival skills workshop in the therapeutic outcomes they report. The primary intent of the survival skills workshop is to reduce family stigma and guilt. We prefer to accomplish this goal using a rehabilitation-oriented program of treatment.

Socializing

The first 15 minutes and the last few minutes of each MFT group are devoted to socializing. Casual social topics of interest to group members, such as current news events and recreational activities, are discussed. Structuring the group to engage in socializing serves several purposes. First, it demonstrates the idea that although therapists, families, and patients each have many significant issues to discuss, such issues need not completely dominate their time together. Given the tendency for families to become overly focused on problems, it is helpful that they learn how to focus on other aspects of life.

This social time also provides an environmental structure that facilitates the development of a supportive social network. Socializing gives family members and patients the opportunity to get to know each other in a nonclinical sense. Often, families wish to follow up with each other regarding interesting issues that arose during the more formal problem-solving work. A brief end-of-group socializing period (held over remaining coffee and cake) can serve well as a staging arena for extragroup contact. Getting to know others in this personal, social way leads to the development of acquaintanceships, friendships, and ultimately a social network.

Another purpose of the social period of the MFT meeting is to teach families (primarily through modeling and demonstration) adaptive socialization behaviors. Therapists must be able to step out of their group leadership role and socialize. In this process they join in conversations about many topics, including current news events, vacations, and recreational activities. They are expected to relate to group members as social equals, that is, to relate to other group members as people, not patients. In addition, therapists must disclose information about themselves, sharing opinions and information about activities, interests, likes, and dislikes.

This is a unique way of relating to patients for many group leaders, and we have found socializing to be very difficult for some therapists. They have difficulty moving from leading a discussion to participating in one.

When the therapists are successful in relating to group members as described above, a bond is formed among the therapists and group members that is healthy and beneficial to the group. The socialization period can have a normalizing effect on patients and families that is remarkable and uplifting for all.

Monitoring Progress Toward Goals

After the socialization period, the leaders make a clear, decisive shift to what is referred to as the "go-around." This name comes from the fact that the families are usually assembled in a circle and the leaders go around the room, focusing on one family at a time.

In the early weeks of the group, members are asked to report briefly on important developments that have occurred during the week since the last meeting and on problems they would like to work on in the problem-solving phase of the group. A here-and-now focus is maintained by the leaders since there is often a tendency for families to dwell on historical problems and conflicts and to discuss them in such a way that they are not resolvable. While group members need some opportunity to express feelings based on long-standing conflicts, the leaders gradually shape the focus to current issues. During this portion of the group, members address the group as a whole. There should be minimal interfamily exchange. In an orderly manner, each member gets an equal share of the time devoted to this activity. Part of the leaders' task is to listen carefully to the problem situations presented in preparation for helping to determine which problem will be selected for extensive consideration in the last phase of the group, which involves problem solving.

After the group has met for several weeks, some families will have engaged in problem solving and will have identified solutions to be implemented outside of the group. Consequently, the focus of the go-around portion of the group may shift to family reports on efforts to implement various problem solutions. These routine progress checks help to motivate families to act on their identified problem solutions. Each week in the go-around, members will experience group pressure and support for attempting to engage in adaptive problem-solving activities. This feature of the MFT group is very important since families will often develop an excellent plan of action in the group but not follow through on implementing it outside the group. Also, it is frequently the case that the course of action proposed to solve a problem must be revised and modified once attempts at implementation have been initiated. Revision is often called for as new information becomes available about client skills and environmental reaction to the plan. A brief discussion during the go-around can help a family make minor modifications in their plan so they can proceed with implementation. Sometimes, however, families report that the planned course of action is not feasible or has failed. In this case families are encouraged to again bring the problem to the group so that it can be reanalyzed and a new solution developed.

After the routine of the group is well established and members are bringing an ample number of problems to the group for processing, the time spent on the go-around may be shortened to allow more time for problem solving. Shortening can occur by limiting reports on problem-solving activities to those that need immediate attention. Also, the go-around can be reduced in frequency to every second or third group meeting.

Problem Solving

One of the primary goals of MFT is to teach families an effective process of problem solving and to encourage the implementation of solutions outside of the group. Knowledge of an effective problem-solving process has been shown to be extremely effective in helping individuals cope with a wide variety of psychological conditions (Bedell, Archer, & Marlowe, 1980; Bedell & Michael, 1985; Bellack, Morrison, & Mueser, 1989; D'Zurilla & Goldfried, 1971; Hogerty et al., 1986).

Problem solving begins with a consideration of the various problems presented by members during the go-around. We require that the group decide which problem to work on. This is often a difficult task for the group and takes considerable time. Most group members would prefer the leaders to decide which problem to focus on. However, giving the members a problem such as this is a way to encourage ownership of the group and leadership, and to demonstrate empathy and altruism.

We prescribe a general formula to group members to help them decide which of the presented problems to select for solution. Members are prompted to consider (a) how urgent a problem is, (b) how similar it is to any problems they themselves are having, and (c) how long it has been since the presenting member has worked on a problem in the group. Thus, an urgent problem shared by other group members and presented by a person who has not solved a problem in a long time would get the highest priority. These guidelines greatly facilitate what could otherwise become a long, confused group decision process. Also, use of these guidelines provides some assurance that members are considering appropriate dimensions in their selection process.

Once a problem is selected, it is submitted to a problem-solving process similar to those described by D'Zurilla and Goldfried (1971) and Bedell and Michael (1985). A work sheet is used to guide discussion, and the following steps are followed in the problem-solving process: (a) identify cues that help one to recognize the existence of a problem, (b) define a problem in a way that it is solvable, (c) generate alternative problem solutions, (d) select the best alternative solution, and (e) implement the solution.

This model of problem solving has been well described in the literature and need not be presented here. To facilitate problem solving, we have developed a list of general principles to assist families in an overall evaluation of their problem, and to establish a positive "set" regarding problem solving. Establishing a positive set is considered to be fundamental to problem solving (D'Zurilla & Goldfried, 1971). These guiding principles are briefly presented below.

Seven Guiding Principles of Problem Solving

The guiding principles are given to families in written form and are discussed in the family meetings. We even suggest that they be posted in the home and referred to often. Having a written list of guiding principles seems to be useful to establish a positive philosophy of problem solving and to help families avoid common pitfalls. Families learn that when they are stuck in trying to solve a problem, it is often because one of these seven principles has been violated. The seven principles are as follows.

1 Problems are natural. It is important that problems be accepted as a natural part of life. It is not "bad" to have problems; it does not indicate a weakness or failure to have a problem. Accepting problems as a natural part of life helps families to be more open and less "defensive" about them.

2 Think before jumping to a solution. Frequently, once families decide that a problem exists, they act on the first solution that comes to mind. But it is more adaptive to do some thinking about the problem before a solution is attempted. This thinking should involve defining the problem, formulating at least three possible solutions, evaluating each solution, and then selecting the best one.

3 Most problems can be solved. Another characteristic of many families seems to be the tendency to give up on a problem before trying to solve it. Families often assume that they cannot solve the problem, so they don't try. This kind of thinking leads to poor problem solving. Families can solve a problem only if they assume they can solve at least part of it and make an effort to do so.

4 Take responsibility for problems. Families can solve only those aspects of a problem for which they are able to take responsibility. Taking responsibility for a problem does not mean blaming oneself for everything that goes wrong in life. Nor does it encourage feelings of self-criticism or guilt about problems. Rather, it is a positive philosophy that identifies one's responsibilities and separates them from those of others. It is a philosophy that there is something you can do about any problem that is your responsibility, but that there is little you can do about problems that are the responsibility of others.

5 State what you can do, not what you can't do. Sometimes families decide to solve a problem by stopping certain behaviors. For example, if one family member argues with another, the family might decide to solve the problem by "not arguing any more" or not talking about certain topics. A more adaptive approach would be to learn how to deal with differences of opinion in a constructive way. If families solve problems primarily by stopping some behavior, it is possible that after a period of time they will have eliminated a large portion of their social activities. Generally, avoiding problems is not considered the most adaptive way of handling them. Having a goal in mind that one can work toward provides direction and incentive, while merely avoiding tends to leave one with the dilemma of what to do in its place.

6 Behavior must be legal and socially acceptable. When trying to solve problems, families often extend themselves in new ways. Sometimes, these new behaviors push the limits of what would be considered legal and socially acceptable. For example, if a family decides to deal with the neighbors by "telling them off," this probably involves being rude and discourteous and ventilating anger. A more socially acceptable solution should be sought.

7 Solutions must be within our power and ability. Families sometimes identify solutions that are beyond their ability and power to implement. Such solutions are doomed to failure. The most common error is to forget that individuals generally can control only their own behavior. It is difficult, if not impossible, to control the behavior of others. Families cannot make others behave in a certain way. The most that can usually be done is to attempt to influence someone to behave in a certain way. If that person responds positively to the influence, families can further help the person behave in a certain way by providing feedback, guidance, and support. For example, a family may want a member to get a job. They can explain the benefits, offer encouragement, and even establish contingencies based on progress toward finding work. But ultimately, the individual is the only one with the power to actually gain employment. Once this principle is accepted, frustration is reduced and families learn to establish appropriate expectations about changing another's behavior.

Of course, families are aware of the fact that they can exert power to force members to behave in certain ways. Everyone knows of cases where individuals (often children) have been forced to behave in a certain way to solve a problem that was identified by another person (often a parent). We also know that unless an individual also wants to change the behavior in question little is typically accomplished. The use of power to change behavior is less likely to have positive long-term outcomes than most people expect.

Thus, the agenda for each MFT group meeting is set. First, there is a socialization period, followed by a review of progress on problems previously considered by the group and a presentation of new problem situations. A problem is selected from among those presented, and the group engages in a structured process of problem solving. Within this process, the goals of MFT can be accomplished and the therapeutic elements are actuated. While this process enables members to receive support and assistance for immediate ongoing problems, it also provides a strong environment for the development of a social support network.

Development of a Social Support Network

The potential to facilitate the development of supportive social networks among families and patients is one of the unique features of the MFT modality. The presence of an extensive social support network has been shown to be a buffer against stress and is associated with adaptive coping behaviors. The networks of families with psychologically handicapped members tend to be small and offer little social support (Beels, 1978). Thus, it is important that the unique environment created by the MFT group be used, if possible, to develop a social network among members.

Attention to network development is important throughout the duration of the group and must be a clearly specified goal from the onset. In practice, networking will be more likely to occur after families become familiar to one another, establish trust, and develop a desire to both seek help from and assist other group members.

The groundwork for social network development is established by the activities of MFT. The various elements of MFT are facilitative of network development. The "joining" phase helps select families that are willing and motivated to develop a social network and to be involved in the various therapeutic activities of the group. The socialization period encourages the development of friendships.

Learning common methods of communication provides a universal language and group identification. And similarly, learning a process that allows for a common approach to problem solving encourages cooperation of members outside of the group.

In addition, the therapists structure opportunities for families to function together toward the accomplishment of clear goals and reinforce interfamily communication and problem solving. Networking is also facilitated by letting families take progressively more responsibility in dealing with problems as their skills improve. Families ultimately begin to expect support from each other, and therefore in future times of need seek out their peers, rather than depending solely on assistance from the therapists. Anderson et al. (1986) describe a technique called "interfamily management," which is one of four primary intervention techniques recommended for use in MFT groups. Using this technique, the therapist encourages interfamily conversation and group-based problem solving. The therapist purposely reflects problems back to the group rather than getting involved. The use of techniques such as interfamily management allows therapists systematically and gradually to turn to group members for leadership and decision making and to minimize their own input. Therapists give up, as much as possible, their roles as leaders and become consultants to the families, eventually becoming unnecessary or optional components to the group.

CASE REPORTS

The following examples draw on multiple-family group work done at the Albert Einstein College of Medicine, Department of Psychiatry, during 1989–1991. The intention of presenting these case reports is to provide the reader with illustrations of how some of the major therapeutic concepts discussed in this chapter have been actualized in our practice and to provide a feel for what it is like to conduct an MFT group using the rehabilitation-oriented design described in this chapter.

Briefly, MFT groups meet once per week for 90 minutes and comprise four to six families and two leaders. Families consist of an identified patient (aged 15–25) and one or more accompanying family members (persons actually part of the family or a parental surrogate who has daily patient contact). Patients and their families are mostly Black or Hispanic and of lower socioeconomic status. Patient diagnoses include oppositional-defiant disorder, conduct disorder, schizophrenia, bipolar disorder, schizo-affective disorder, and mild autistic disorder.

The vignettes presented provide a composite of experience from several multiple-family therapy groups, organized to illustrate three specific therapeutic factors: learning from another family, using the problem-solving model, and networking.

Learning by Interacting with Another Family

Sally Tinley (all names have been changed) is unhappy with her 25-year-old chronic schizophrenic son, Ralph, who has recently been having serious recurrences of negative symptomatology. Ralph stays in bed and smokes cigarettes all day, has not gone to his job for 2 weeks, and has become unwilling to help Sally around the house. She is at her wits end. Despite problems with Ralph, she maintains an active role as a leader in community youth affairs, is the functional family head because of her husband's disabling illness, and babysits each day for three local families. She is extremely effective in all areas of life except managing her son. Particularly, she questions his right to lounge around all day while she works so hard to make ends meet.

Sally cocks her head incredulously and then draws back into her chair upon hearing how another parent in the family group, Dee, shrieks, screams, and even smacks her son Jack when he fails to complete school assignments. Jack is 15 years old and a very likable young man, but so painfully shy and withdrawn that during conversation he is unable to engage in even minimal eye contact. He reminds the therapists of a whipped dog. "Jack doesn't know how to take care of himself," Dee complains bitterly. "He won't tell me things. He needs to learn to trust me more and be able to ask for help. After all, I am his mother." Sally appears confused. She is not sure what to make of what she is hearing from Dee, but clearly doesn't seem to like it.

Usually Sally is in command, but now she is saying nothing. Whatever Dee has just communicated about her son Jack has had the effect of disabling Sally, who is slumped wide-eyed and sheepishly in her chair.

Suddenly, from across the room, Ralph speaks out in Jack's defense, "Maybe Jack isn't getting the respect he deserves from his mom. Maybe Jack's doing the best he can. Maybe it's just his way to be a little slow."

At once, Sally is reengaged, and for the first time in weeks seems supportive of her son. "Ralph might have something," she adds emphatically. "There might be more to this than meets the eye. Maybe the problem is that Jack doesn't know the best way to communicate his feelings. I've seen that happen at times with my kids too."

What followed was a sharing of ideas and approaches among the families about how to cope constructively and assertively with the situation between Jack and his mother. And Sally learned that her son was not as worthless as she thought.

Using the Problem-Solving Model

The Carsonton family, comprising a 22-year-old patient, Reggie; his mother, Charleen; and three younger school-aged brothers, Kip, Keith, and J.R., had attended all eight of our communications skill training sessions, which are presented routinely at the beginning of each new MFT group. As hoped, the instructional sessions were engendering a preliminary sense of group cohesion and acceptance of our philosophy of treatment. The Carsonton family's ready participation was exemplary, and so it came as no surprise that Reggie volunteered to present a long-standing conflict between himself and J.R. over the use of bedroom space. This was the group's first real-life test of the problem-solving approach. The families were already beginning to use some of the communication skills at home. J.R. reported experimenting with primitive forms of the empathic request to prevent conflicts with his brother. Charleen Carsonton admitted she was learning a thing or two herself about being assertive, and reported she was using emphatic requests with feedback to deal successfully with unreasonable demands made by her in-laws.

Following the standard procedures of our model, we first helped Reggie identify a host of cues that had allowed him to recognize he was even having a problem. These cues included (a) his unmet want to have space at home to relax, (b) fear that arguments between J.R. and himself would result in permanent hard feelings between them, and (c) a recent increase in his smoking behavior, which coincided with the recent escalation of the arguments, and his yelling at the family dog. Charleen was able to help Reggie describe the problem situation using techniques learned in the group.

Reggie had little difficulty expressing his wants, which basically amounted to a need for privacy he never had at home. However, J.R.'s needs were more complex and he stumbled in his attempts to explain them. Reggie rallied to the aid of his younger brother and helped him articulate his needs by recalling what he himself had wanted when he was that age. Reggie's recollections and empathic efforts seemed to moderate his own wants. The engagement focused on this problem was contagious, and the other group families also joined in, spontaneously proposing a compromise for the brothers. Reggie was to have the bedroom to himself each day from one o'clock to six o'clock, except if J.R. needed to get something, and he was to recommend J.R. to his employer for a weekend job. Both brothers accepted the group's solution eagerly. In the weeks directly following the compromise, Reggie and J.R. sat together in the circle for the first time and agreed during go-arounds that any conflicts between them had decreased in both frequency and intensity. J.R. met the boss, was offered a job, but did not accept it. Reggie is happy now having the bedroom to himself during the afternoon.

Networking

Case 1   Liz, a 21-year-old patient with bipolar disorder, was having difficulty getting to work on time. Her history showed a pattern of having to leave jobs because of stress, even though she had always been strongly motivated to work. She had been employed for about 5 months in our sheltered clerical site at the mental health center, but was invariably half an hour late each morning. At the group leader's request, it was decided to problem solve for Liz's dilemma. Liz indicated a number of cues of depression, and ultimately an alternative solution was selected, that members would take turns calling Liz at home in the mornings to help her awaken.

Liz explained that her grandmother, the head of Liz's household, would be opposed to the solution as she herself had been trying in the mornings to help Liz awaken. Additionally, her grandmother frowned on strangers having her telephone number. Other group members agreed it was worth the try anyway, and with Liz's reticent consent, they enthusiastically mapped out a schedule of turns for the first 2 weeks. In the go-around at the beginning of our next session, Liz reported feeling an emotional lift from the calls each morning. It was "different" she said because it showed that others cared, not just her grandmother. The calls were helping her get back into the routine of getting up on time, and she had been late leaving the house only once. All of the group members congratulated Liz, and they agreed to continue the morning calls.

Enthusiasm for continuing the networking project ran high at the beginning of our next meeting, and Liz reported she was now waking up prior to the phone calls because she wanted to be able to prove she could do it on her own. Members confirmed that Liz was answering the phone by the middle of the first ring. Liz, somewhat embarrassed, thanked the group members for their caring and assistance but requested they no longer call her. Some members said she wanted the calls stopped because she was afraid of her grandmother. Others adopted the more positive interpretation that Liz had expressed and thanked her for having let them be of help. The group reaction was supportive and accepting of her decision. There was no further lateness to work. Two months after that, Liz gained outside employment as a clerical assistant at a law firm. To date there has been no reported problem with her punctuality or attendance.

Case 2 Wallace, a 23-year-old paranoid schizophrenic patient, was extremely apprehensive about beginning his new data-entry job at a local graphics shop. He had trained successfully for over a month doing clerical work in the sheltered program at our center, but beginnings were difficult for Wallace. His nascent employment history was already replete with jobs from which he had withdrawn because of frustration and performance anxiety.

Wallace wished he could be like Victor, another patient in the group whom we had placed at the same company months earlier. Victor was a hard worker, quick and experienced at the data-entry terminals. The job was easy for Victor, and he saw Wallace struggling. But Victor, diagnosed with neurotic depression, had his own problems, which were mostly interpersonal. He had always been afraid of making friends and had particular trouble warming up to people his own age.

Our job coach reports he isn't sure if what happened next was due to Wallace's being reprimanded by his supervisor for making too many errors, or due to the three of them having lunch together at the end of Wallace's first week of work. But suddenly, Wallace began asking Victor a lot of questions, like how he'd felt when he first came on the job, how he liked it, and how long he thought he'd be sticking around. And Victor, probably flattered by being in the expert role, began creeping out of his shell and started giving Wallace advice about how to tell one signature from another on the invoices, what especially to look for on the manifests, and the best places around work to eat and cash his checks.

Two months later, Wallace and Victor are still supporting each other on the job. They are, however, somewhat suspicious of one another. Wallace is much more confident at the job now, and he attempts to get closer to Victor when he can. Victor responds to Wallace's overtures by joking spontaneously with him and providing him with encouragement when it's needed, but he's threatened by the severity of Wallace's psychiatric disability, and he keeps his distance. At weekly meetings, we continue our attempts to facilitate a friendship that we believe has already brought significant gains to them both.

SUMMARY AND CONCLUSIONS

This chapter has presented the goals and therapeutic elements associated with rehabilitation-oriented multiple-family therapy. While sharing many features with group and family therapy, multiple-family therapy provides a unique setting for members to learn from other families, and establish a social support network. Factors important to the structuring and operation of this type of therapy were presented, along with a detailed presentation of the rehabilitation-oriented multiple-family therapy currently in operation at Einstein. This rehabilitation model of multiple-family therapy is based on a set of positive learning principles and procedures that can be applied to heterogeneous family groups with members having a variety of types of mental disabilities. Because of this enhanced approach, the program described has several important philosophical and procedural advantages over the more traditional models presented in the literature.

Our clinical experience with multiple-family therapy has shown it to be uniquely effective with the families of seriously emotionally handicapped young adults. This experience, coupled with the powerful effects reported for multiple-family therapy in the literature, suggests that it should be considered an essential element of psychiatric rehabilitation programs.

REFERENCES

Anderson, C. M., Hogarty, G., & Reiss, D. (1980). Family treatment of adult schizophrenic patients: A psychoeducational approach. *Schizophrenia Bulletin, 6,* 490–505.
Anderson, C. M., Reiss, D. J., & Hogarty, G. E. (1986). *Schizophrenia and the family.* New York: Guilford Press.
Barrowclough, C., Tarrier, N., Watts, S., Vaughn, J. S., Bamrah, J. S., & Freeman, H. L. (1987). Assessing the functional value of relatives' knowledge about schizophrenia: A preliminary report. *British Journal of Psychiatry, 151,* 1–8.
Bateson, G., Jackson, D., Haley, J., & Weakland, J. (1956). Toward a theory of schizophrenia. *Behavioral Science, 1,* 251–264.

Bedell, J. R., Archer, R. P., & Marlowe, H. A., Jr. (1980). A description and evaluation of a problem-solving skills training program. In D. Upper & S. M. Ross (Eds.), *Behavioral group therapy: An annual review.* Champaign, Il: Research Press.

Bedell, J. R., & Michael, D. D. (1985). Teaching problem-solving skills to chronic psychiatric patients. In D. Upper & S. M. Ross (Eds.), *Handbook of behavioral group therapy.* New York: Plenum Press.

Beels, C. C. (1978). Social networks, the family and the schizophrenic patient. *Schizophrenia Bulletin, 4,* 512–521.

Bellack, A. S., Morrison, R. L. & Mueser, K. T. (1989). Social problem solving in schizophrenia. *Schizophrenia Bulletin, 15,* 101–116.

Brown, G. W., Birley, J. L. T., & Wing, G. H. (1972). The influence of family life on the course of schizophrenic disorders: A replication. *British Journal of Psychology, 129,* 241–258.

Drake, R. E., & Osher, F. C. (1987). Using family psychoeducation when there is no family. *Hospital and Community Psychiatry, 38,* 274–277.

D'Zurilla, T. J., & Goldfried, M. R. (1971). Problem solving and behavior modification. *Journal of Abnormal Psychology, 78,* 107–126.

Falloon, I. R., Boyd, J. L., & McGill, C. W. (1984). *Family care of schizophrenia.* New York: Guilford Press.

Fisher, J. D., & Farina, A. (1979). Consequences of beliefs about the nature of mental disorders. *Journal of Abnormal Psychology, 88,* 320–327.

Hardcastle, D. R. (1977). A multiple family counseling program: procedures and results. *Family Process, 16,* 67–74.

Herz, M. I. (1984). Recognizing and preventing relapse in patients with schizophrenia. *Hospital and Community Psychiatry, 35,* 344–349.

Hogarty, G. E., Anderson, C. M., Reiss, K. J., Kornblith, S. J., Greenwald, D. P., Javna, C. D., & Madonia, M. J. (1986). Family psychoeducation, social skills training, and maintenance chemotherapy in aftercare treatment of schizophrenics: One-year effect of a controlled study on relapse and expressed emotion. *Archives of General Psychiatry, 43,* 633–642.

Hogarty, G. E., Goldberg, S. C., & Schooler, N. R. (1974). Drug and sociotherapy in the aftercare of schizophrenic patients. *Archives of General Psychiatry, 31,* 609–618.

Kaufman, E., & Kaufman, P. (1977). Multiple family therapy: A new direction in the treatment of drug abusers. *American Journal of Drug and Alcohol Abuse, 4,* 467–478.

Laqueur, H. P. (1972). Multiple family therapy. In C. J. Sager & H. S. Kaplin (Eds.), *Progress in group and family therapy.* New York: Brunner/Mazel.

Leff, J. P., & Vaughn, C. E. (1976). The influence of family and social factors on the course of psychiatric illness. *British Journal of Psychiatry, 129,* 125–137.

Leichter, E., & Schulman, G. L. (1968). Emerging phenomena in multi-family group treatment. *International Journal of Group Psychotherapy, 18,* 59–69.

Leichter, E., & Schulman, G. L. (1974). Multi-family group therapy: A multidimensional approach. *Family Process, 13,* 95–110.

McFarlane, W. R. (1983). Multiple family therapy in schizophrenia. In W. R. McFarlane (Ed.), *Family therapy in schizophrenia.* New York: Guilford Press.

McFarlane, W. R. (1990). Multiple family groups and the treatment of schizophrenia. In M. I. Herz & J. P. Docherty (Eds.), *Handbook of schizophrenia, Vol. 4: Psychosocial treatment of schizophrenia* (pp. 167–189). Amsterdam: Elsevier Science Publishers.

McFarlane, W. R., & Beels, C. C. (1983). Family research in schizophrenia: A review and integration for clinicians. In W. R. McFarlane (Ed.), *Family therapy in schizophrenia.* New York: Guilford Press.

Mills, P. D., Hansen, J. C., & Malakie, B. B. (1986). Psychoeducational family treatment for young adult chronically disturbed clients. *Family Therapy, 13,* 275–285.

Minuchin, S. (1974). Structural family therapy. In S. Arieti (Ed.), *American handbook of psychiatry.* New York: Basic Books.

O'Shea, M. D. & Phelps, R. (1985). Multiple family therapy: Current status and critical appraisal. *Family Process, 24,* 555–582.

Searles, H. F. (1965). *Collected papers on schizophrenia and related subjects.* New York: International Universities Press.

Steinglass, P., Gonzalez, S., Dosovitz, I., & Reiss, D. (1982). Discussion groups for chronic hemodialysis patients and their families. *General Hospital Psychiatry, 4,* 7–14.

Strelnick, A. H. (1977). Multiple family group therapy: A review of the literature. *Family Process, 16,* 307–325.

Szymanski, L. S., & Kiernan, W. E. (1983). Multiple family therapy with developmentally disabled adolescents and young adults. *International Journal of Group Psychotherapy, 33,* 521–534.

Tarrier, N., & Barrowclough, C. (1986). Providing information to relatives about schizophrenia: Some comments. *British Journal of Psychiatry, 149,* 458–463.

Wallace, C. J., & Liberman, R. P. (1985). Social skill training for patients with schizophrenia: A controlled clinical trial. *Psychiatry Research, 15,* 239–247.

Yalom, I. D. (1970). *The theory and practice of group psychotherapy.* New York: Basic Books.

Index